T0156922

What Kind of America

.....Do You Want to Leave Your Kids?

R. EUGENE SPITZER

iUniverse, Inc.
Bloomington

What Kind of America
.....Do You Want to Leave Your Kids?

iUniverse books may be ordered through booksellers or by contacting:

iUniverse
1663 Liberty Drive
Bloomington, IN 47403
www.iuniverse.com
1-800-Authors (1-800-288-4677)

ISBN: 978-1-4759-4280-4 (sc)
ISBN: 978-1-4759-4281-1 (ebk)

Library of Congress Control Number: 2012914040

Printed in the United States of America

iUniverse rev. date: 08/08/2012

Contents

Acknowledgements

I couldn't have written this book with God's help. It was He that gave me the inspiration and persistence to write craft it. I also want to thank my wife for putting up with me during this long journey. I didn't let it interfere with our weekly golf game, but I spent a lot of time squatting in front of my computer. She's a very tolerant woman.

I want to thank my two editors for their invaluable help, and thanks to my website and Facebook page designer, too. I couldn't have done this without them.

I also want to thank Rick Anderson of AndersonImages.net for his excellent photographic skills for the front cover.

And finally, I want to thank all of the politicians who, because of their false promises, and inept performance, gave me incredible amounts of fodder that helped so much in the writing of this book.

Mr. Spitzer and his wife have five children, 14 grandchildren, and will soon welcome their third great grandchild. This book is dedicated to all of them, and those to come, and to all of the parents, grandparents, and great grandparents everywhere.

Foreword

First of all, I'm not some elitist from a famous college, someone who has a bunch of degrees and membership in a few think tanks. I'm not a politician, nor am I the host of a radio or TV show, and I'm not a consultant for some organization. No, I'm "just" an American citizen, like you. Unlike many folks, I pay a lot of attention to what is going on in our country and around the world. I pay attention to the mores and folkways we used to observe, and the destruction of them over the decades. I've spent over 40 years watching and studying people, learning how to read people and their motives. I'm seldom wrong in my assessments of people. Much of what is in this book has been building up for many years. I hope you can relate to the topics I've included here. You may not agree with my analysis and assessments, but I hope you will get a good refresher course in America starting in the 1940's through today, and some prognostications for tomorrow.

I wrote this book for many reasons. Yes, I know that many people who have read my articles and columns find me inflammatory. For the most part, that is my intent. I've been invited to give speeches several times with the instruction to be, "Fire them up." That I can do. I am not a person who believes in shades of gray. A person's behavior is good or bad, right or wrong. There are no shades of gray to cloud the issue. I don't subscribe to the term nuance. I simply write or speak what I believe. What I believe is that the left, the Progressives, the Liberals, the Communists, are all intent on "Transforming" America into a Communist form of government where all rights come not from the Constitution, not from God, but from a government ruling class. My hope is to inspire, or inflame people into taking action to fight back.

Another reason, connected to the reason above, is that like you I want my kids and grandkids to grow up safe and free with the opportunity to pursue their dreams without the government standing in the way.

What do I mean by safe? Well, my kids are all grown and have become productive citizens of society. For me, then, the book is targeted more towards my grandkids and my great grandkids. But you get the idea.

- I want my grandkids born drug free.
- I want my grandkids safe at home, at school, on the street, and at play.
- I want my grandkids to be free of indoctrination by one philosophy or the other.

- I want my grandkids to learn how to think, not what to think.
- I want my grandkids taught how to think, not what to think.
- I want my grandkids to receive a quality education that includes all of the subjects necessary to prepare them for higher education and employment. These subjects would include reading, writing, arithmetic and mathematics, and life skills.
- I want my grandkids imbued with good moral values.
- I want my grandkids to have good role models to emulate as they grow.
- I want my grandkids to be self-reliant, prepared to live their own lives, not to be dependent on handouts or other government programs in order to survive.
- I want my grandkids to grow up free from government intervention or control.
- I want my grandkids to receive their sex education from their parents, not from some government school bureaucrat.
- I **don't** want any government school feeding my grandkids any meals, or using my tax dollars to feed any other children. Parents, if you have kids, feed them yourself. Taxpayers aren't responsible for feeding or clothing your children. Take some responsibility.
- I want my grandkids and great grandkids to beel and know that they are loved.

That's probably not an all-inclusive list, but I would hope that you agree with these desires for our kids, grandkids, and great grandkids. This book covers topics that relate to this list. Some topics are targeted at some terrible things I believe are being foisted upon all of us. One thing I learned that I'm sure you've learned as well is, "If you give people things, they will become dependent on those things and the people that provide them." And don't forget, "If you want less of something, tax it more." And I adopted this one, "You can tell the character of a man by his actions, not by his words."

Getting Started

First, let me make a few things quite clear. I am not related to the disgraced former Attorney General from New York, Elliot Spitzer. You can quit wondering about that now. I am not a politician, nor do I play one on TV. I am an American, just like you. I have no desire to "enhance" my career by writing a book. I'm writing this book because We The People have to pay attention, stand up, and fight back in order to restore our great country to what it has been for over 200 years, that "*Shining City on the Hill.*" My perspective is that of a citizen, not a professor, not a legislator, not a biased reporter, and not an elitist lecturer. I pay attention; I write things down; I do research; I remember things, just like you. I'm a conservative; I believe in the Constitution; I believe in God; I love our American flag; I've worn the uniform and been to war; I fought for this country, and I bled for this country. I do not respond well when people denigrate America. I struggle to become a better man every day. People who know me understand that I am the most politically incorrect person they've ever encountered. Cultural Marxism, from which political correctness was derived, is used by some to censor free speech. I won't participate. I call'm as I see'm. So let's get going.

The current administration is carrying out the President's pledge to "*Transform America.*" I believe him to be a Communist, and what I labeled him some years back, a Manchurian President. I think there's a book out now with that title. Most of us weren't quite sure what was meant by "transform," but we've certainly experienced what he meant when he shouted those words. That "*Shining City on a Hill*" under this administration, is fast becoming "*That Miserable, Third World Cesspool I Always Wanted.*" For nearly two centuries the United States has been the most glorious country in the history of the planet, yet this president says our system of government has never worked. Never worked? If that's true, why does everyone want to come here? If that's true, why does every country suffering a disaster call on the United States for help? This president wants to sign the "*Law of the Sea*" Treaty. This treaty gives the United Nations control of all the oceans. This president grants himself sole authority to declare martial law, which is an absolute violation of our Constitution. He has a noticeable habit of taking personal credit for everything good that happens in America—not that much when you think about it in nearly four years—and blames everyone else, especially former President Bush, for anything that goes wrong—like just about everything in nearly four years. As George Will said some months ago, "*This President has used the personal pronoun so often that if he stopped, there would be nothing but silence.*" Everything is "I" or "As President I ordered . . ." This is truly a self-aggrandizing little man. This president constantly says that we have to be fair so that everyone has an equal opportunity for greatness, then beats on small businesses like a drum. Sounds good, Mr. President. But if that's true, why are nearly 50% of the people who can work on welfare and unemployed, and paying no federal income tax? If the "rich" have to pay their fair share, why won't you tell us the definition of "*Fair Share?*" Is fair share 60%, 70%, 90% in income taxes? Is that fair? And why is giving money to the government to redistribute "*fair*"? That's right out of the Karl Marx playbook, isn't it? This president intends to "transform" America into a Communist state where the government runs everything, confiscates the money you earn, and then redistributes it as they see fit. You are supposed to work, if you can find a job, and then give nearly all of your money to the government, which will then give back to you what they decide that you need. That's the Ruling Class / Working Class model. "*From each according to his ability, to each according to his needs.*" For those who don't remember, Karl Marx wrote it in "*The Communist Manifesto.*"

I no longer focus any attention on this president's fraudulent birth certificate. His birth certificate is a fraud, his social security number is a fraud, and his selective service card is also a fraud. His entire education record is hidden, by his order as well. We all know he's a fraud, but neither the politicians nor the lame stream media is going to seriously challenge it. The lame stream media is 100% in favor of this President. They didn't investigate him in 2008, and they're not about to investigate him now. Republican politicians don't want the media to call them racists. So, out of fear, an unqualified man is serving as President. Let's forget about what's been done to us, and focus on defeating him. The lame stream media could more accurately be called the *Goebbels* propaganda arm of the government. This only applies when a Democrat is President. When a Republican is in the White House, the Goebbels media becomes a pack of pit bulls. Goebbels, by the way, was the Minister of Information for the Nazi regime. The lame stream media refuses to report the news in any kind of objective manner. Everything is distorted so as to make the current president look good, and opponents look bad. Dan Rather, formerly of CBS, actually manufactured or accepted manufactured documents, in an attempt to smear President George W. Bush's National Guard service. He got caught and was humiliated. Not too long afterward his debacle, he retired. To this day he says the documents have never been proven false, which was yet another lie. Within four hours of Rather presenting those documents, the Internet went nuts and dozens of people provided proof of falsehood.

In late April, NBC edited an audio tape of a 911 call by the shooter, George Zimmerman, to make it sound as if he was a racist. NBC got caught, too. The CNN network has lost so many viewers that they are now getting less than 350,000 people to tune in during prime time. MSNBC, which is the "I love the President if he's a Democrat" network, makes no attempt to report anything accurately on any of its shows, and their ratings are in the toilet as a result. They finally got rid of Keith Olberman, who never should have been hired anyway, and replaced him with Al Sharpton, the English language-challenged race baiter. And there's always Chris Matthews, who gets thrills up his leg every time the president speaks. Reporting and Journalism are dead professions; they're nothing but propagandists for the Communists.

Here's an observation you may have already made regarding leftists during a debate. If you check your watch when the debate starts, I can almost guarantee that within five minutes the leftist will run out of facts or opinions, and begin the name-calling phase. It only takes about five minutes for the leftis to run out of intelligent arguments, and then the politics of personal destruction begin. Just recently I watched and listened to Tamara Holder, a guest on a TV show, and a devout leftists. She called Darrel Issa, chaimanr of the Oversight Committee, a "*Mall Cop,*" within three minutes. That's got to be a record, but she had nothing intelligent to say. Pay attention the next time you're watching a political TV show, or listening to a debate on radio. The name calling comes pretty quickly. Civil discourse seems to apply to others, but not to the left. If you've ever watched "*The Five*" on FoxNews, you'll hear Bob Beckel, a leftist buffoon, call just about everyone a punk, a nitwit, you name it, if they disagree with him.

I have flown across the United States several times over the years, and have visited almost all of the 50 states—57 if you believe this President's count. More importantly, I have also visited and/or lived in several foreign countries. After all those trips, I have to agree with all those who say, "*The United States is a terrible country.*" They left out the rest of the statement, however. They should have included, "*except when compared to all the rest.*"

Like you I watch the news. Some time back there were a lot of news stories devoted to the Occupy Wall Street people—I prefer the word mob, but I'm trying to be nice. These anarchist thugs told us that they intend to destroy this country. They say that they are fighting for a new country, but only after they do their drugs, rape a few women, and defecate on some police cars. People claiming to be members of the Occupy Wall Street "movement" have been linked to riots, attempted bombings, and rioting. Is this the new country they're trying to form?

Some members of government seem to be doing their best to undermine our way of life. Our freedoms seem to be disappearing, one by one, day by day, year by year.

The twin towers fell on September 11, 2001, and we all saw it. Law enforcement determined that there were 19 hijackers who flew those passenger jets into those towers, into the Pentagon, and, or into the ground in Pennsylvania, thanks to some brave passengers. It was also determined that all 19 were Islamic terrorists, and all male. The 20th hijacker was caught before he could board the jet to which he had been assigned. Besides the terrible loss of life, this was an act of war, but a very unusual war. The terrorist fight under no flag of a country, and wear no uniform. In essence America is fighting a war against an invisible enemy scattered around the world.

Those hijackers got away with the planning, training, and execution of their heinous plan because our government can't or won't enforce laws regarding visas, and certainly don't seem to care about protecting our borders. This whole process has been shown to be a joke. People get a visa to come here for all kinds of reasons, and then just disappear. The government has no idea where they are, and they aren't looking all that hard to find them.

The United States, which has brought freedom to more people than any other nation in recorded history, is threatened with extinction in favor of Communist rule and, to a lesser extent, by Islamic rule. Every time there has been a major disaster anywhere in the world, America is first on the scene with food, medical care, and rebuilding efforts. You don't see Russia, China, France, Italy, Saudi Arabia, Iran, Cuba, Venezuela, or other countries responding, but America has always tried to be anywhere people are in trouble, or disasters strike.

When Japan attacked us in 1941, a great Japanese Admiral said, *"I fear we have awakened a sleeping tiger."* He was right. We defeated Japan, but with a great loss of life. We call August 14, 1945 *VJ day* for Victory Japan. Times were different then. America was united in its fight with both Japan and Germany. America is no longer united about much of anything.

When the U.S. got involved in the war in Europe, at their request, to stop the advancement of Hitler's Germany, we fought and won that war, too. America had help, of course, but without our involvement, European countries might well be speaking German today. Anyone who ever read or saw documentaries on the landing at Normandy understands how costly that war was to the United States. We celebrate that day as *VE day* or Victory Europe. The exact date is difficult to determine since German forces surrendered in various countries on different dates, but the first week of May, 1945 would seem close enough.

In early 2012, on the one year anniversary of the death of Bin Laden, some leftists said that we should equate the date of Bin Laden's death with VJ or VE day. The U.S. tracked down and killed one man, and the left wants to call it a day as significant as the surrender of Germany and Japan? I would call it a stretch, but when you think about it, you know that the leftists are attempting to draw moral equivalence between the events in order to make the current President seem tough on terror. He didn't kill Bin Laden; our military did. All he did was say, "OK" and his part was over. You would think that the war on terror ended in 2011 with Bin Laden's death. It's not. There are terrorists all around us, some plotting on foreign soil to come and destroy us, others right here in America planning to destroy us. During the past four years, more and more people lost their jobs. More and more homeowners lost their homes. More and more people have gone on welfare just to survive. The number of people on welfare today are the most since the depression. Yet this President says that his plan is working. Well, if his plan is to destroy America and turn it into a Communist state, he's right. This isn't America, and this isn't a country I want my kids and grandkids to inherit. America is nearly $16 Trillion in debt with no end in sight. For nearly four years the unemployment rate has remained over 8% although we were promised it would be down to 5.7% by now. All we had to do was spend spent $784 billion on *stimulus*. Yeah, right. Some on the left say we should get used to it, that 8% unemployment is the new "normal." Is this what you want for your kids and grandkids? Nearly 50% of working Americans pay no federal income tax. Is that their fair share? A recent statistic stated that approximately 50% of college graduates today will not find a job, and will move back in with their parents. Getting a college degree used to be the entry into the good paying job market where the dreams can materialize, but no longer. Yet this President keeps saying that "everyone should have the right to go to college." Why? If going to college means acquiring a huge debt, but having no job when you graduate is what kids have to look forward to, why go? What about trade schools? Do we no longer need plumbers, electricians, construction workers, and the other tradespeople? Is this what you want for your kids and grandkids?

Americans used to invent all kinds of things and, to some extent, we still do. Americans used to start new business and provide goods and services to customers, and jobs. Do you see that happening today? The regulations imposed on businesses today are so onerous that small business star-up ventures are at their lowest point in decades. A member of Congress spoke in the Well of the House, and carried the 1,100 pages of regulations, new regulations, imposed on small businesses in the past three and a half years. Americans used to know that they had the opportunity, not a guaranteed outcome, but the opportunity to pursue their dreams. Can you honestly say today that your kids and grandkids are going to be better off than you are?

Most politicians lie a lot. They also make promises, counting on you to have a very short memory so you'll forget them once the election is over. Once in office many politicians continue to lie, misrepresent, and obfuscate. And yet, every two or six years, these same politicians come back home to a) make more empty promises and b) beg for your money. Far too many people, desperate for some good news, actually believe these politicians. Just look at how many people this President fooled with all his "Hope and Change" rhetoric. His list of lies would fill a book. Folks, don't believe a thing they say, but pay very close attention to what they actually do. They'll promise you anything, but will forget about you when they get to the clubhouse.

How many promises did the current President make during his campaign? There were dozens and dozens of them. He targeted those promises towards the young because they didn't own anything, didn't pay taxes, and most of them are in school. And, most importantly, many young people are easily indoctrinated and manipulated.

In 1928 when Herbert Hoover was running for President, and said, "*I promise a chicken in every pot, and a car in every garage.*" He didn't keep that promise, either. The lies from presidential candidates date back even farther than 1928, but you get the picture. Candidates make all kinds of promises without a thought as to how they will keep them. Always assume that they are lying, and you will usually be right.

The man who now occupies the White House as President made promise after promise, before he was elected, and continues to make them.

Single-Payer Healthcare is On the Way

Although the President promised that you could keep your doctor, and your healthcare insurance if you were happy with it, the reality is that nothing could be further from the truth. If you think you'll be able to keep your doctor and your healthcare insurance through individual purchase on through your employer, you're fooling yourself. All of this silliness about whether ObamaDoesn'tCare is a tax or a penalty, now that the Supreme Court has spoken is just smoke and mirrors. The leftists refuse to use the word tax because the President had vehemently stated that his Affordable Care Act (ACA) was not a tax. The Supreme Court, in a 5-4 decision, declared that the act was Constitutional because it levies a tax, and Congress has the power to levy taxes. That the tax is levied for NOT buying something seems not to matter. The ACA is not Constitutional under the Commerce Clause because the government does not have the authority to force people to buy a product. I don't understand the difference since now it's a tax if you DON'T buy health insurance. This is where America is today. If you recall, starting back in 2008, the intent was to include the "public option," or single-payer insurance program, but that idea was shelved because the American people would not support Socialized Medicine which is what the single-payer stems is when you open the kimono. It should be noted that the President was seen in a video, before he became President, saying that the ultimate goal for health care was the single-payer program.

There are 21 new taxes in the ACA, and new requirements for current insurance companies. For smaller companies, it most probably means that they'll have to drop coverage for their employees, and send them to the government exchanges. These exchanges, under government control, will offer healthcare coverage at a very high rate. For larger companies it will be a cost-benefit analysis. If the cost of providing the coverage, and all of the additional coverage and cost outweighs the benefit to the company they, too, will have to drop coverage for their employees. Eventually, no company will offer healthcare coverage to their employees. Then what? You see where this is going, right? We will end up with single-payer healthcare, run by the federal government. America will become Canada or the United Kingdom. If you don't know what that means, you should start checking out the reality of government-run healthcare. Rationing, long, long waits just to see a doctor, denial of care; it's all in there. Yes, there are death panels in ObamaDoesn'tCare. Older people will not receive the quality of care they receive today. The elderly will also be denied certain operations, like a new heart, kidney, or liver. They will also be denied a hip replacement, and so on. The elderly may well be told, as the President alluded to in one of his speeches, that "Maybe it's better to give her a pain pill," when asked about an elderly woman who needed a heart transplant.

The young will wake up one day and realize that they can no longer avoid buying health insurance because, if they attempt to do so, they will receive a fine from the government. And you can't hide from the government when you owe them money. The government always gets paid, even if it means garnishing wages, attaching a checking or savings account, or by whatever means they decide to use. However, as the President has said, for those young men and women who can't afford to buy insurance, the government will "assist" them. Yes, they'll assist them alright, with our tax dollars. Even the Congressional Budget Office (CBO), has raised its assessment as to the cost of ObamaDoesn'tCare, now estimating it at over $2 Trillion over ten years. 2014 may well be the year when America becomes a socialized medicine country, and healthcare quality and availability will suffer greatly.

Closing Guantanamo Bay

What was one of the first things that the new President did after inauguration? You guessed it. He signed an executive order calling for the closure of the military's Guantanamo Bay prison facility for terrorists within one year. Whew, glad that's done. This should have been easy pickings for the President and his cabal. Just close it, folks. OK, Mr. President, let's close it. Uh, Sir, I have a question. What do we do with all of those terrorists currently being held in Gitmo? Turn them loose? Make them citizens? Please help us understand, Mr. President. As usual, this President acted without thinking it through, politically or logistically. Now, in 2012, Gitmo is humming along. Having the terrorists there is better than putting them in some prison in the United States. The President, along with his lackey, Eric Holder, thought they could hold civilian trials for each terrorist in New York. That idea was discarded when the citizens screamed their outrage. In the end, the President's executive order was just a piece of paper destined for the dust heap of history.

We Have to Defend Labor Rights

In 2007 the President said this: "Understand this. "If American workers are being denied their rights to organize and collectively bargain when I'm in the White House, I will put on a pair of comfortable shoes myself, and I'll walk that picket line with you as President of the United States." That line was funny. Has anyone seen the President keeping that promise? No, and of course he never will. It was just more rhetoric for the weak-minded.

Unions make up only about nine percent of the working population in the private sector, and their numbers are decreasing. No one has ever stopped a union from attempting to organize. No one stops a union from attempting to bargain for pay, benefits, and retirement. The problem is that more and more people don't want to be a part of a union. They've discovered that unions are not really about the workers; they're about power and control for union bosses. The left loves unions. And union bosses live very, very well. Lavish lifestyles on the backs of union workers. When unions go on strike, the union bosses keep on making those huge salaries while telling the workers to walk those picket lines, without pay. The leftist politicians love the money that union leaders pour into leftist candidate campaigns.

I've worked at companies where some union representatives came and wanted to get the employees to vote as to whether they wanted to unionize. They were given that opportunity, and opposed unionization in large numbers. The union organizers left with their collective tails between their legs.

Get Rid of or Reform the Patriot Act

Since elected, this President has never called for a reform of, or abandonment of the Patriot Act. His leftist buddies keep whining about it, but nothing has been done. It's a divisive issue with large numbers favoring it, and large numbers opposed to it. The Patriot Act came about after the atrocities of 9/11. In effect, this act gives law enforcement more latitude in its pursuit of suspected terrorists here in America. Law enforcement can monitor phones, and conduct surveillance of suspected terrorists without having to always get a warrant beforehand. This was done because of the fluidity of the situation. Many terrorists switch cell phones and cell phone numbers almost daily in an attempt to evade law enforcement. Terrorists also move around a lot, never staying in one place for long. Law enforcement needed a way to monitor and keep track of them, and the Patriot Act served the purpose. There are also permissions that allow the FBI to research library use by suspects, warrantless searches, and similar authorities. This President has done nothing to curtail the provisions of the Patriot Act, and I doubt that he will. We have to remember that it is almost impossible to infiltrate a terrorist cell here, or in other countries. These cells are almost always comprised of people who have known each other for years and years, and outsiders are never let into the cell.

I Will End the Wars

During the campaign season, this President said that he would end the war in Iraq in 2009. Oops. That didn't happen. He said that he would support the war in Afghanistan because that was the "*right war*" to be fighting. I'm not sure how he determined that Afghanistan was the right war, but we'll take his word for it, NOT. We've been in Afghanistan for over a decade, and have no clue as to what victory means. The President said he would have us out of Afghanistan in 2012, then 2013, and I believe that now he says we'll be out in 2014. The military doesn't agree with him, but the military doesn't have a vote. We're leaving Iraq, but the violence continues. We're going to leave Afghanistan, but the violence continues. Just what is the trigger that says, "Now we can bring our warriors home." It can't be when we win, because there was never a strategy for winning anything. We went to Afghanistan to capture Bin Laden. He was already gone, but we stayed. If you're paying attention, you'll notice that the President never mentions Iraq or Afghanistan now. Our warriors die, but he's oblivious.

Reduce the Debt and Revive the Economy

This President's campaign promises were pretty specific when it came to the economy. He said that Americans would go back to work again, unemployment would drop back to 5.7%. Well, after over three years the stated unemployment rate is about 8.2%, though some would tell you that the real unemployment rate is about 15%. He said that by spending all that stimulus money, the national debt would be cut in half in his first term, or it would be a one-term proposition. Instead, the national debt has risen by over $5 trillion dollars. He's been wrong on everything but, as he tells it, it's all George W. Bush's fault. Really? After nearly four years, it's still the former President's fault? Recently, the number of people applying for social security disability outpaces the number of people that went to work. Why is that happening? Could it be that some people having been unable to find a job in over a year or two, have come up with a way to get some money by applying for disability? If that's true, what does that say about our economy? Every budget that the President has proposed contains over $1 Trillion in new debt. It's interesting to note that none of the President's proposed budgets got even one vote of support from any member of Congress. It's sad to note that the Democrat Senate has not put forth a budget in over three years—though the Constitution calls for it. Harry Reid does what the President tells him to do, and the plan is to not have a budget, and keep on spending. The House, however, has offered several budgets, but the Senate, has refused to even allow those budgets to be brought to the floor for debate and a vote.

What Has Happened to Justice and Freedom?

Since this President has been in office, the American justice system has everyone confused. Far too often what I see and hear just make no sense. Here are just a few examples.

- A U.S. Army Major, on an Army base in Texas, shouts "Allahu Akbar," and then opens fire with multiple weapons, murdering over a dozen soldiers and civilians, and injuring more than 30. It's been over three years, yet this man has yet to come to trial. The

Homeland Security secretary decided that this was not an act of terrorism. Wow, you could have fooled me. No, Ms. Napolitano referred to this mass murder as an act of workplace violence. Really? Mass murderers have been put on trial faster than this terrorist. What's the holdup, Mr. Holder?

- In 2008, members of the Black Panther party stationed themselves right in front of a polling place in Philidelphia. They were dressed all in black, and carried black police-style batons. Many people did not attempt to go around them and enter the polling place because, as they said, they felt intimidated. This was clearly a case of voter intimidation, but it was intimidation by black Americans, and the Attorney General did nothing. One former member of the Attorney General's office said that it was understood that there would be no prosecution of black Americans for behaviors that white Americans would be charged with. To me, anytime you put that much authority in the hands of one person, justice will not be well-served. I felt, back when Eric Holder gave his speech after his appointment, that the American people were cowards for not having a discussion of race, that he, Eric Holder, has behaved as a racist. Nothing has happened since then to change my mind.

- There was a comment made by the Homeland Security Secretary that sounded, in effect, like the labeling of people with politically objectionable bumper stickers as domestic terrorists. Really? I wonder if she would say the same thing about someone who had a bumper sticker supporting the current President? I'm taking bets on that one.

- An American citizen has a Dump Obama bumper sticker, and can be branded a Domestic Terrorist by the Homeland Security Secretary? What happened to free speech? Oh, wait, I've got it; it's free speech if you have a Dump Romney bumper sticker because he's on the wrong side, you know, the conservative, Republican side.

- If a person in a vehicle is stopped for a driving infraction, and can't provide a driver's license, proof of insurance, and a legal registration document for the vehicle, the police may investigate whether or not the person is in the country illegally. However, if he or she is an illegal alien, ICE will not take custody and deport them. This happens even though federal law calls for the deportation of all people in this country illegally. Is that justice, Mr. Holder, or are you just courting potential voters for the Democrat party?

- Just as an aside, what about the recent news story stating that Homeland Security and ICE are buying 950 <u>million</u> rounds of .40 caliber ammunition over five years? Whom are they planning to shoot, us? In general, the Border Patrol and ICE don't use weapons very often, although they do have to practice and qualify with their weapons on a regular basis. That being said, 950 million rounds of ammunition of one caliber is odd, don't you think?

- The country is currently in debt to the tune of about $16 Trillion. The last three budgets the President has proposed called for an increase of the debt by over a Trillion dollars each year. The President says that his ideas and policies are working. If I may be so bold, Mr. President, is your policy, and your ideas, intended to bankrupt the country, and turn America into a third-world cesspool? If so, well done, sir.

- The Supreme Court has ruled that, for clarity on the issue of the separation of church and state, lower courts cannot display the Ten Commandments. However, the Supreme Court can display the Ten Commandments prominently in their building. Please, someone, explain this one to me. The whole issue of the separation of church and state is a red herring, anyway. The purpose of the First Amendment was to ensure that the government did not <u>establish</u> a religion, as was done in England. Putting the Ten Commandments on the wall of a courthouse, or putting a nativity scene in a public display, or children singing Christmas carols in a school pageant is not the establishment of religion. If you understand the Communist left, then you understand why they have to, in essence, "kill" God. In Communism, god is the government. Nancy Pelosi said as much some years back: "People don't need God anymore; they have us Democrats."

- A child can't read a Bible at school, but the school can put on a presentation of how homosexuality is just as normal as heterosexuality, and that's OK. How is a child bringing a Bible to school to read during lunch, or praying in the morning at school, a violation of the First Amendment? If you take nothing else from this book, take this: Democrats are liberals. Liberals are Progressives. Progressives are Communists. These Communists are determined to do whatever it takes to get God out of the public discourse, and out of sight. Don't let them.

- Everyone wants fair elections. Only citizens, registered to vote, should vote, one time. "*One Man, One Vote.*" Remember that? Knowing that, why has the Attorney General sued multiple states from implementing a mandatory photo ID when people show up to cast their ballot? When Florida wanted to clean up their voting rolls, to get rid of dead people, and people not legally registered, they asked for access to the federal government's database to help accomplish the task, the Attorney General fought vigorously to stop them. Fortunately, he lost. One interesting note here: This Attorney General is trying to stop any use of photo ID at the polls to verify the identity of the people casting their ballot. In my view, he knows that the Communists need every illegal vote they can get, so he's going to try and stop any attempt by any state to clean up its voter rolls. At the same time he was saying he was fighting to keep people from being disenfranchised through the use of a photo ID, entrance into his speech required that everyone show a photo ID. This is hilarious. He doesn't want photo ID used to vote, but you have to have a photo ID to attend his speeches. Here's my advice to every state regarding elections. In every election, including Presidential elections, there are candidates running for local and state offices. Each state should assert its sovereignty and proceed with the requirement for a photo ID for every voter since local and state offices are part of that election. Once each state does this, send a letter to Attorney General Holder, and tell him to shut up, sit down, and remain mute.

- Why do politicians exempt themselves from laws that apply to us? Is that justice? Why do members of Congress exempt themselves from a healthcare system that is foisted upon us? Is that justice?

- Is it just and fair for a child to be required to obtain parental approval, in writing, to go on a school outing, but needs no approval from anyone in order to get an abortion? I can't figure that one out, can you?

This is where America is today. Couple several factors together and you end up with many people who will vote for anyone who promises them "free" things. We have a government school system that fails year after year, and produces uneducated, nearly illiterate graduates, yet demands more and more money—not for the kids, but for administrators and unions. We have a college system where many students are indoctrinated with the socialism is the salvation of the world mantra. If you look at the Communist Manifesto, you'll see this phrase: "*From Each According to his ability, to each according to his need.*" That statement sums up the policies of the current administration.

In addition to our drug society, we also have an entitlement society, and an illegal alien society, and most of the members of those groups vote. It is our education system, our 'compassion' for the poor, the downtrodden, yadda yadda, that drives many voters to elect people who promise them anything and everything with no understanding of where the money comes from.

Conservatives believe in a hand up; Communists believe in handouts, sufficient to make those people receiving them dependent on those who provide them.

Those paragraphs certainly sum up the mantra of the left (Democrats, Liberals, Progressives, Communists)—vote for us and we'll give you free stuff, which we'll pay for by taking money from other people. With each succeeding generation fully indoctrinated on the beauty of Socialism/Communism, they come to believe that it is the responsibility of others to give them stuff because, well, because they want or need it, but don't want to earn it. This really chaps my hide.

For many years I have watched my country change, and I don't like what I see and experience. I ranted and raved about all of the stupidity and corruption in government, the lust for power of politicians, the increased unruliness of children, and the terrible behavior of many parents. I've watched the government school system turn into an indoctrination system, with too many unqualified teachers, and administrators living large on my money, at the expense of our kids, grandkids, and great grandkids. I've also given dozens of speeches around my state, and written dozens of columns trying, in vain at times, to wake people up.

My family finally told me to "*shut up and write a book.*" When I decided to take their advice, and put my words where my mouth is, I began the research, note taking, building topics and fleshing them out. That decision to write this book was also because of the many people I would come into contact with who voiced their outrage about many of the same things I was upset about. This book is not intended to be all inclusive. It may take another volume or two to cover everything as events unfold almost hourly.

As I saidk, I've given speeches all over the state, on topics such as our education system, our political system, the ongoing war with Communism, and the war with Islamic terrorists. I've also met with several politicians and let them know that I was either happy or unhappy with their performance. I remind politicians that they work for us; we don't subjugate ourselves to them. I've never been accused of being shy or lacking an opinion on just about everything, but my opinions are, generally, based on my reading, my research, and common sense. In many ways what you read here will hopefully turn on a light in your head, and you'll say, "Yep, I need to quit waiting for others to stand up and fight back; it's up to me, too.

The traditions of our society are being taken away. Our taxes rise higher and higher, and our government spends more and more. But the spending doesn't help us, it helps the government. I see moral decay everywhere I look. I see government schools turned into Hitler-like youth camps, indoctrinating our kids and grandkids into being believers in Communist dogma. I listen to or watch the news and it always seems to be slanted or biased against conservatives, Christians, and Republicans. The leftist lame stream media has a vested interest in destroying the underpinnings of our society in favor of some immoral, lazy, shiftless collection of groups beholden to government for their very existence. Wow! Some news stories are ignored completely because those stories don't fit the station's agenda. I hear a coarsening of our language. I hear kids as young as eight or nine swearing like sailors on liberty (sorry, I didn't mean to insult sailors). I watch the nighttime entertainment show hosts using language in the public arena which never existed in past decades, and people laugh. I watch so-called comedians searching for laughs by telling jokes that always demean or smear other people, usually a conservative or Christian, and call it comedy. I see prime time TV shows turn into sex festivals that children are watching, and many of them seem to include a token homosexual in the cast in order to curry favor with the homosexual lobby. I always wonder what values these children derive from these shows. Could it be that women are there for the sexual pleasure of men in a "hook up" for nothing but sex? There are shows dedicated to child sexual predators where little children are wearing push up bras, skimpy outfits, tons of makeup, and doing bump and grind performances for the cameras. There are TV shows celebrating unwed mothers still in high school. There's a TV show where one of the main characters is a short, fat, drunken slut, and kids tune in by the millions. I once heard the owner/manager of *The Bunny Ranch*, a legal whorehouse near Las Vegas, describe casual sex as being on the same level as bowling, playing golf, or going out to dinner and a movie. Sex between two people has now been reduced to a recreational activity. This is sick. For that matter, why are whorehouses legal anywhere?

I read stories and hear tales from parents about how dangerous government schools are, how drugs are readily accessible on our middle and high school campuses, and how the standards of learning are continuously lowered just to try and graduate some students. I read story after story of how many government high schools have day care centers so these unmarried teenage girls with one or more babies, without a father to be found, can drop off those babies and go study arithmetic, or learn how to put a condom on a cucumber. Government schools seem to celebrate their efforts to take care of unwed mothers in their schools, and not only condone sexual activity, but offer free condoms, thus encouraging the promiscuity. The only things missing are a bedroom with a nightstand, a pack of cigarettes, and a refrigerator for the beer.

I look at the price of gasoline and wonder why, when we have over a 150 year supply of oil under our ground and oceans, are we paying such high prices, and buying our oil from countries that don't like us very much. What is our government doing about it? Why is government making more in taxes on a gallon of gas than the oil company is making on that same gallon? I wonder why the environmentalists are so concerned about the sanctity of our lands and waters, but don't have anything to say about the countries where the oil is being drilled. Our government leaders keep telling us that windmills and solar will be along soon, so don't worry. What am I going to do, put a solar panel on the roof of my car? What if it's raining? Do I just stay home because my car won't run? It's insanity. The environmentalists don't seem to care that birds are killed by windmills. When a windmill generates electricity, where is it stored? There is no storage battery technology to support this type of energy conversion. And, just for the record, there is no such thing as "renewable energy." A decent high school class would have taught that, but our government schools can't be bother. What if the wind doesn't blow for a week or two? Does the town go dark, do refrigerators quit working, do television sets and computers quit working, too? There are over ten thousand products we use that are based on oil, and our own government is trying to make oil so expensive that we can't have those products, including gasoline, unless we're rich. At the same time, our fearless government leaders are giving tens of billions of dollars to alternative energy companies, trying to pick winners and losers, while at the same time, ignoring fossil fuel reserves that the world depends upon to function. And remember this, when the government gives guaranteed loans to this company or that company, they're playing with our money, not their own. And it's also curious that this administration seems to give these guaranteed loans to companies that are big supporters of theirs. The phobia some people have of a drilling rig is very curious, and a psychiatrist could have a great career studying this unwarranted fear.

There are many who believe that the earth came into being, and we came into being, because of the "Big Bang." Really? A humongous collision of a bunch of inanimate objects smashed into each other, and animate objects emerged. Really? From nothing, life was created. What are these people smoking? Never mind; we already know. Did you know that despite all of the years that have gone by, all of the technology available, and all of the scientists studying the subject, no one has been able to create life, ever. Others believe that we evolved from monkeys. If that's true, why do we still have monkeys? Has anyone seen a monkey in the process of evolving? They should have all evolved into humans by now, shouldn't they? Nonetheless, monkeys keep breeding and having baby monkeys. Then there are those that say we evolved from fish. Fish evolved by coming onto land, growing legs and arms, and the ability to breathe air, and here we are. If that's true, why are there millions of species of fish still swimming around in the oceans? Did they not get the memo? They could have grown legs and arms, learned to breathe air, and be driving around in a Lexus and working on Wall Street by now.

The current White House occupant is working very hard trying to instill class warfare among the American people, pitting the poor against the rich. That's right, he is encouraging class warfare, pitting one group of Americans against another, and he's proud of it. I was under the impression that the President was the President of all Americans equally, but I guess I missed his memo telling us that that *One America* stuff is over. We have a President who, during nearly four years in office, has seen a decline in employment, a continued decline in home ownership and sales, an increase in bankruptcies, an increase in people on food stamps, has no budget, no plan to revive the economy, added over $5 Trillion to our national debt, and yet spends his time ranting about his opponents, when he's not playing golf. He has been to over 100 fundraising events, but he hasn't met with his Jobs Council in over six months. He does manage to get in a round of golf, or then, during that time. I see a problem here, don't you? He is a failure by any measure, except to those people who are getting "free" stuff. You can see him on TV, nearly every darned day, up on a stage somewhere, ranting about how rich people need to pay more, to pay their fair share. Pay more? Fairness? Are you kidding me?

Nearly half of working Americans pay nothing in federal income taxes, and he's talking about the rich not paying enough? The President says that Americans should give more of their money to the government so government can spend it on what they know is best. I learned a long time ago that the politicians in Washington were not the sharpest pencils in the box. What they are is a group of people hungry for power and control.

When the President wants us to pay more, to pay our fair share, is it so he and his cronies can give more billions to failing alternative energy companies, like Solyndra, which just happened to be run by one of the President's biggest campaign bundlers? How about the GSA spending our tax dollars on lavish "conferences" in Hawaii, or Las Vegas? There are millions and millions of Americans whose tax dollars are wasted by this government, and their answer? Give us more of your money so we can live it up.

Millions of Americans are fed up with this wasteful, corrupt, hidden government. Enough is enough. These bums need to leave, now, or we need to throw them out in November.

Are you as tired as I am of this "fair share" gibberish the leftists are always spouting? Not one of them will ever tell us what a "fair share" is; they just want more money to spend as they see fit, with no accountability. In the President's class warfare strategy, this administration denigrates success, and almost quotes the Communist mantra of "Workers Unite." What workers, Mr.

President? May it should be, "All you unemployed Americans should unite against successful Americans. Success must be punished. That's our President. Is that the American dream you want to pass on to your kids and grandkids?

It's a political campaign slogan, not a policy. The current administration is spending well over $3 Trillion of our tax dollars each year, plus additional hundreds of billions of dollars we don't have, and our economy is getting worse by the day. That's the definition of insanity, to keep doing the same thing over and over, looking for a different result. This President preaches envy, not aspiration. This President tells people to envy and hate rich people. He never tells people to get off their collective butts and go get a job doing something, even if it's not a CEO position. He says every kid should be able to go to college without having a big college loan debt when they graduate, but never tells these kids that working their way through college is a good idea. If mom and dad don't pay, and they need a student loan, how do they pay it back if they can't find a job? Right now, about half of college graduates can't find a job when they graduate. When you read about these and many other topics, I hope it makes you as angry as it makes me.

There was a time in America when kids could see, feel, and taste the American dream. They could dream of inventing the next Microsoft®, Facebook®, or Apple®. They saw their parents pursue their dream and achieve it by working hard, saving their money, buying a home in a good neighborhood, putting food on the table, putting their kids in good schools, and enjoying the life that can be America. Some parents started their own businesses, hired employees, provided a good or service people wanted without the government trying to either shut them down for some unknown violation, or adding more fees and taxes to their business.

It wasn't fair for all, to be sure. There was discrimination across the nation, and some racism. It wasn't as big an issue, primarily because back in the 1960's the media wasn't covering nearly as many stories as they do today. We may not have read about clashes in the streets, or fights between races until the 24-hour news cycle and cable television and race-baiting haters like Jesse Jackson and Al Sharpton came along.

With the introduction of all the news every minute of the day and night, there was a need for reporters to come up with something, anything, to talk about. Reporters began rounding up any story that even looked like it met the "*if it bleeds, it leads*" standard, and any racial conflict was a perfect fit. If a "news" event didn't have racial components, some reporters would imply that it did—like NBC in the recent Zimmerman/Martin shooting case; anything to fan the flames to cause more incidents which fed more news stories. Look at the Rodney King and O.J. Simpson cases. Both cases were turned into individual circuses, by the media. Children, and most adults, didn't accept the status quo on racism. Attitudes have changed, and laws have been enacted to prevent it to the extent possible. These laws are intended to control behavior, not attitudes. As schools opened their doors to all races, and as jobs were accessible to all races, the conflict diminished even further. But some racism still exists, and there are some that want to swing the pendulum all the way in the other direction as if that makes it all equal.

I can tell you that as a hiring manager for over 20 years, I always looked to hire the best candidate for the job, that fit within my budget constraints. When I fired someone it was because they couldn't or wouldn't do the job they were hired to do, not for any other reason. I fired friends because their personal lives had taken over, and they weren't producing. But, in every hiring manager's head, wheels are spinning when they make a hiring decision. It doesn't or shouldn't make any difference if job applicants have black, white, or yellow-colored skin, or if they're male or female. That's the way it used to be. Hire the best person for the job with a salary or rate that falls within the budget. But, today the Human Resources departments are more in control of hiring than are the managers. I had one incident where the HR manager asked me to choose a minority candidate because it would look good to clients and the board of directors. I explained that although that particular candidate was pretty good, I had two candidates with better skills and experience. He asked me to make an exception and hire the minority. I declined. My budget was cut the following year.

Hiring managers are looking for the best candidate who can hit the ground running, and produce results quickly. They typically don't look for someone to fill a quota, or look for someone whom they want to give a chance to become a good performer, someday. It's not in the best interest of the department or the company to do that.

Today, too many people believe that companies exist primarily to provide jobs, a lot of benefits, and a lot of time off with pay. Whatever product or service that a company provides is secondary. Whether the company makes a profit or not is no longer a consideration. Many people believe that if a company makes a profit, it's shameful. This seems to come straight from the Karl Marx playbook.

R. Eugene Spitzer

What is The American Dream?

When America became a country, with its Constitution and its Bill of Rights, people with a yearning to be free couldn't get here fast enough. At Ellis Island, New York immigrant officials screened and processed millions of immigrants. They arrived, presented identification papers, were screened for communicable diseases, and were welcomed. These immigrants immediately went looking for work. They couldn't wait to learn English, and loved being free to worship as they pleased, to work as hard as they wanted, and to be rewarded for it. They invented new things, they worked in cities and on farms; they saved money, bought homes, married, had children, and loved America.

Now, let's examine how college kids today believe the American Dream to be for them. Several colleges have conducted experiments to determine, as objectively as possible, how students view "The American Dream" today. The general process is as follows: The professor gives the students an assignment to write a short essay on what the American Dream means to them.

When the essays are returned, the instructor or professor takes them home, reads them, classifies them, and develops some statistics on their responses. In general, about 80% of the students explained the American Dream as follows:

- Free college tuition for as long as they attended school. If they wanted to stay in college until they received a Doctorate, it should all be free. And included with that free tuition is free healthcare.
- A well-paying job, guaranteed.
- Plenty of money they could invest for their retirement.
- Free money, taken from rich people, so they have enough.

That result appalled me. This is the American Dream for many of our children today? They want entitlements, guaranteed income, plenty of money to invest and retire on, and money taken from rich people so they have enough for what they want.

Where did they learn this? The answer is as true today as it has been for over 50 years; government schools and college professors who live, love, and preach the Socialist model.

The American Dream for illegal aliens seems to be one where we allow them to break into our country, and then get America to provide them with welfare, food stamps, subsidized housing, free medical care, and free education for their children. We need to guarantee them a job, too; a good paying job. Just because they broke the law and crossed our border illegally is no reason to discriminate against them, right? What's worse is that there are many people in this country that support that approach to illegal immigration. Another insanity

The Differences Between Capitalism and Communism?

Today, there is a major, fundamental conflict going on between whether we're a Capitalist society, or moving closer to being a Communist society. For those of you who don't know what the fundamentals of Communism are, let me provide a brief summary. In a Communist society the state (the government) runs or controls everything. That means that the government controls transportation, housing, radio, television, print media, jobs, communication, agriculture, farming, factories, all businesses, everything. You live where you're told to live, work where you're told to work, and are paid whatever the state wants you to receive. You are told how many children you can have—marriage is optional—and the list goes on. In a Communist society you are a member of the working class. The state (government) is the ruling class. Laws that apply to the working class don't necessarily apply to the ruling class.

It's important that you understand the differences because the direction that this county chooses to follow will most assuredly affect your kids and grandkids. Let's explore, briefly, the principles of Capitalism and Communism.

Principles of Communism, (summarized from the 1848 publication, *The Communist Manifesto*.)

- Abolition of Private Property. This means that under Communism no one can own any land except the state. As you've seen over the years, the federal government has confiscated more and more land, declaring it a natural wilderness or something similar. Even up in Alaska, the federal government owns millions and millions of acres. The

Alaska Natural Wildlife Reserve (ANWR), has been put off limits for drilling, even though there are billions of barrels of oil under the ground, and not a human within hundreds of miles. Just about every state has land that is off limits to that state because the federal government owns it. However, they do not pay property taxes to the state for this land. The government continues to confiscate more and more land every year. Private property rights are one of the principles of our society, but now that's being attacked. Remember back when the Supreme Court ruled that a city could take private property away from its owners in order to allow a developer to build office buildings and other tax-revenue producing businesses? This was the outrageous Kelo decision in Connecticut.

- Progressive tax; the more successful you are, the more the government takes. This is one method by which a Communist system punishes innovation, inspiration, hard work, and success. It, more or less, putts a ceiling on the American dream. Not that long ago a concentrated attack was made by the Democrats, again, against the *"rich."* Things like, "The rich have to pay their fair share" echoed throughout the land. The definition of fair share has never been stated, but we have a clue. When the President talked about families making over $250,000 a year as rich, we discovered what the ceiling is for the American dream. How will your kids accept that they should not aspire to be rich, to achieve success?

- The First Lady once said publicly that our youth should not aspire to enter the workforce but, rather, volunteers to help others. Very noble goals, but just what do these young people use for money? Why should our kids be told to lower their expectations and aspirations? The First Lady and the President certainly didn't lower their expectations. If you consider the following, you can gain some perspective on just what $250,000 buys you. First of all, what is the cost of living in Wyoming versus New York? Is it the same? Of course not. What if your family has three children who want to attend a good college? That could cost a family nearly $90,000 each year. When you factor in a house payment, a couple of car payments, the various insurance costs, food, gasoline, what do you have left of that $250,000? Not much. After that family pays local, city, state, and federal taxes, there isn't much left is there?

- Abolition of Rights of Inheritance. The so-called *"Death Tax"* has been the center of dispute for many years. The government wants at least 55% of any inheritance forfeit to them, not to the heirs. Remember now, that any money, land, or other things of value have already had a tax paid on them, but government wants more. Actually, they would like to get it all, but the rate goes up to 55% in January. The basic question to ask is, why should the government be able to confiscate the inheritance at such a rate in the first place? Is the government saying, in effect, that when you die, the state takes the assets of the deceased? It's not theirs to confiscate in the first place, but under Communism that all changes.

- Confiscation of the property of all emigrants & rebels. This is pretty much self-explanatory, but essentially it means that the government confiscates all personal property, transferring ownership to the state.
- Central Bank (like the Federal Reserve Bank?) With only one bank, a central bank, under the control of government, manipulation of the currency is very easy. Money lending is under the control of government. Those favored by government can get special deals from that central bank. People and businesses out of favor with the government may, no, will, have trouble accessing capital.
- Government Ownership of Communication and Transportation. When the government controls communication, control can mean anything. Government can control newspapers, magazines, periodicals, the telephone, television stations, radio stations, cell phones, the Internet, as well as CB and amateur radio. If you look at some countries around the world, like Cuba, Germany, China, Russia, North Korea, and others, the people only get the information the government wants them to get. It can censor every communications medium with impunity. Government can, in essence, indoctrinate our kids and grandkids, feeding them only the "news" that extols the benevolence of the government. This is not, by any stretch of the imagination, freedom.
- Government Ownership of Factories and Agriculture. With this control the government run unions are put in control of every business that produces anything, and control what crops are grown and not grown, and set the prices for those products. If the government decides that you don't need to eat corn, corn production stops. If the government decides that you don't need new technology gadgets, they shut down those companies that produce them. If the government believes that eating meat is unhealthy for you, the raising of cattle and pigs is stopped. Government can decide how many companies produce a particular product. Government can determine how many farms there will be, and what they will produce and sell. There is no more competitive market. Is this something that appeals to you?
- Government Control of Labor. Again, when the government controls education, it can indoctrinate our kids and grandkids. Go watch that old George Orwell movie, "1984." That's a pretty well done depiction of what a Communist system can do to you. At the

same time government can select students for various jobs the government wants filled. It can also determine which students may be allowed to go to a government college. In the workforce, wages will be set by government. There will be no incentive for anyone to work harder or smarter. Workers do the job the way the government wants it done. Our children will have no inspiration, no aspiration to improve their lives because the government controls all of that. What new technologies or medicines will be created? About as much technology and medicine as North Korea has developed.

- Corporate Farms and Regional Planning. Central planning has never worked in the history of the world, but the Communists of today will tell you that it's because those who came before just didn't know how to make it work. The Communists of today state that they know how to make it work. Ask self-admitted Socialist Ed Asner, retired movie actor. With all farms owned or controlled by the government, what crops will be allowed; which crops will be denied? Remember, the government is not full of the best and brightest minds. A Communist government is run by connected people, people who belong to the right groups or classes—the ruling class.
- Government Control of Education. In a Communist society the government takes our children as soon as they're weaned and toilet trained, and "educates" them as the state sees fit. The government decides if our kids or grandkids can go to college and, if they're allowed, what they will study. Most of our kids and grandkids will be trained for factory or farm work; there will be no free choice involved.

You may remember that during the years 1972 through 1984 the Communist Party of America had a candidate on the Presidential ballot, Gus Hall. In the 1984 Presidential election, Gus Hall had as his running mate, Angela Davis, of Black Panther and Socialist Party fame. If you don't remember that far back, visit *Wikipedia* and other online sources for a refresher. After the 1984 election Gus Hall announced that the Communist party USA would no longer submit a candidate to run for President under the Communist party banner. Hall said that it was no longer necessary since the Democrat party held the same principles and goals as the Communist party. Mr. Hall encouraged all of his Communist party supporters to vote for Democrats. No Democrat I've ever met or heard from will acknowledge those statements, but they're a matter of record.

Many of our kids and grandkids now espouse much of the Communist dogma as the way of the future for America. The reason for this view is that they've been indoctrinated to think, speak, and act that way by government schools, and Socialist-preaching college professors. This is very similar to the method by which Communist doctrine dictates. The Communists believe that if they take control of the following, their victory is assured:

- Infiltrate and take control of the education system
- Infiltrate and take control of the media
- Infiltrate and assume positions of power in government
- Disarms the population

How are they doing so far?

Our kids and grandkids are in school for a reason, to learn. Students in school are easily influenced and manipulated. These young men and women don't really have any idea what a Communist country looks like, or how it really operates. Where does Communism really work anywhere in the world? If advocates start citing Cuba, China, North Korea, or Russia as models, then you know that you're dealing with someone who has no understanding of Communism.

What our children don't understand is that in a Communist society, as in any form of government, there must be people who set policies and make laws. These people are called the ruling class. Those who enforce those rules or laws are just working class folks following orders. The media, all forms of it, are the information—propaganda—arm of the ruling class. The rest of us are called the "working class." This is the model set forth by Karl Marx, and illustrated in George Orwell's movie, "*1984*." Our children and grandchildren should have that book or the movie on their reading or viewing list of subjects to study in school. Don't hold your breath.

Many young people have this utopian view of everyone sharing everything as equals. The concept of rich people disappears. This view couldn't be further from the truth. Under Communism the people have no rights, no Constitution, no freedom. Citizens, now called the working class, do what the government dictates and, in return, the government "*takes care of them.*" Is that what you want for your kids and grandkids? Wasn't that something former President Bill Clinton once said, many years ago? "I have to get back to taking care of the American people." Yes, I think it was.

Principles of Capitalism

Individual Rights (as opposed to collective rights or collectivism). The most basic and widely understood principle of capitalism is that of individual rights to life, liberty, property, and voluntary contractual exchange. Individual rights encompass not only the right to control one's own life, liberty, and property, but also to defend those rights.

Limited Government. The limited role of government solely to the defense of the rights of individuals is also an important and almost universally understood principle of Capitalism.

Equal Justice under the Law. The principle of equal justice is critically important to the function of capitalism. Government must treat all individuals and organizations equally, refraining from giving any legal support to popular discriminatory practices. Government must also never succumb to the temptation to reward unsuccessful businesses_and individuals, with special benefits, or heap additional burdens on successful business.

Spontaneous Order. The tendency for Capitalist markets to order themselves naturally through the laws of supply and demand is one of the most familiar principles of Capitalism. When individual rights are respected, unregulated competition will naturally tend to reduce costs and increase the abundance of products that are in demand. This principle is also referred to as the *invisible hand of the marketplace.*

Private Ownership. The principle of private ownership is the Capitalist belief that property that is owned by the state, or is communally owned, is not respected or preserved as effectively as that property which is owned by private individuals or corporations. This principle is also commonly referred to as the *tragedy of the commons.*

Subsidiarity. Many free market organizations believe the principle of subsidiarity is essential to keeping capitalist markets competitive and dynamic. Subsidiarity is the principle that authority should always be vested at the lowest, most local possible level, where local knowledge and concerns can best guide decisions. The natural tendency is often to pass the buck, expecting higher authority to take responsibility for too much.

The Golden Rule. The principle of fair treatment of others is considered a core principle of the Capitalism by organizations such as the Heritage Foundation. Capitalism requires some level of mutual honesty to function best. We <u>achieve</u> this not only by dealing honestly with others, but by requiring honesty in return and holding those accountable who misrepresent or negotiate in bad faith.

If you look at the principles of Communism, you can see that nearly everything is controlled by the state (government). Under Communism, the government controls all education. Can you see a problem with that idea? With a ruling class, there would be no political party concept; it would disappear. Our current Constitution would, necessarily, have to be eliminated in favor of a new Constitution that is based on Communist principles. Rules, laws, and freedoms all become subject to the consent of the ruling class. We're seeing some not-so-subtle moves in that direction today.

State sovereignty is being subjugated more and more in favor of federal rule and, sadly, too many states are sitting on their collective hands. The Department of Justice is one arm of the federal government that carries out challenges to state laws that do not conform to the wishes of the federal government. If, or whatever reason, the control of the ruling party changes, then what is taught in schools could change, too. Wow, wouldn't that screw things up for those professors, huh? The result of all this stupidity is that our kids and grandkids will be indoctrinated; it's just that the form indoctrination would vary. Is that a good thing?

When government controls labor, the government can control the wages for every person. Merit and performance no longer matter. We—you me, your kids and grandkids—are just members of the working class; we're all the same. The ruling class has total power and control.

There was a time in America when people wanted to work, get married, have a few children, buy a home, save for retirement, and live the American dream. The government wasn't involved except in the most obscure ways. We expected the government to keep us safe from attack, get the mail delivered on time, and keep the roads, highways, and bridges in good shape. Otherwise, we didn't want to hear from them. The founders believed that government should be small, limited, nonintrusive, and out of the lives of the people.

People were free to pursue their dreams with no guarantee of success, but the freedom to try. I once read about a man who had been a millionaire several times, and been bankrupt several times. His advice to people was, "*If you're going bankrupt, do it in a hurry so you can get busy on your next business.*" The country's foundation is based on hard work, honesty, ethics, and instilling good characters and moral values in their children. Man oh man, has that changed. Has it changed for the better? The short answer is no. The government is now involved in almost every aspect of our lives, and parents seem to be losing the ability to parent their children, choosing instead to try and be friends with them.

There was a time when a handshake between two men or women was a contract, and it was honored. Now there are legions of lawyers, writing contracts that are so complicated that each side has to hire other lawyers just to figure out what is written. Today, honesty is the subject of scorn. Honor and honesty have been replaced with, "*If I don't get caught, it's not illegal.*" Honesty may mean that someone else will take advantage of you. Even high school and college kids believe that cheating on tests is acceptable if it gets them the grade they want. Their parents seem to agree with them. Advertisers use bait-and-switch tactics to get people to buy something they don't want. Politicians make promises—give their word—but have no intention of keeping them. A man's word today is of no value; it used to be his "*bond.*"

Politicians swear an oath when they take office, then completely ignore that oath in order to enrich themselves, and to gain power and control over others. This is America today?

America used to be the "melting pot." Immigrants came here to join and become part of America. Honest immigrants are still lining up today to come here because this is, or was, the land of the free. Those who immigrated back then became part of the fabric of America, its culture, its work ethic, and its dream. Now, America has become a "*stew pot.*" People come here legally and illegally, and bring their culture with them. They want to fly the flag of the country they left in order to come here. They demand that America adapt to them, not that they willingly adapt to America. And the strangest thing is, we let them.

As far as I'm concerned, if you immigrate to America, you should become an American, not someone from another country and culture demanding we accommodate you. If you don't like our culture, feel free to go back where you came from. If you're going to stay, adapt to and accept the American culture. When you became a citizen you swore allegiance to America. Act like it. You can have private ceremonies to honor occasions in your former country, but don't ask American to have some public celebration to appease you. If you want to wear clothing from your culture, feel free so long as you abide by our laws, like not covering your face when your driver's license photo is taken. This is America. You're not bringing your culture here; you've taken an oath to become an American, live that oath.

Today, we have Little Vietnam, Chinatown, the Barrio, Little Italy, and so on; enclaves of people who may be citizens, but remain tied to the very culture and customs they fled in order to come to America. There are millions of people that come to America illegally, and immediately want you and me to give them money, housing, medical care, and education for their children. They have no allegiance to our flag, our culture, or our country. They just want free stuff, or want to work here to get money to send home, but pay no taxes on what they earn. Many have been caught because they stole the social security number of a citizen. In addition, others come here illegally and become gang members, selling drugs, committing crimes, and filling our state prisons. Unfortunately, there are some Americans that believe this is fine. Over 21% of Arizona's state prison inmates are illegal aliens who have committed felonies, and some Americans think this is fine? What kind of America are we leaving our kids and grandkids?

There was a time when voting was a civic duty, and Americans looked forward to going to the polls, showing their identification, and voting for the candidates of their choice. Now, people are so "busy," they can't be bothered. Many of us want early ballots, absentee ballots, provisional ballots and, soon I fear, Internet voting. Even registering to vote has become oh so tedious for some Americans that they demand an Internet-based method, which is wide open to fraud. There are demands now to no longer require to present a photo ID in order to vote. Our own Attorney General is suing states that require a photo ID in order to vote, claiming that this requirement disenfranchises too many poor people. You have to show identification to rent a movie, drive a Chevvy Volt, get on an airplane, but don't have to show identification to vote? Really? Hey, Eric Holder, what are you smoking? Did you know that when Eric Holder appears at some function to give a speech a photo ID is required for everyone entering the hall? But he doesn't think you should have to show a photo ID to vote. Someone explain that to me.

For many, voting has become a chore they can't be bothered with, which is why, in a major general election, only about 55-60% of those eligible to vote bother to do so. Is that what American has become? We don't care who is elected to SERVE us? Boy, have times changed. Based on this response at the polls, it seems that many people would just as soon have a dictator in charge of the country as long as he or she throws them some free stuff. Is that the legacy you want to leave your kids and grandkids?

What Does the Government Do Well?

I know we grumble about government all the time. There seem to be so many government employees, all paid for by you and me. There are a seemingly endless number of agencies, designed to solve one problem or another, or to create a problem so they can solve it, that never seem to get solved, but with more money spent. There are currently about—are you ready for it—2.65 million Government employees. Wow. With all those employees, the government must be doing all kinds of swell things for us, right? Let's see.

Let's begin with Head Start, a government program, started in about 1965 says *Wikipedia* and other sources. Thus far this program has consumed about $180 billion tax dollars. Head Start is a sort of summer school for underprivileged kids to prepare them for kindergarten and beyond. Recently the government conducted an audit of the Head Start program, using about 20 data points. At the conclusion of the audit the government determined that Head Start had absolutely no positive effect on the children who participated in the program. That is to say, kids that didn't go through Head Start did just as well as the kids who did. From its inception until 2005 about 22 million children had gone through this pre-school program. That works out to about $8,100 per child for a summer school before kindergarten. That seems a little expensive to me. What have the past few administrations, Democrat and Republican, done about Head Start? Well, they increased the budget, of course. As recently as April, Congressman Ellis from Minnesota was stunned to learn that there had been no positive results. The first thing he said after he managed to get his jaw off the floor was, of course, to say, "*The program is underfunded.*" Why not, it's not his money, it's our. From my perspective this is just a very expensive daycare center that serves no other purpose. We have to give the government an "F" for this program.

One of the primary responsibilities of government is to secure our borders and protects American citizens. This is a government responsibility, and is so important that it's in the oath of office for the President, the Congress, and the Supreme Court members. They are, to the best of their ability, preserve, protect, and defend the Constitution of the United States. Members of Congress take an oath that's a little more detailed.

The oath of office for members of Congress says, in part, "*I do solemnly swear (or affirm) that I will support and defend the Constitution of the United States against all enemies, foreign and domestic . . . . so help me God.*" For some members of Congress, like the Muslim Congressman from Minnesota, or the Socialist member from New England, that last phrase must kind of stick in their craw.

Are U.S. borders secure? No. Has the government built the fence it authorized and funded? No. Has the government done all it can to remove people here illegally? No. Has the government deported those here illegally even if they have committed no crime? No. Of all the people that have entered this country illegally, how many are terrorists? No one knows because the government does not control our borders. Does the government pursue and deport people who overstay their Visa? No. The 19 foreigners, Middle-Eastern Terrorists, were all here legally at the time they carried out the murder of over 3,000 citizens. Give the government an "F" on protecting us from all enemies foreign and domestic.

We can't leave out the very important TSA, the people who seem to enjoy legally groping you. It was discovered earlier this year that there are over 50,000 employees of TSA, and of that number there are over 4,000 "administrators." Each of those administrators receive, on average, a little over $100,000 per year. The TSA budget is about $8 billion. I've read stories about how easy it is to get through TSA security checks with various weapons with no problems. We also learned earlier this year that a warehouse was discovered in Texas that is housing over $184 million in TSA equipment, much of which has never even been unwrapped. It's just sitting there. We paid for that. Just another government bureaucracy that is mismanaged, incompetent, and bloated, and absolutely unconcern with how they waste our money. After all, it's not their money. I've going to be benevolent and give this government agency a D.

Let's look at our borders, North and South. Are they secure? People who live in border states would give a big resounding NO on that one. Despite the lies from the Homeland Security Secretary, people who live in Texas, New Mexico, California, or Arizona know that illegal aliens are still pouring across the border. Are less of them invading America? Yes. That's because our economy is down so far, illegal aliens can't find illegal jobs if they manage to sneak into our country. Many years ago the Congress approved funding to build a double-fence, 12-feet high, across the entire border. But over the years, the funding was cut off for that fence. There are estimates of between 12-20 million illegal aliens in our country. Contrary to what some will say, they didn't all come here to get jobs. If that were so, why is over 21% of the Arizona state prison system populated with illegal aliens who have committed felonies? The statistics are similar in other border states as well.

In Arizona, the incidents of domestic violence, child abuse, rape, murder, robbery, and carjacking have increased, and a large percentage of the incidents can be attributed to illegal aliens. The illegal alien invasion doesn't stop with border states. Illegal aliens can be found in all or nearly all states in America. You have to ask yourself, why would the federal government refuse to build the fence so the border can be controlled? Does it really matter if three million illegal or five million illegal aliens come into America each year? The shear cost of dealing with people illegally entering our country is staggering, but the government is spending our money, not theirs.

If you get cable TV, you can watch shows such as "Border Wars," "Border Wars Texas," and "Drug Wars" on the *National Geographic* and *Discovery* channels. Evidently the Secretary of Homeland Security can't find those channels on her television because she thinks border security is just fine. Or does she know better but has to spout the government propaganda?

In summary, our southern border is still a sieve despite the tremendous efforts of our Border Patrol. In Arizona the drug cartels now come across the border from Mexico and there have been numerous armed conflicts with them inside Arizona.

I give the federal government an F on protecting our borders.

Let's look at delivering the mail. Starting back in 1775, before we declared our independence, mail service began. That's impressive. The United States Postal Service (USPS) is described as a business-like semi-governmental agency. Under that definition the USPS is a non-profit entity. Although the USPS operates somewhat autonomously now, it is still under the regulatory control of the federal government. I guess that means if the mail is late or not getting delivered, it's the government's fault.

I can remember the '50's when a postage stamp was 3-cents, and a postcard was a penny. Postage fees have gone up over 1,500% since those days. With the advancing technology, the need to mail letters has diminished considerably in favor of sending an e-mail, or the use of Facebook®, cheap phone rates, Skype® and Twitter®. The response from the USPS was not to innovate but, rather, to keep raising the cost of postage. I think it's fair to say that there are no smart business people running the USPS, but since they're a government entity, they're wasting our money, not their own.

In my neighborhood there are days when the mail should be delivered, but isn't. If the regular postal carrier is on vacation or out sick, and no other carrier picks up the route. Oh, well. I've also experienced situations where I was sitting in my kitchen and saw the mail truck go by. When I go out to get the mail I find a notice that a package wasn't delivered because no one was home, which was a lie. The mail carrier couldn't be bothered to get out of the truck. I then had to wait until the next day and drive to the local post office, stand in line, and present the notice to pick up my package. When I complain, the person at the counter just kind of rolls his or her eyes, and says, "Will there be anything else?"

Given the tremendous rise in prices, and the chaotic delivery schedule, with no one you can complain to, I give the government an F.

There have been times when our government has ordered our military into combat for various reasons, none of which were declared wars. That alone would give the government an F, but there's more. The United States has never "won" a war or conflict since WWII. We send our military into combat with no definition of what victory looks like. The government has now added the "national-building" component to incursions into foreign countries. Take your pick—Korea, Vietnam, Iraq, and Afghanistan. None were declared wars, not in the sense that the Congress votes on a declaration of war. As far as Korea goes, we're still there, 57 years after "hostilities" ended. Why are we there? If you look at Vietnam, you can only conclude that we lost even though the military never lost a battle during all those years. We quit and came home because the politicians didn't have the will to win. If you look at Iraq, we invaded, captured or killed all the bad guys in charge, and then we stayed, and stayed, and stayed to help rebuild Iraq into something approaching a "democracy." How has that worked out? It's a big fat zero. Iraq is a country with centuries of tribal culture governance. They don't understand central government, and aren't all that keen on building one. You can say the same thing about Afghanistan. We, more-or-less, invaded the country to kill, capture, or drive out the Taliban and Al Quada, and capture or kill Bin Laden. We kept our warriors in this third-world country, trying again to build a democracy based on central government. Have you seen a map of Afghanistan? It's a collection of wide open dirt patches, and almost impossible mountains containing thousands of huge caves. This is also a tribal culture that really didn't want us there in the first place. These countries do not equate to Germany or Japan in 1947. Iraq and Afghanistan will never be first-world cultures, and will never adapt to a central government democracy. How many more of our combat warriors have to die before our government figures it out? Is there a grade lower than F? If so, assign it to our government.

The federal government is supposed to build and maintain our interstate highway system and its associated bridges and dams. How has that worked out? In just the past three years I've listened to federal government officials talking about how we need to "invest"—that means more of our tax dollars—in our "infrastructure." They were supposed to be keeping our "infrastructure" in good shape all along, but somehow they just didn't get around to funding it, and now need more of our money to fix the infrastructure. To me this is a dereliction of duty by our federal government, and they should all be ashamed of themselves. They're so busy giving away our tax dollars to social programs, they forget their prime directives. I have to give the federal government a D on infrastructure.

How about the General Services Administration (GSA)? This agency, with a staff of about 12,000 people, and a budget of about $20 billion, is supposed to save the government money as they rent, lease, and buy buildings. They also negotiate the purchase of supplies and related equipment. We all watched the stories of how this agency, from the top down, took our money and threw themselves a big party in Las Vegas—the town that the President said we shouldn't visit during hard times. They spent tens of thousands of dollars on multiple "site-selection trips" to Las Vegas. They had parties, shot videos, hired clowns and magicians, gave out all kinds of gifts, consumed a big pile of $4 shrimp, and all in all, had a wonderful time to the tune of nearly $800 million of our tax dollars. Another bunch of GSA employees flew to Hawaii for a dedication ceremony, which lasted about one hour, but took them five days to complete, on our money. The top GSA employee then takes the Fifth Amendment when asked questions about the expenses in front of a Congressional committee. So, a couple of sacrificial lambs were told to resign. Congress is conducting an investigation—we all know how that's going to turn out—and the rest of the GSA employees just keep showing up and drawing a paycheck. A fellow named Bob Beckel, who appears on a Fox News show called *The Five*, stated in April that "Hey, this kind of stuff has been going on forever. It doesn't matter if it's Republicans or Democrats in charge; waste is a part of government." That makes me feel all warm and fuzzy. How about you? So, what grade do you give the government for this agency? I'm opting for an "F" this time.

Let's not forget the Secret Service miscreants. Any person in their right mind would question the standard line uttered by agents once the plane takes off for a foreign country mission—"*Wheels up, rings off*." Isn't that classy? But, let's not throw the baby out with the bathwater here. By and large the Secret Service does a magnificent job. In this prostitute case it was about 10-15 agents, plus a few military personnel and, maybe, some administration officials. They were the ones that took part in this drinking, prostitution acquiring escapade. Many have, and more will, lose their jobs and their careers. My question is: where were the supervisors and where was the leadership of these agents while they were in Cartajegna, Columbia? I'm going out on a limb and giving the Secret Service a B-.

I'm still looking for something the government does well. Unfortunately I haven't found anything, but I'm still looking.

How Many Members of Congress are Also Members of the Socialist Caucus?

I have been calling Democrats out as socialists for a long time, as have many of you. Take a look at this. The following is a list of name of 70 Democrat members Congress clearly identified as members of the Socialist Caucus. There are no Congressional Republicans that are members of this caucus. What does this mean to you and me? It means that these 70 people support the principles of Socialism. It is based on a 2009 report, so some Democrat members were defeated and are no longer on the list, but there are newer members who may well be signatories on this caucus.

The Socialist Party of America releases the names of members of their caucus periodically to, I suppose, brag about their influence. There are several places you can look to see the most current list of names.

According to The Socialist Party of America newsletter, back in 2009, it touted the names of these70 Congressional democrats as being current signatories to their caucus. This admission has been posted in several places.

Co-Chairs Raúl M. Grijalva (AZ-07), Lynn Woolsey (CA-06)

Vice Chairs Diane Watson (CA-33); Sheila Jackson-Lee (TX-18); Mazie Hirono (HI-02); Dennis Kucinich (OH-10)

Senate Member Bernie Sanders (VT)

House Members:

Neil Abercrombie (HI-01)h; Tammy Baldwin (WI-02); Xavier Becerra (CA-31); Madeleine Bordallo (GU-AL); Hon. Robert Brady (PA-01); Corrine Brown (FL-03); Michael Capuano (MA-08); André Carson (IN-07); Donna Christensen (VI-AL); Yvette Clarke (NY-11); William "Lacy" Clay (MO-01); Emanuel Cleaver (MO-05); Steve Cohen (TN-09); John Conyers (MI-14); Elijah Cummings (MD-07); Hon. Danny Davis (IL-07); Peter DeFazio (OR-04); Rosa DeLauro (CT-03); Donna F. Edwards (MD-04); Keith Ellison (MN-05); Sam Farr (CA-17); Hon. Chaka Fattah (PA-02); Bob Filner (CA-51); Barney Frank (MA-04); Marcia L. Fudge (OH-11); Alan Grayson (FL-08); Luis Gutierrez (IL-04); John Hall (NY-19); Phil Hare (IL-17); Maurice Hinchey (NY-22); Michael Honda (CA-15); Jesse Jackson, Jr. (IL-02); Eddie Bernice Johnson (TX-30); Hank Johnson (GA-04); Marcy Kaptur (OH-09); Carolyn Kilpatrick (MI-13); Barbara Lee (CA-09); John Lewis (GA-05); David Loebsack (IA-02); Ben R. Lujan (NM-3); Carolyn Maloney (NY-14); Ed Markey (MA-07); Jim McDermott (WA-07); James McGovern (MA-03); George Miller (CA-07); Gwen Moore (WI-04); Jerrold Nadler (NY-08); Eleanor Holmes-Norton (DC-AL); John Olver (MA-01); Ed Pastor (AZ-04); Donald Payne (NJ-10); Chellie Pingree (ME-01); Charles Rangel (NY-15); Laura Richardson (CA-37); Lucille Roybal-Allard (CA-34); Bobby Rush (IL-01); Linda Sánchez (CA-47); Jan Schakowsky (IL-09); José Serrano (NY-16); Louise Slaughter (NY-28); Pete Stark (CA-13); Bennie Thompson (MS-02); John Tierney (MA-06); Hon. Nydia Velazquez (NY-12); Maxine Waters (CA-35); Mel Watt (NC-12); Henry Waxman (CA-30); Peter Welch (VT-AL); Robert Wexler (FL-19);

I have a quick comment on this list. The word, "honorable," was removed from each of those names, by me. I've become so disenchanted with politicians that I can no longer refer to many of them as "The Honorable . . . ." So many of them have done such dishonorable things while in office that I think they've lost the right to that title, but that's just me.

It's a big list. As an Arizonan I'm not surprised at all to see Ed Pastor and Raul Grijalva's names on the list. They've done everything they can to destroy Arizona and America since they've been in office. Grijalva even went on the record to encourage everyone across the country to boycott Arizona as a protest against the immigration enforcement law, SB1070. He's not that bright, but very loyal to illegal aliens and all things Socialist. Ed Pastor has been actively working against America for decades. Not surprisingly, both men are from very Hispanic districts.

You might want to look through this list and find those representatives from your district. If your representative is on the list, you may want to attend one of their campaign speeches, or a town hall, or even send them an e-mail, and ask them, "Why did you sign on to the Socialist Party of America Caucus?" Then listen to them wiggle and squirm, and deny, deny, and deny. But you now know better. These 70 should all be defeated and sent packing. When you have 70 members of Congress supporting Socialism, it has to affect their votes. Take a look at the voting records of your representatives and see if they're voting FOR or AGAINST America.

The Government and The People—Not a Love Story

When I was growing up, I vaguely remember President Truman and President Eisenhower. :I remember President Kennedy very well. While in the military I served in Vietnam in 1969-1970. I did indeed remember President Nixon because in 1970 he announced to the nation that no American combat troops were in Cambodia. At the time of that statement I was sitting on what was called a Tango boat, 21.7 kilometers inside Cambodia, providing communication support to some U.S. Marines that were further down the way cleaning out bad guys. I remember learning that President Kennedy was a very rich man, living off a $1 Billion trust fund set up by the Kennedy family. Mostly, I remember not seeing or hearing from the President much at all. Today, however, it seems as if this President is on television almost every day. Enough already, Mr. President. Go spend some time actually being President.

I notice one very important thing about politicians, and that is technology. Yes, technology changed everything. Some of the changes were good. Many of the changes were not so good, especially for our military warriors.

When Harry Truman was President, after the end of WWII—the last war this nation ever won—television was just coming into commercial use. What we knew about the President or Congress was sparse, and it generally came from the radio or newspapers. I know that my parents, like most parents in the neighborhood, rarely ever mentioned politics or politicians. For the most part the federal government was that bunch of suits way back in Washington, D.C., mostly staying out of our lives. Parents trusted that the government was doing its job, and citizens went about their lives. In those days the people trusted their government. How about now?

If you think about it, what is the government doing that is good for you? Well, if you're on food stamps, getting unemployment checks, and your kids are being fed at school, you'd probably think the government is doing just fine. And you probably don't care much about who is really paying the bill for you. Another thing that we now know is that far too many people have no idea, nor do they care, that the government has no money except the money it confiscates from taxpayers. Remember that quote from some woman who was standing in line for a chance to get a handout? When asked where the money came that the President was giving away, she said, "*I don't know, from the President's stash?*" That speaks volumes.

If you remember back several years, the government took away many of our deductions from our tax reporting. We could no longer deduct interest on credit cards for one. In return, the government promised to keep the income tax rate low. Anyone remember what the rates were then? No? I don't either, and that's what they counted on. They took away deductions and, within a few years, raised tax rates. And tax rates have been going up ever since. This brings up a good question, the answer to which has never been given by the government. "Just how much of the money I earn will you allow me to keep and spend as I want?" We hear story after story of waste, fraud, and corruption in government, and yet so-called investigations never result in any arrests, convictions, or firings of government employees. They've figured out that if they just say they're investigating, people will forget. And we do forget. It never stops. So many of us are paying income taxes to subsidize that waste, fraud, and corruption while the government sits on its collective backsides and talks and talks about how this has to stop. But the waste, fraud, and corruption continue unabated. The government is so large that it's impossible to provide enough oversight to stop all of this wasted money, and the Congress doesn't really try. They talk about it; politicians are really good at posturing and talking, but very poor at actually getting anything done.

Our government officials in Washington seem to be living large, don't they? They have lavish offices, large staffs, lots and lots of time off, and wear $3,000 suits, all paid for by you and me. Up until recently they also were allowed to receive inside trading information and act on it, something you and I would go to prison for if we did it. Wouldn't you like to have a job where you work three, sometimes four days a week, sit in a bunch of meetings that resolve nothing, then go meet the boys and girls in the bar, or in their private dining room; maybe take a swim in your private pool, or workout in your private gym, all paid for by you and me? They live well, work very little, and get automatic pay raises every year, even while we're unemployed, on food stamps, scratching for something to eat, and a way to pay our rent or house payment.

It doesn't seem to faze them, though. Oh, they'll get in front of a TV camera and talk about feeling our pain, but then do nothing about it. Government is the ruling class.

I have heard people in government talk about creating jobs at least 5,000 times. Time out. The only jobs the government creates are government jobs, and wow, have they created a lot of them. The government cannot create one private sector job, not one. What they could do is reduce regulations and restrictions on businesses, reduce all of the additional taxes heaped on businesses so they could grow and prosper, expand, and hire people. But government refuses to do what needs to be done. The government believes, in the aggregate, that they are the solution to all problems. Despite decades of failure, each new crop of politicians believe that they are the brightest and smartest, and know how to fix things, and they usually fail. But they keep on drawing those big salaries. U.S. Senators and U.S. House Reps earn around $170,000, plus or minus, with a built-in raise each year, while voting not to give cost of living allowance (COLA) raises to people on social security. They also vote not to give COLA raises to retired military personnel. They get theirs, though.

Has anyone ever looked at the financial statements of a U. S. Senator or Congressman when they go into office, and see what their net worth is at that time? Then, when they leave office, check their financial records and net worth? Why are so many of these people becoming millionaires while serving in public office? How can that happen? I'm sure it's not because they vote for bills that carve out some land for a special project, and by sheer coincidence, discover that the Senator or Congressman happens to own a few thousand acres right in the path of the development. And getting that insider trading information and using it to enrich themselves is all perfectly legal, right? Yeah, and I've got beachfront property in Arizona I'd like to sell you.

Why do many Senators and Congressmen and women lease very expensive cars? Oh, I remember. They don't pay the monthly lease, but charge it to the taxpayers of their state or district. There was a story about on House Rep who drove some high end vehicle, and the monthly lease payment was over $1,000, all paid for by his constituents. He couldn't drive a Honda Civic, no, no. He had to have that luxury SUV so he could travel in style. Does that sound like a public servant or a con man? I think every member of Congress should drive a Chevy Volt, selected from the motor pool each day.

Why aren't elected public servants subject to the same laws that we live by? Charles Rangel, a Harlem, New York Congressman for about 100 years, got caught evading federal income taxes, by not reporting income from a condo he owned in another country. Did he get arrested? No. Did he even get censured by the Congress? No. He walked after paying the back taxes. Do you think we'd be treated the same way? If so, why not talk to Wesley Snipes, who went to prison for evading taxes? When Barney Franks, a Massachusetts Congressman, was caught by the police for running a male prostitution ring out of the basement of his town house, did he get arrested? No, of course not. All he did was say that he didn't know his male lover was running this male prostitution ring out of the basement of a townhouse he owned. I thought ignorance of the law was no excuse. Oh, that's right. That only applies to us, not to the rulers in Washington. He got off without any charges being filed. Ain't America grand?

Senator Chris Dodd was proven to have gotten a sweetheart deal from a mortgage company for a home he bought. The deal was blatantly a favor or, as I would call it, a bribe. It screamed for an investigation. Did anything happen? Of course not. Now Duke Cunningham, a San Diego, California Republican Congressman was a crook, and really stupid. He took bribes. He was selling his vote all over the place. And then the idiot didn't have the common sense to hide the money. Oh, no, he spent and spent. He bought a fancy house, a luxury boat, vacations, great clothes, and then he got caught. He as tried, and convicted. He is now serving several years at Club Fed, the prison for the ruling class.

Of course, Anthony Weiner, a real weenie, had to resign his office as a Congressman from New York because he liked to take pictures of his genitalia and send the photos to various women with whom he was communicating. This married man lied about it, but as usual got caught. He tried new lies and got caught again. Finally, in utter humiliation, he resigned. But since he served several years in Congress, he'll get a nice paycheck when he reaches retirement age. Then he'll be able to afford a better cell phone camera. What he did is a felony, but he was never prosecuted. He is now making noises that he might want to run for Mayor of New York City. They should elect him. New York City deserves him.

Chris Lee probably holds the record for the fastest resignation. He was a Republican Congressman, married with kids, and for some reason took cell phone photos of himself with his shirt off, and went trolling on dating web sites, sending this photo to a few prospects. Unfortunately, someone recognized him and turned him in to the House of Representatives. When Speaker Boehner got word, and saw the photo, he called Lee into his office, asked him if he had done what was reported. Lee said that he had. Speaker Boehner said he wanted Lee's resignation on his desk by the end of the day, and got it.

There have been homosexual Congressmen who got caught tapping their foot in a men's room at an airport, Congressmen who got caught sending graphic messages to House Pages and got caught. Is this really where the best and brightest are residing? I don't think so.

In Washington our public servants insulate themselves from the people they represent. Actually, these politicians believe that they rule their constituents, not serve them. I was once in a heated debate with my Congressman at a local state function. He was about eight inches taller than me, so I would have needed a step stool to look him in the eye, but we were going at it, arguing over CAFTA, the Central America Free Trade Agreement. I wanted to know why a free trade agreement takes 1,200 pages to describe, and he was telling me it was too complicated for me to understand, and I was in his face, but it was just arguing, not fighting. One of his "handlers" came over, inserted himself between us, and informed me that the Congressman had to go. I've been to town hall meetings with Congressmen and women, and when I ask a tough question, I get the same answer you have probably received if you ask pointed questions. "I'm investigating that situation and expect to have an answer within a few weeks." And you never hear from him or her again.

Some years ago, here in Arizona, Senator Jon Kyl agreed to meet with several of us who were members of the County party's Executive Guidance Committee after one of his Coffee Klatches with constituents. We filed in to the meeting, and I ended up right across the table from the Senator. Within a few seconds, one of his "handlers" came over and whispered in his ear, whereupon he got up and moved to the end of the table. Gee, I showered and wore deodorant; what was the problem? He was ostensibly there to listen to our concerns over a proposed Amnesty bill that he and Senator McCain, along with Senator Ted Kennedy were pushing. But instead of listening to us, the Senator launched into this silly slide show of how wonderful the immigration reform bill he was championing would be for all Americans. He just rambled on for about 20 minutes, and I finally got fed up. So, I interrupted his presentation and told him there was no way this bill was going anywhere. It was stupid, ill conceived, and put all responsibility on law enforcement to respond to all these *"triggers"* scattered throughout. The bill was, as usual these days, hundreds of pages long. I told him to pack up his show and start listening. When I finished my rant, the lady next to me—a very nice woman—told the Senator that with a stupid bill like this we could end up with blood in the streets, and it would be on his hands. Within minutes the Senator packed up his slide show and exited stage left. He wasn't there to listen; he was there to lecture. To be fair, Senator John McCain isn't like that. No, Senator McCain just doesn't lower himself to meet with people who might talk back, not unless they are donating a lot of money to his campaign. If you give him a lot of money, he has time for you. If not, you'll never get within a mile of the guy. Don't be fooled.

As I have said dozens of times, Senator McCain is no war hero. No, Senator McCain is a survivor, and he should be celebrated for withstanding over five years of torture—real torture—in the Hanoi Hilton, a North Vietnam prison camp. But he wasn't alone there. Over 500 other combat warriors also served time in that horrendous prison, and Senator McCain was one of them. After all the torture he endured he did break down and made a video condemning the U.S. involvement in Vietnam. The Senator did survive and come home. He was busted up, in poor health, but he survived. I admire him for his ability to survive all those years. His wife stayed faithful during that entire ordeal. Once Senator McCain came home, he finished his military service and then decided that a political future was not that far away. He needed money. So, our beloved hero, John McCain, divorced the wife who had stood beside him all those years, and married a woman with money. Maybe he got some advice from Senator John Kerry, who has a history of marrying rich women. Heck, Kerry wouldn't be worth squat without a woman supporting him. And Kerry now gets his ketchup for free!

We need to remember that John Kerry served in Vietnam, for 83 days. He shot himself in the foot with his own weapon, and received a Purple Heart. That's the character of Senator John Kerry. Senator John Kerry is the only military man I've ever heard of—and I served 20 years in the Navy—who received a Purple Heart for a self-inflicted wound. Senator John Kerry wrote himself up for all kinds of medals, and got out of Vietnam because of them. He served about the same amount of time in Vietnam as Al Gore. When Kerry returned, he supposedly threw his medals over the fence of the White House in protest of the war. It was discovered later that he threw someone else's medals over the fence. He kept his medals, and displays them proudly in his Senate offices. This traitor also went to Paris to insert himself into the peace talks being conducted there, though he was still on active duty, and had no authority to be there. There's no doubt in my mind that John Kerry is a traitor to his country, but he's a sitting Senator. His picture hangs on the wall of a memorial building in Ho Chi Minth city (formerly known as Saigon), and has the thanks of the North Vietnamese for assisting them. He should be in prison.

Back in May the Democrat members of Congress held a weekend training session to learn how to take almost any news event and make it a racial charge against Republicans. They had to be trained on how to manipulate a news story so as to make themselves look good and opponents look bad. I was surprised. I thought the Democrats had already mastered the art of media manipulation.

Republicans also need some fresh faces in leadership. The Speaker of the House, and the Senate Minority Leader, need to be replaced. Republicans need fighters in leadership positions, not go along to get along milk toast people currently occupying those positions. All of us need Senators and Congressmen and women who listen to their constituents, and represent them. The clubhouse mentality currently in place is, literally, killing our great country.

It's way past time for Americans to stand up and fight back. It would be a wonderful thing if every citizen who gave a damn would start confronting these politicians, and demand answers, votes, and behavior that represents constituents, and do it again and again and again, at every opportunity.

Truth In Journalism is Dead in America

While I do believe that this President is a Communist, he is essentially a puppet of the manipulators. The biggest enemy of America is, in my view, the media. Over the past 60 years television has become more and more prominent, and intrusive, in our lives. It should be noted that a poll of the media, taken just a few years ago, revealed that approximately 85% of journalists vote Democrat. Do you think that bias towards the left influences what they write and speak? When you couple in the more recent advancements in the Internet and now Twitter, the amount of news, real and invented, has risen even more dramatically. I remember seeing President Eisenhower on television a couple of times. Generally, he was just talking about how good things were, the Korean "war" was drawing to a close, and we moved on with our lives. With the passage of time, newspapers seemed to get larger with a lot more advertising. The headlines became more sensational, and the old cliché of "*If it bleeds it leads*" became more prominent each year.

As television was on the air more hours each day, the need for shows and news reporting seemed to increase exponentially. Interestingly, it seems that as the quality of journalism declined, so did the quality of non-news television shows. It must be a coincidence. I've watched lots of local reporters giving us the news, and many of them seem to be challenged by the English language. As time went on, television shows needed more news "anchors" to serve up the stories each night. I remember Edward R. Murrow, Walter Cronkite, and Chet Huntley and David Brinkley. What I remembered most about them was that they just reported the news, and if they had a bias one way or the other, I never knew it from their broadcasts. They were articulate; they knew how to weave the story, and it kept your interest. Today, news reporters and reporterettes bring their agenda and their bias with them. It's usually pretty clear which side of the story they favor. Now we have the likes of Brian Williams of NBC, who is one of the worst news broadcasters around now that perky Katie Couric has been dispatched. Then there's a cable channel, MSNBC, run by NBC, which is a major propaganda arm of the Communist (oops, Democrat) party. They have people on that show that, by my unofficial count, spout 80% more lies about all things religious and conservative than any other network. One, a guy named Schultz, seems to enjoy calling conservatives, like Laura Ingraham, *right wing sluts*. At first I thought he was talking about "Snookie." That's objective journalism to him. Now, to be fair, MSNBC, like CNN, only has a few viewers, mostly relatives and friends of the employees, which seems fitting. One of those MSNBC hosts, Chris Matthews, cannot discuss any story without slandering or demeaning a conservative, a Republican, or a Christian. He's just compelled to do it because, as he tells it, "*I get a thrill up my leg*" when Obama speaks. That says it all.

Then there's Jon Stewart of MTV. Yes, Jon Stewart reports the news so that children can understand it, even though most of it is manufactured so Stewart can get a joke in there somewhere. But Mr. Stewart thinks very highly of himself, and he gets a lot of money to spew his childish baloney. There have been a few surveys that show that young people watch Stewart's show to get "*the news*," even though it's a comedy show with made up news stories. I'd mention Stephen Colbert but he's of so little importance, I don't want to waste the ink.

As newspapers got larger and larger, with more advertising and more departments, management had to hire writers and reporters. It is very clear to me that today there is a dearth of quality people from which to choose to fill these jobs. And don't forget the politically correct quota system at newspapers and TV stations. If you read a newspaper now, you can probably find multiple typographical errors, incomplete and one-sided stories, and opinion articles based on nothing but the vacuum that exists between the ears of the author. Who, what, when, where, and why is long gone now. The number of advertisers has gone way up, seemingly lead by automobile dealerships. I see the same auto advertising, some of which fill up an entire page, running two, three, four times a week in my local paper. Is it possible that Arizonans have an auto fetish? We do like our pickup trucks.

Television news has deteriorated into a poorly written, poorly produced, and poorly directed reality show, with the primary parts being played by females who are blonde haired, leggy, big breasted, and have trouble speaking a proper sentence. Maybe that's the checklist for hiring TV reporterettes today. There seems to be a quota on a lot of local television shows. In Arizona there appears to be a demand for more Latino reporters, reporterettes, and weather guessers. Some are pretty good, most are very bad. There's this one lady on a local channel who cannot give a weather forecast while looking at the camera. Her eyes are glued off camera at the monitor to the side, out of camera range, so she can find various cities and counties in the state, and she's been doing this for many years. You would think she could figure out where the cities and counties are by now. She does however fill a quota.

Back in the '60's and '70's, news reporters reported the story without injecting their bias. They went out, interviewed all of the principle players, took notes, got the who, what, when, where, and why, came back, wrote the story, and when it was their turn, gave the report. It just doesn't work that way today. Other than some reporter or reporterette standing out in a windy, rainy storm telling us that it's windy and rainy, using terrible grammar, everything else seems to be scripted from some other news source. They're more like ventriloquist dummies.

I've read several articles, and heard from many people, that the newsroom at a newspaper is staffed with like-minded people. Since at least 85% of the media votes Democrat, you can guess where their allegiance lies. In those newsrooms, the boss assigns stories and, it appears, tells the reporter to whom the story is assigned how that story is to be written, or presented if it's going to be on television. Some newspapers have writers who are so "famous" that they decide what they're going to write about, and they already know what their slant will be, so the boss just leaves them alone.

At the New York Times, there's Paul Krugman, a self-identified Socialist, who hates all things conservative or Christian, writes lies, but he does it so well people actually pay attention to him. I think he's received a few awards, too. They're tarnished because he's such a liar, but he no doubt looks at them lovingly each night. Another is Maureen Dowd, this spinster who can't seem to find a man who will put up with her, if she's even interested, writes these occasional screeds that condemn Republican women, conservatives, and you know the song. What's interesting is that many newspapers around the country take their news stories from the pages of the New York Times. The thinking evidently is, if the New York Times wrote the story, that's good enough for them, and they ran with it. It's a major case of laziness if you ask me. Independent research, investigation, and a search for the truth, are no longer part of the equation for the print media. There are exceptions, of course. The Wall Street Journal is essentially a financial newspaper that runs a lot of stories that seem to be down the middle. They praise what they believe is good, and condemn that which they believe is bad.

We can't leave out the nighttime comedy show entertainers like Jay Leno, David Letterman, Jimmy Fallon, and Jimmy Kimmel. Every one of them seems to relish the opportunity to slander, demean, and insult conservative women, and Republican politicians. Probably the worst is Dave Letterman. This guy, for years, was having sex with his female employees, almost all of them. It appeared to be a condition of employment. He did this while he was living with a woman who gave birth to his child. She eventually married him. It didn't seem to slow him down a bit. Where were the feminists? They were nowhere to be found. After all, Letterman loves the leftists so the feminists aren't going to say a word. Letterman has also had some very crude, rude, and obscene things to say about Sarah Palin and her children. On one show he said that while Palin and her family were at a Yankees baseball game in New York, Palin's daughter was "knocked up" by Alex Rodriguez in the seventh inning. That's what passes for humor in Letterman's peanut brain. He's not capable of telling a joke that isn't crude or attacks some other person. Yet CBS pays this little man about $30 million each year, so he must believe he's really important and relevant. The truth is that he's an empty-headed moron whose only claim to fame is that he can be counted on to carry the water for Democrats, and attack Republicans.

Jay Leno is slightly better. He doesn't stoop as low as Letterman, but he rarely misses an opportunity to try and get a laugh by making fun of other people. That's the formula for so-called comedians today. He knows a lot about cars, but not much else. He has been outspoken in his support of homosexual marriage.

Jimmy Fallon is just a teenager in an adult body. His show is truly insipid and is often outrageous. When he invited Michelle Bachman to appear on his show, the band struck up the tune, "*Lying Assed Bitch*" to serenade her as she came on stage. That's the crudeness of Jimmy Fallon. No, nothing was done about this slanderous act. He's funny if your brain quit growing when you reached puberty. His target audience is uneducated, stunted-growth drunks and drug addicts. He always seems happy to talk about the joy of getting drunk, or doing drugs.

Jimmy Kimmel isn't worth many words. He used to be a comical football forecaster for a cable TV NFL sports show. smf then ended up on ABC with his show, Jimmy Kimmel Live. He also suffers from a lack of maturity, and a desire to make fun of other people just to get a laugh, and he calls it comedy.

A lot of young people watch these shows, but today that's not saying much. There are a lot of weak-minded people splayed out on the couch, eating chips, and drinking beer between hits off their bong pipe, and they occasionally show up and vote.

There are print magazines like Time and Newsweek that have pretty much gone the way of the dinosaur. With the advancement of the Internet, which was invented by Al Gore I believe, reading a weekly or monthly magazine is so yester-decade.

There are always those incidents occuring that make you scratch your head and wonder, what the heck was he thinking? Take for example, CBS News anchor, Dan Rather.

Dan Rather was exposed as a liar and a fraud. This stemmed from his actions in 2004 during the presidential campaign between sitting President, George W. Bush, and Senator John Kerry, who served 83 days in Vietnam in case you didn't remember. During a broadcast, Rather actually presented some documents that he intended to use to smear the sitting President, George W. Bush. He stated that these documents proved that George W. Bush was AWOL from his National Guard duty, didn't complete his required time with the National Guard and was, therefore, unfit for reelection. Within a few hours there were nearly 1,000 people who sent feedback showing that the documents were complete fabrications. But Dan Rather refused to admit it. Some of that feedback came from high school kids who found these documents laughable. Rather left CBS News within a few months. To this day he refuses to admit that he tried to fool the American people and cause them to vote for John Kerry.

We have television news reporters presenting the news, as they interpret it, and we have politicians who will lie to mislead and slant opinion to serve their own purposes. There is a dearth of character in the media and politics. There are exceptions, of course, but in the aggregate, more and more people have come to understand that if they want accurate news, don't read the so-called mainstream media. That's not news; that's propaganda. One of the biggest offenders is the *Old Gray Lady*, the New York Times. This paper is dedicated to supporting and helping Democrats, and running stories to slander Republicans. Senior management often pretend to be objective, but several of their employees make no bones about it; they don't like conservatives; they deny that there is a God; they don't like Republicans, and they intend to slander them at every opportunity.

Gun Control and the Second Amendment to the Constitution

A lot of people in our great country don't like guns, don't own a gun, and are afraid to have guns around. That's fine. There's no law that makes anyone own a gun. However, there is a pesky Second Amendment to the U.S. Constitution that says, in part, ". . . . the right of the people to keep and bear arms shall not be infringed." That portion of the Second Amendment really bugs some people, mostly leftists. These folks, many politicians among them, try to do everything they can to restrict or deny gun ownership by law abiding citizens. They don't do much to stop criminals from getting guns, but I guess that's because it's a lot harder to accomplish. Going after lawful citizens is much easier.

Our own U.S. Attorney General has said that he doesn't believe that the Second Amendment gives citizens the right to keep and bear arms. What? I hate to tell you this, Eric, baby, but you are required to respect and defend the law, and the Constitution. Does it really matter what the Attorney General thinks? His job is to enforce the law as written. The Attorney General takes an oath to protect and defend the Constitution, and the Supreme Court has said that the Second Amendment means what it says, and the Attorney General says, not so fast? This Attorney General is another one of those people who is living proof that there's a large chasm between education and intelligence. In the Attorney General's case, there appears to be a big chasm between what the law says, and what he intends to enforce.

A reading of the founder's documents tells us that the reason for putting that amendment in the Constitution is simple; citizens should have arms so they can, if necessary, rise up against a tyrannical government. Ahhh, the plot thickens. Government doesn't want citizens armed because an unarmed citizenry is much easier to control. The government fears that citizens might finally get fed up and throw government officials out on their . . . . ear?

There are many cities that ignore the Supreme Court, and ignore the Second Amendment. Some state governments, and some city governments, impose all kinds of laws on their residents when it comes to their ability to buy and own firearms. These governments make it nearly impossible to get a permit in order to buy a gun. They impose limits on a citizen's ability to carry a gun anywhere. There was even a case in New York where a man's home was invaded by criminals, armed criminals. The owner was able to get to his gun and shoot one of the invaders. As it turned out, he didn't have the right permits and permission to even own a gun. So, he was arrested and charged with unlawful possession of a firearm. What he should have done, evidently, was allow the invaders to terrorize and maybe kill him and, if he survived, call the police for help. Does that sound like a good plan to you? Me neither. When three businessmen obtained a permit to open a gun store, abiding by every restriction, the city then decided that although they had issued the permit, they revoked it because they had changed the rules. The case is in the courts. Fortunately for Arizonans, we have no such restrictions. People are free to buy, possess a firearm on their person or in their home without government permission. All that is needed is to obtain a background check at the time of purchase. Other states, like California, New York, Illinois are doing everything they can to deny citizens to exercise their Second Amendment rights.

Why would some states and, more specifically, some cities, pass laws they know can't stand up to a court challenge ? That's easy. They're counting on the fact that most citizens can't afford to hire lawyers and bring a lawsuit. It's not an illegal law if no one sues them, right? Even police departments have confiscated weapons from a citizen during an investigation, and then refused to return them, telling the gun owner to sue if they want their guns. In most cases, city, state, and police officials are right. Criminals are big supporters of states and cities that ban gun ownership. If only the police and the criminals are armed, the odds are pretty good that the criminals get away with whatever crimes they commit.

Some state and city governments believe that citizens dial 911 if a crime is committed, and let law enforcement go catch the criminals. Tell that to a woman being assaulted and raped. Tell it to a homeowner whose home has been invaded by thugs. They never talk about the criminals who have access to and do carry guns in order to commit their crimes. The police respond to a call for assistance because a crime is in progress or has already been committed. Police are a reactive agency, not a proactive agency. Our laws are such that police can't arrest someone because they believe he or she might be thinking about committing a crime. If anyone saw that movie, "Minority Report," please don't believe it. The police can only respond to a crime if it is happening or has been completed. Now, if I'm the victim, and I'm unarmed, the criminal knows that if they kill me, and remove evidence, and then take off, chances are they will get away with it. If, however, a criminal comes into my home and attempts to assault or kill me, and I have a gun, I can ruin his or her whole day, or life. There will be one less crime committed, one less criminal on the street. This looks like a win-win to me.

Here in Arizona, guns are a way of life, and our murder rate is a lot lower than New York, Washington, D.C., Illinois, and many other states. In Chicago, Illinois, there have been nearly 40 shooting deaths, many of them children, in just the past month. In Arizona you can buy just about any weapon you want, up to and including a .50 caliber machine gun. For that weapon, however, you have to fill out extra paperwork for the federal government, pay a fee, and send it in. If your background is clean, and you pose no risk—not sure what risk means—you get permission to purchase the weapon. I've purchased handguns and "long" guns (rifles) by showing proper identification, filling out the background check application, and within just a few minutes, I've been cleared, paid for the weapon, and I'm on my way. I personally own four handguns, three of which are semi-automatic, a .44 caliber revolver, a 12-gauge shotgun, and a 7.62x39 semi-automatic rifle. I also have about 1,000 rounds of ammunition. I always have one handgun in my vehicle, and the others are strategically placed around the house. If I'm going to be out at night, I carry a handgun in a holster on my belt. I have taken my wife to the shooting range, and she's very accurate with her revolver, which she keeps near her side of the bed. None of those weapons have ever been fired except at the range. We have those weapons because we'd rather have them and not need them than need them and not have them. I pose no threat to anyone who isn't threatening me or my family.

There are very few instances of people being robbed on the street if the criminal knows that the intended victim is armed. A book was written several years ago, "*More Guns, Less Crime,*" wherein the author includes charts, graphs, statistics, and real life stories of how an armed society is a polite society.

Yes, we need laws to prevent felons from purchasing weapons. We need laws to prevent people with mental diseases from buying weapons. But there have been several cases where someone with a mental problem was able to legally purchase a gun. Why? Well, in the case of the murderer of six and the wounding of 13, near Tucson, Arizona, no one who knew the shooter was unhinged bothered to notify law enforcement. The schools where he sometimes attended, had removed him from classes because he was unstable, but "didn't want to get involved" with reporting that behavior to law enforcement. So, when the shooter went into a gun store and bought a gun, the background check was performed, and it came back clean. Now, who is at fault here? Is it the fault of the gun shop owner? He followed the law. Unfortunately, there are a lot of places where a mentally unstable person works, attends classes, and the employer or the school won't report erratic or unstable behavior to law enforcement. Then you get things like the shooting in Tucson. The situation in Aurora, Colorado has yet to be fully revealed. But it appears that even though the alleged shooter was seeing a psychiatrist, doesn't mean that he revealed anything that would cause the psychiatrist to contact authorities.

It is true that guns don't kill people; people kill people, and sometimes a gun is used. But people have been known to kill people using kitchen knives, baseball bats, golf clubs, tire irons, you name it. But we don't pass laws banning those weapons. For a time we had a law banning the sale of "assault" weapons. In all of my years around guns, I never saw one that wasn't an assault weapon. If a gun can fire one bullet, it can be used to assault someone else. If a weapon is semi-automatic, it's called an assault weapon. What is an assault weapon? All guns are assault weapons even if they're only used for defensive purposes, or used at a gun range. The problem is the nature of the people calling for this ban on assault weapons. They have probably never owned a gun, or fired a gun. They just look at a gun, and if it looks menacing then it must be an assault weapon. One political hack said that any gun that looks like a military style weapon is an assault weapon. Have you seen some of the air rifles being sold today? They look just like the Russian AK-47 automatic rifle.

Unfortunately, city and state leaders, and a lot of our elected leaders in Washington are afraid of guns. For those people afraid of guns, I have a piece of advice: Don't buy a gun, but obey the Second Amendment to the Constitution.

An essay was written not too long ago. The author of the essay was originally attributed to a Major L. Caudill, USMC, Retired. It was discovered later that there is no such person. Many searches revealed that the original author could have been any of three or four authors. To ensure that I don't step on any other author's toes, I'll paraphrase the essay. You can read the entire essay in rocker Ted Nugent's new book, "*Ted, White, and Blue.*" Just understand that there is no Major L. Caudill, USMC, Retired, but if there were, I'd like to buy him a beer.

"The Gun Is Civilization"

- There are two ways that humans deal with one another, (persuasion) reason and force.
- If you want to convince me to do something, you must choose between reason and force.
- Typically, people convince each other through persuasion (reason).
- If I am carrying a gun, you cannot deal with me by force.
- When I carry a gun, you have to deal with me through persuasion because I have the means to repel the use of force.
- A gun puts a 100-pound man or women on equal footing with a 250-pound man or woman carrying a gun. The gun puts the senior citizen on equal footing with a criminal.
- There are those who believe that removing guns from all citizens. They are foolish. Such an act would make the criminal element very happy because those criminals know that their potential victims are not on equal footing.
- Those who advocate for the banning of all firearms are automatically give the young, the strong, and those with evil intent who can overpower citizens. These people have an automatic advantage over the elderly, and the weaker citizens.
- Those who believe that baseball bats, knives, tire irons, or stones don't constitute lethal force need to quit playing video games or watching television.
- The gun is the equalizer between the 300-pounder as it is in the hands of an 80-year old senior citizen.
- A citizen carrying a gun takes force out of the equation. Persuasion is now the only means one has to cause another to comply.

Why Does Government Cost So Much?

I'm only including a few of the areas where the bloated government bureaucracy wastes so much of our money. There is a book by Tracy Coyle, titled *"The Apocalypse Plan: A Federal Budget Alternative."* This is an excellent book that covers our government waste from stem to stern, with excellent alternatives. It's a good read, and very enlightening.

The first thing to understand about why government is so wasteful and bloated is that they're spending our money, not their money. When government talks about money, they talk billions and trillions. They believe that their role in government is to spend other people's money. As many people often say about socialists: "Sooner or later they run out of other people's money to spend." The whole concept of a balanced budget is lost on our government officials, and especially our President. They don't have to worry about balancing a budget. If they run out of money to spend, they'll raise taxes somewhere, and the spending continues. If you've been paying attention you know that our nation is about $16 Trillion is debt, and government borrows $0.40 of every dollar that it spends. You, as a person, don't exist to them; you are just a wallet or purse from which they extract money. If every member of Congress were forced to sit down and read through a list of every federal tax levied on the American people, they would first be shocked, and then they would look for other areas where they could tax you even more. That's what Congress does, spend your money on things they want, and look for ways to raise a tax or invent a new one. It should be said that not all members of Congress behave this way, but those who don't are by far the minority. Congress no longer believes they are accountable to you and me. They believe they are in Washington to rule the country, not serve their constituents.

The fault for our bloated government is not party-specific. Both Republicans and Democrats contribute to the massive, bloated, behemoth we call the federal government. The federal government is the largest employer in America, and we all pay for it. There are so many departments, doing so little, but costing so much, that it's a tragedy. Take, for example, the Department of Energy.

The Department of Energy was created by then President Jimmy Carter—that tells us a lot. This department had one primary job—reduce our dependence on foreign energy, like oil. The budget for the DOE is $24.2 BILLION per year. There are 16,000 employees in the DOE, all getting paid with your money, and receiving great healthcare benefits. There are also an additional 100,000 contract employees.

Has this government department accomplished anything in 35 years, like reducing our dependence on foreign sources of energy? No. I see $24.2 billion in spending cuts right off the top, don't you? And all those unemployed government workers could be trained as McDonald's employees. Repeat after me: "Would you like fries with your order?"

Let's look at the Department of Education, shall we? This department, another brainchild of you know who, Jimmy Carter, is called the DofED, not the DOE, had a budget of about $70 billion in 2011. That budget was increased this year. There are approximately 5,000 employees, making it one of the smallest government sinkholes. A government department with 5,000 employees is one of the smallest departments in the federal government. And with all of this money, and 5,000 employees, what have we gotten in return? Not much. We have students failing at higher rates; we have many schools failing so badly that parents are fleeing those districts. The federal government usurped education decisions from the states and drives government schools across the nation from its perch in Washington. This is a travesty, and our kids and grandkids are the victims.

If you look at K-12 education today, it's a failure, and has been getting worse for decades. What can 5,000 employees with $70 billion each year do to help improve our education "system"? The first thing I would recommend is to get rid of the entire department, and return education back to the states. You and I know, though, that once some agency or department is created by Washington bureaucrats, it never goes away; it continue to grow and swallow more and more of our tax dollars. But there is no return on investment, and we all know it. Heck, even Congress knows that the DofED is a failure, which is why most politicians send their kids to private schools. Bbut they will never disband the DofED. Considering that education is found nowhere in the Constitution, what gives Washington the authority to create and run this department?

It's difficult to find out just what this department is a) supposed to be doing and b) is actually doing. With $70 billion and an increased budget every year, why is every state spending more and more of its budget on education? In Arizona, 53% of every state tax dollar goes to K-12 education, plus whatever the federal government tosses in, and student performance continues to plummet. Something just isn't working here, Martha. Here's a novel idea; disband this failing department and return education to the several states. The government saves $70+ billion each year and, when combined with the savings from disbanding the DOE, we've reduced spending by over $110 billion, and we're just getting started. These unemployed government employees could become employees at movie theaters. Repeat after me: "Would you like to make that a large for only 25-cents more?"

We can't leave out the Department of Homeland Security (DHS). The Department of Homeland Security works in the civilian sphere to protect the United States from within, at, and outside its borders. Its stated goal is to prepare for, prevent, and respond to domestic emergencies, particularly terrorism. On March 1, 2003, DHS absorbed the Immigration and Naturalization Service (INS) and assumed its duties. In doing so, it divided the enforcement and services functions into two separate and new agencies: Immigration and Customers Enforcement (ICE), and Customs Enforcement and Citizenship and Immigration Services (CECI). You can see this bureaucracy getting bigger and heavier by the hour. Their budget is about $40 billion, with another $5.5 billion in disaster relief funds. This behemoth has over 200,000 employees, which includes Border Patrol and Customs Enforcement officers. This is the third largest cabinet department in the federal government. Do you feel safer now? Me neither. With $40 billion dollars and over 200,000 employees, why are our Northern and Southern borders so porous? Why hasn't that double-fence securing our southern border been completed? Other than salaries, where is all the money going? Here in Arizona we've had sheriff's deputies killed, and a border patrol agent killed by drug cartel thugs—IN ARIZONA! If you pay attention, then you know that the drug cartels pretty much run Mexico, and have spread into the desert areas of southern Arizona. Where is Homeland Security? They're nowhere to be found. The Border Patrol works long, dangerous hours every single day, trying to stem the flow of drug, human, and cash smuggling, but hundreds of millions of dollars in drugs, and hundreds of thousands of illegal aliens cross that border every year. The amount of cash that crosses the border is unknown because law enforcement can't stop it. The current Secretary of Homeland Security, Janet Napolitano—whom we lovingly call Janet Incompitano—has been nothing but a shill for the open borders crowd. She keeps spewing the party line about how safe the borders are, and how many illegal aliens have been deported. But the truth is that the border is not safe, and it sure isn't secure or under control. For a long time—before the media started reporting it—there were signs erected by the federal government along many roads in Southern Arizona warning people not to venture into the desert area because it wasn't safe (from drug and human smugglers). The government puts up signs along Arizona roads, warning citizens not to enter the desert area, that doesn't make me feel safe. They removed the signs, but did nothing to secure the area.

Here's an excerpt from a Washington Post article published earlier this year:

"You know things are bad for workers when a bipartisan congressional hearing is called to examine a department's drooping spirit. It ranks 31 among 33 large agencies in The Best Places to Work in the Federal Government survey published by the Partnership for Public Service. (The Partnership has a content-sharing relationship with The Washington Post.)

"Why Is Employee Morale Low?" asked Thursday's hearing by the House Homeland Security panel's subcommittee on oversight, investigations and management.

"DHS employees strongly believe in their work and mission," said Chairman Michael McCaul (R-Tex.). Citing a federal employee survey, he asked: "But what does it say when only 37 percent of DHS employees believe senior leaders motivate them and only 37 percent are satisfied with their senior leaders' policies and practices?"

The report states that there is a problem with leadership.

Ya think? It's as true in the private sector as it is in the public sector. Anytime you get a company, government, or government agency comprised of thousands and thousands of employees, there will be dead wood, inefficiencies, and waste. With the DHS, when they have these kinds of issues, and you add in very low morale, is it any wonder our borders are wide open? The buck stops with the head of DHS, Janet Napolitano. This department needs a serious audit, and major changes in senior management. We citizens wouldn't be so upset with the budget of this department if it would do its job. But with all that money, and all of those employees, why are we not safe? I've got it! Fire all the senior management and their exorbitant salaries, and turn it over to a private sector security company. They'll do a much better job, with less people, and spend less money. All in favor say Aye!

Look at the Environmental Protection Agency, please. This government organization spends over $8.5 billion dollars a year protecting the environment from you and me. The EPA has over 17,000 employees, paid for by you and me, while they go about fighting you and me.

This is the agency that defines wetlands. You might have a mud bog in the back of your property, decide to dredge it up, build a damn to prevent the water from seeping back in. But wait. The EPA can order you to leave your land alone because it is now a wetland. There really is no appeal. There was a couple who bought a large lot in a beautiful Idaho area, about a mile from a lake, and decided to build their dream home. They got all the permits necessary—permission from the government to build on their own land—and started clearing the land. Hold on there, pardner. The EPA came in, declared that lot a wetland—there was no water anywhere around—and ordered them to restore the land to its original condition, and add non-indigenous plants or face a fine of over $30,000 per day until they complied. They appealed and appealed, and finally ended up in the U.S. Supreme Court, which told the EPA to go fly a kite. But the financial side was a disaster for this couple. It cost them hundreds of thousands of dollars during this whole process. What did it cost the EPA? Absolutely nothing. They use government lawyers, and we pay for them. That's our EPA. There are hundreds of stories just like this one. The EPA apparently decided that they are a law unto themselves, and are drunk with the power. They can just wave their magic wand and stop citizens from using their own land. This agency is making a frontal assault on private property rights, and we let them. This whole agency needs to be blown up and started again, with adult leadership and management.

There are numerous other agencies that are a complete waste of money. There are some agencies that would like to do a good job, like the Department of Defense, but their Secretary is under the thumb of the President. The President snaps his fingers, the Secretary of Defense jumps. As a result of the politicization of this department, combat warriors die.

Political Correctness—Scary Stuff

If you care to do a little research, you can easily find out where this term, *politically correct*, comes from. Never mind, I already found out. This term is derived from another term, *Cultural Marxism*. Wow, no wonder those that push its use don't want you to know where it came from.

Cultural Marxism means, in effect, censoring speech that is in disagreement with the state. Proponents of political correctness have taken it several leaps forward. They invoke political correctness when it comes to any spoken or written that may offend someone, or cast aspersions upon someone or some group. Essentially then, political correctness is censorship of free speech. Is the push for political correctness becoming clear now? Through this obsession, the use of many words can be banned from public discourse for fear of "offending" other people. Here's a simple example. In greater Phoenix a parkway was built many years ago. The initial name was the "Squaw Peak Parkway." No one had any issues with it. Then, from almost nowhere, a group of people, a small group, started speaking to the media, saying that the term "squaw" was offensive to Native Americans (American Indians before political correctness). Very few of the group were actual American Indians; most were busybody folks with way too much time on their hands. They kept up their badgering of the media, demanding that the legislature change the name of that parkway. Well, as it so happened, a female American Indian woman, who was serving in the Iraq war, was killed in action. So, just like that, the Squaw Peak Parkway became Piestawa Parkway. The law didn't allow the name of a deceased person to have their name enshrined on a building or a road until five years after their death, but the then governor couldn't be bothered with that law. So, voila, the Squaw Peak Parkway became Piestawa Peak Parkway. That road is actually, officially, call highway 51, but most people still refer to it as the Squaw Peak Parkway or the 51, but the politically correct folks won that one. Actually, the devotees of political correctness win a lot of fights. Many Americans are now afraid to take any chance of offending someone. I'm not one of them.

In April of this year, MoveOn.org, a infamous socialist organization with major funding from George Soros, a noted socialist, started a campaign to make the term Illegal Alien a hate crime, stating that people cannot be illegal, and a human cannot be an alien. This is, more or less, a favorite for the most stupid ideas of the year, but they got some media coverage, and some appearances on television, mostly on CNN and MSNBC. Fortunately, few people saw them. They did get one appearance on Fox News, and the host eviscerated the guest because her claims were so specious. This is what political correctness comes down to. Nothing can be said that might offend someone. Do you know how hard it is to say anything that won't offend someone? Heck, I offend people all the time just by speaking the truth. But making use of the term Illegal Alien a hate crime is too stupid to ignore.

Even the homosexuals got into the politically correct business. They took a word from the dictionary, gay, and insisted that all homosexuals now be called Gay. They did this because they knew that if people referred to homosexuals by that term, homosexual, it would immediately call attention to their sexual behavior. I refuse to participate. I have nothing against homosexuals as people, but I abhor their sexual practices.

Political correctness has invaded television shows, too. There's a show on one of the alphabet soup channels, and some people don't like it. So, they all start writing to the TV station demanding that the show be taken off the air. I guess the idea of just changing the channel never occurred to them. This is a case where maybe 200-300 people demand the show be taken off TV because they find it offensive, but the show draws an audience of three or four million. This is typical leftist behavior. If they don't like a TV show, it must be taken off the air. If they don't like a radio show, it must be taken off the air. If they don't like some political candidate, they must be destroyed by whatever means necessary. And they call this behavior . . . . fairness!

People have demanded that a radio show host be banned from a station because they are offended by what he or she says. Anyone besides me see a theme here? People get offended if anyone says anything that is politically incorrect. The whole concept of changing the radio station, like changing the TV channel, is a foreign concept. You have to wonder if their light ever comes on to full brightness. Or, to be politically incorrect, are they just mental midgets?

I gave one of my 'fire them up" speeches, which was very well received. Afterwards, one person came up and said they were offended about one thing I said about another person. My response was to tell them that they may want to work on their "getting offended syndrome" because getting offended is a choice you make; it's not my responsibility. I doubt I've given one speech, and I've given close to 100 of them, where someone in the audience didn't get offended about something I said, but that's not my responsibility. One thing I hate to hear people say is, "Now I don't want to offend anyone, but . . . ." It's moronic. Just by starting a sentence in that way is the surest way I know to ensure that someone will choose to be offended. My philosophy is, you being offended is your problem, not mine, so go work on it, and leave me alone.

You can see political correctness in the office, too. Some employees have been called into the Human Resources office because someone filed a complaint to the effect that they were offended at seeing a Bible sitting on another person's desk. I have two possible solutions to that problem: 1) don't look on the person's desk—it's none of your business, anyway, and 2) don't walk by that desk, and you won't run the risk of seeing the Bible. We could add a third option, resign.

And, for goodness sake, don't ever tell a joke that has any of the now forbidden politically incorrect words involved. Someone told a joke one day, about Davy Crockett, you know, the famous early American hero? He wore a hat that is now famous. But the speaker couldn't refer to the hat by the name used for the past 150 years or so. That would be offensive. So, he said, ". . . . and Davy put on his raccoon-skin hat and . . . ." If had said the word, "*coon-skin hat . . .*" I can imagine millions of people fainting all over the place. That's how bad it's gotten in America. Do you want an America where your children can only use "approved" words?

We can't have a nativity scene at Christmas (am I allowed to say Christmas?) because those who aren't Christian or Jewish might be offended. There is also this specious argument that having a nativity scene on public property is a violation of the First Amendment. That Amendment says, in part, that the government may not establish a state religion. The Amendment also says that the people shall not be prevented from the free exercise of their faith.

Are you kidding me? Hey, if you're offended at the sight of a nativity scee, don't look, you idiots. If you don't think we're founded on Judeo-Christian principles, take a look at our founding documents. If you don't think America is founded on Judeo-Christian principles, where did "We are endowed by our creator with certain unalienable rights, among them . . . ." At the time that was written, our founders, for the most part, believed in God, and many of our laws are derived from the Ten Commandments, as well as from England's common law. Those Ten Commandments, for those of you who don't know, are proudly displayed at the entrance to the U.S. Supreme Court building. Some people are so afraid of offending someone of some other faith, that they subordinate their own faith. And let's not leave out the atheists from the discussion. These people, and there aren't that many of them, though they are loud and tend to get media attention, desperately want the word, God, removed anywhere it exists because they don't believe in any god. My advice to the atheists is to take a deep breath, get on with your life, and avert your eyes if you see the word God around you. Over 80% of the population professes to believe in a god, be it the Christian God or some other god. They all believe in a higher power. Get over yourselves. If you choose to be offended, please do it quietly so as not to disturb the adults.

But the attack on the Christian God is not limited to the private sector. Oh, no. Government schools are working feverishly to get the Christian God out of every classroom. Kids have been told they can't read their Bible, even on their lunch breaks. Kids are told they can't write an essay or tell a story if the word God is mentioned. However, if you want to mention Allah, please feel free to do so. It's just that pesky Christian God that offends school leaders. Well, that and their fear of reprisal if they banned anything related to the Islamic faith.

Let's be clear about one thing. No one should use words that can hurt people. Calling people names is a pretty natural thing that people do, but if those words you use are slang words to describe someone's race, don't. However, if you say something that you believe someone might "feel" offended about, go for it. It's their problem, not yours.

What Are the Principles of Liberals and Conservatives?

When you read definitions of liberal, you can get confused. Some of those definitions refer to open-mindedness, equality for all, tolerance, and are often mixed with the term, Progressive. This can get very confusing until you look at behaviors of people who have self-labeled themselves. Let's simplify things a bit. Here are some differences that make it pretty easy to understand the difference between liberals and conservatives or Democrats and Republicans.

If a Republican doesn't like guns, he doesn't buy one.

If a Democrat doesn't like guns, he wants all guns outlawed.

If a Republican is a vegetarian, he doesn't eat meat.

If a Democrat is a vegetarian, he wants all meat products banned for everyone.

If a Republican is homosexual, he quietly leads his life.

If a Democrat is homosexual, he demands legislated respect.

If a Republican is down-and-out, he thinks about how to better his situation.

If a Democrat is down-and-out, he wonders who is going to take care of him.

If a Republican doesn't like a talk show host, he switches channel.

If a Democrat doesn't like a talk show host, he demands that the show host be fired.

If a Republican is a non-believer, he doesn't pray or go to church, but doesn't concern himself with what others do.

If a Democrat is a non-believer, he wants any mention of God and religion silenced.

If a Republican decides that he needs health care, he goes about shopping for it, or may choose a job that provides it.

If a Democrat decides that he needs health care, he demands that the rest of us pay for his.

If you review these differences and think about them for a while, does this list pretty much sum up the differences? If you use some of the same logic that a liberal uses regarding guns, wouldn't you also want to ban all knives, baseball bats, golf clubs, crowbars, tire irons, hammers, and screwdrivers? After all, those items have been used to kill people, haven't they?

Here are some famous—well, famous to some—quotes from Democrats.

"One man with courage makes a majority."—Andrew Jackson

"The only thing we have to fear is fear itself."—Franklin D. Roosevelt

"The buck stops here."—Harry S. Truman

"Ask not what your country can do for you; ask what you can do for your country."—John F. Kennedy

And here are a few quotes from Democrats in the past few years.

"It depends what your definition of 'IS' is?"—former President Bill Clinton

"That Obama—I would like to cut his nuts off."—Reverend Jesse Jackson

"Those rumors are false. I believe in the sanctity of marriage."—John Edwards

"I invented the Internet"—Al Gore

"The next person that tells me I'm not religious, I'm going to shove my rosary beads up their ass."—Joe Biden—Speaking of plagiarists, Joe had to drop out of a political campaign in 1988 because he got caught plagiarizing and the publicity—at the time, anyway—was humiliating.

"America is—is no longer, uh, what it—it, uh, could be, uh what it was once was . . . uh, and I say to myself, 'uh, I don't want that future, uh, uh for my children'"—Barack Obama

"I have campaigned in all 57 states."—Barack Obama

"You don't need God anymore, you have us democrats."—Speaker of the House Nancy Pelosi (said back in 2006)

"Paying taxes is voluntary."—Senator Harry Reid

"Bill is the greatest husband and father I know. No one is more faithful, true, and honest than he."—Hillary Clinton (said back in 1998)

There are thousands more quotes, but you get the idea. The Democrats, that I call Communists, are not trustworthy people. Their hyperbole is the stuff of legend. Their political campaigns are chock full of promises, none of which they intend to keep. They just think you're too dumb to catch on. Once they get elected, they go about tearing the country down, turning it way to the left, so they can assume their rightful positions as rulers of the socialist state called America. It's time to wake up.

If your child is a believer, does a school have the right to ban that child from praying at school, or reading their Bible during recess or during the lunch hour? In this case it is the government imposing its non-believer opinion on every child in every government school. Is that even constitutional? But it goes on every school day all across the country.

I have heard Hillary Clinton refer to herself as a Proud Progressive. As near as I can determine, she believes that the Constitution is a document we should edit whenever the president or the Congress believes it's necessary. They just don't have time for that silly Amendment process—it takes too much time, and the little people could stop us. Hillary believes that even if you're a Catholic, you should support a woman's right to choose to kill that unborn child if it's inconvenient to be pregnant. As a progressive, you also believe that everyone should make an equal amount for their labor, from janitor to rocket scientist, except of course for the rulers of the country. They should not be subject to the laws of the working class, and should be proud to be as rich as they want to be, by whatever means necessary. Progressives believe pretty much what the Communist Party of the USA believes. Maybe that's why Gus Hall, the perennial candidate for President for the Communist party said, in 1984, that he would no longer run for President because the Democrat party held the same principles and policies as the Communist Party, so he encouraged all Communist to vote for Democrats. You can read more about these statements by Gus Hall at *Wikipedia* and from other sources. I'm not sure, but I think the Progressives are proud of that. Progressives believe that government should "*take care of*" the people because, essentially, the people are too stupid to take care of themselves. Only the elites, educated in those Ivy League colleges, are smart enough to decide what the little people need. Gee, how's that been working out so far?

Racism in America

Is there racism in America? Yes, there is. Is racism as prevalent as it was 50, 100, 150 years ago. No it isn't. Will there always be some racism in existence during the next 20, 30, 40 years? There probably will be some forms of racism.

During the years of slavery, it was lawful worldwide. The U.S. didn't invent slavery, but did participate in it. In some countries today slavery still exists. In the Sudan as one example, tribal warfare continues unabated. When one tribe conquers another tribe, the victors take the losers as their slaves. We're still waiting for Jesse Jackson and Al Sharpton to show up over there and start protesting. Don't hold your breath. Sudan doesn't have much money, so Jesse and Al aren't really interested. America fought a civil war over, among some other issues, slavery. Over 500,000 Americans died in that war to "free the slaves." Many of those who died were white men, fighting to stop slavery. Some people often forget that fact. The southern states seemed to want to keep slavery intact, but the war ended that desire, on the surface.

I remember an incident when I was visiting Virginia, with one of my uncles.

When I was in my early teens, my parents shipped me off to Virginia to spend a few weeks with my mother's sister, her husband, and their daughter. This couple had lived in Virginia all their lives. Virginia has a strong racist past. My uncle had been taught to hate black Americans, really hate them. It all stemmed from the late 1800's when my uncle's grandfather was a member of the KKK. The attitude towards black Americans was virulent. My uncle father carried on the tradition of black American hatred. It was a part of their past and their learning from those who came before them. But I remember vividly my uncle walking to the other side of the street to avoid black Americans. He wouldn't speak to them, but spoke of them in the most pejorative way possible, and there was no discussion to be had with him on the subject. He hated black Americans as did his wife. When I asked why they believed this way, the only answer I ever got was that they're just no damned good, end of discussion. What do you think they taught their daughter about the races? You guessed it. Their daughter, who was about 18 at the time, and on vacation before going to college, spoke of black Americans in exactly the same way she had been taught by her father, who had been taught by his father, and so on. You were never going to change their minds, never. Pass whatever laws you want, their belief system won't change. They had been indoctrinated by their fathers and grandfathers, absorbed it all, and then acted it out.

What Congress doesn't understand is that you cannot legislate thought. You can only legislate behavior. That deep-seated racism takes many generations to overcome despite what some would want you to believe. That brings up this stupid idea of reparations. When I think about it for a while, it really ticks me off. Black Americans today want to receive money from all other races for slavery that ended a long, long time ago. Is that what black Americans really want, to be paid for what their great, great, great grandfather may have suffered from slavery? That somehow some money makes everything even now? It's a stupid idea. It could never happen, anyway. How many black Americans have you met that say they're African-American, but when asked what country in Africa their ancestors came from, they have no clue. Many of these black Americans believe that Africa is a country, not a continent. My other issue is that they are Americans unless they have dual citizenship. Should every person who has ancestral roots in some other country—which is all of us—start hyphenating their name? If so, then I'm a German-Austrian-American. It just rolls off your tongue, doesn't it?

During 20 years in the military I never experienced or saw acts of racism. To be fair, there is a lot of harassment of each other; no one is exempt, no race is exempt. But overt or covert acts of racism just didn't happen. Now, I never served on very large ships like aircraft carriers. The ships on which I served generally had crews of less than 400 men—there were no women on warships at that time. I have heard that on aircraft carriers, which can have a crew of about 5,000 crew men and pilots, and I assume some women, too, some races chose to segregate themselves. But I worked with, for, and supervised men of all races, and there was never a problem. On my first ship my boss was a black American named Fred. We spent a year together, 10 months of which were on a lengthy cruise to the Far East. Fred and I became good friends, and stayed in touch for over 17 years. I'd had Fred to my house for dinner, and I'd visited his home. We went drinking together, and there was never any problem. I just didn't see race in the sailors with whom I served. I saw men, dedicated to their job and going on liberty with whoever was available.

In civilian society, however, racism seems to be everywhere, but it's hard to nail down just what is causing it. There are the usual suspects, people like Al Sharpton, Jesse Jackson, Charles Barron (New York), and some others. These people keep talking about slavery, inadequate compensation (restitution or reparatons), and handouts. If you listen to their rhetoric, you can tell that they don't believe that black Americans are very smart, they're unable to get a decent job, stay off drugs, and on and on. It's interesting to hear a successful black American talking about how black American men and women just don't have a chance in life because the white man is putting them down. That's been going on for over 50 years now, and it's still a lie. If it weren't we wouldn't have black American CEO's, black American professors, a black American Secretary of State, and a black American Supreme Court Justice. These successful men and women, and hundreds of thousands more, worked hard, got an education, and rose within the income structure. For Jackson and Sharpton, telling black Americans that life isn't fair for them, that they'll never make it in a white society is red meat for them. It's the source of their livelihood. If black Americans would wake up and realize that life is right there for the taking, just go get it. Don't listen to the race-baiters. If you work hard and educate yourself, you can make the American Dream a reality. Our founding documents tell us very clearly that each and every one of us is endowed by our creator—not government—with certain unalienable rights, among them are life, liberty, and the pursuit of happiness. It doesn't say that some of us are endowed with unalienable rights, and the rest of us are screwed. But to hear Jackson, Barron, and Sharpton, with their hateful rhetoric, you'd think no black American can be successful in this racist America. If that were true, how did Jackson, Barron, and Sharpton become successful? The picture begins to take shape. Telling black Americans that they're victims is, in their view, how they gain support from them. Do you have to become ordained, have no church, start alphabet soup organizations, and fool people into giving you money to be successful? Any black American who becomes successful and doesn't fall for their rhetoric is called an "*Uncle Tom*" or a "*Traitor.*" There are black American athletes that are by any measure, very successful. There are black teachers, black professors, black scientists, black generals, all of whom are very successful. But to hear Jackson, Barron, and Sharpton tell it, they're not real black Americans. So just who is a real black American? Are the young men and women who excel in school, have a dream, work hard, and become part of the mainstream "Uncle Toms" or successful Americans?

If you want to fan the flames of racism, here are some ways to do it.

First, tell Universities that they have to admit more black students, regardless of grades, and exclude more white students despite their higher grades. Isn't that reverse racism? Naw, couldn't be. If black Americans make up 14% of the population, then 14% of students admitted each year have to be black Americans. Notice that this policy has nothing to do with merit, but is all about quotas. There seems to be no concern as to how many of those black American students are prepared and ready, how few graduate, and what the experience can do to them. The black American students are just pawns in the racism game.

You will be hard pressed to find the percentage of black American students that graduate. That's not the point to the race-baiters. In the private sector, if companies don't have their 14% black American employee quota met, people like Jesse Jackson have a meeting with them. It's kind of like a "Godfather" meeting, where the leaders of the company will receive an offer they can't refuse. Some call it extortion, but it doesn't matter to Jesse Jackson. He tells those companies that they will hire more black American employees AND make a generous contribution to Jackson's coalition, or there will be protests, strikes, and/or walkouts at the company. Gee, what a deal. It has nothing to do with a need for more employees, or employees of a different color, or any opening being filled with the most qualified applicant. No, no, no. It is about quotas, and Jesse Jackson, and others, are pushing it, hard.

If you want to fan the flames of racism create a business atmosphere where government contracts are not given to the best company, lowest bidder, and most able to perform the work. Instead, government grants contracts to a minority bidder based on race rather than competence. Just what do you think that does to the attitude of those companies that were rejected in favor of filling a quota? Does this behavior improve race relations?

In the NFL, it is now a law that any team looking to replace its head coach or member of its coaching staff must interview at least one black American applicant, regardless of qualifications. So, the NFL teams play the game. They're looking for the best coach they can afford, but they have to make sure they interview at least one black American candidate. Does this make sense? It's like telling black American football coaches they're not good enough to get a job on their merit. No, Jesse Jackson has to get you a coaching job. It's stupid, but that's the pendulum swinging the other way.

Some years back at the University of California, Berkeley, the school admissions department decided that too many Asian American students were getting into the university. Their grades and achievements were so high, huge numbers of Asian Americans were at the top of the admissions list. The school decided to discriminate against Asian Americans in admission policies in order to get more school applicants of other races, including whites, into the college. This college used racism to control admission to the school. I didn't follow the story beyond when the Asian American applicants sued the university for discrimination and, I believe, the school caved.

If you look at the number of black Americans playing in the NBA, there numbers are considerably more than 14%, but Jesse Jackson never says that the NBA has to get rid of some black American players and hire more white players. Not at all. Jackson and Sharpton would tell you that in this case, it's merit. Oh, really. And more bad news for black American players; European players are joining the ranks of NBA teams in larger and larger numbers.

We can't leave out the PGA, the professional golfers, or the LPGA, the lady professional golfers. They have to be properly represented as well. We have to get more black American professional golfers on those tours, even if they're not qualified to be there. It's all about quotas, isn't it? The one equalizer in professional golf is that if you don't earn enough money, you lose your playing privileges on the main tour, and have to go play on a lesser tour. In the LPGA there's been a lot of complaining about how many South Korean lady professionals are now on the tour. The problem is that these players qualified to be on the tour at qualifying school, and once there, do a pretty good job of keeping their LPGA players card. In the case of golf, the race-baiters could try and force more black Americans onto the tour, but once there they have to earn enough money or they'll quickly be gone. I think they call that merit when you earn your way onto and win enough money to stay on tour.

If you believe any of this quota baloney, then you'd have to ask the private sector companies, colleges, and professional sports teams to meet the quota for Latinos and Asians as well as black Americans, wouldn't you?

The bottom line is this. Race baiters like Jackson, Barron, Sharpton, and others, depend on inflaming racism to enrich themselves. Jesse Jackson is no paragon of virtue. He is married, but fathered a child with another woman—and dared to call it a love child—and tried to cover it up. He continues to pay child support. Sharpton was responsible for the Tawana Brawley incident where people were killed, and it turned out that Sharpton was wrong, and has yet to even apologize to the family of the person murdered because of his incendiary speech. In April of this year Sharpton was down in Florida, fanning the flames of racism over the shooting death of Trayvon Martin. He spouted all kinds of lies; he had no facts, but that didn't even slow him down. With the passage of time, and more investigation, it now appears that there may in fact have been no murder. It may well have been self-defense. An FBI investigation report stated clearly that there is no evidence of racism in the incident. You'll never hear Sharpton admit that he was wrong. Sharpton and Jackson will never admin any wrong doing. Remember the Duke Lacrosse case? There was Sharpton, beating the flames of racism again. It turned out that the woman who accused several Duke Lacrosse players of rape lied about the whole thing. Jackson, Sharpton, and Barron are not good people. Sharpton is supposedly an ordained minister, too, but seems to have no affiliation to any church anywhere. The same can be said for Jackson. They make money for themselves on the backs of good black Americans, and for that they should be shunned from society. Yet Jackson persists with inserting himself into any incident where he believes he can get in front of a TV camera, and maybe take in some money. Sharpton, who seems to have a perpetual confrontation with the English language, but is very familiar with hair gel, has a show on MSNBC, that network that is ranked about 30th in prime time cable news, so 99.9% of America is able to avoid seeing or hearing him.

Tavis Smiley and Professor Cornell West are also purveyors of continuous racist speech. They can get a willing lame stream media to give them all the air time they want since the media is invested in keeping racism alive and well. It fills the newspaper.

More black Americans need to wake up and realize that they are being used by the likes of these men. They can get out of poverty, but it won't be from some government handout. Those handouts are designed to keep them in poverty, and dependent on that government. Black Americans can get an education if they want one. They can go to college, if they'll work hard, get good grades, and show that they deserve to be there. Black Americans can rise up in the business world, if they want to. If they wait for the likes of Jackson, Sharpton, Barron, and Democrats, they will be confined to poverty forever. And for anyone who believes that the Black Americans today need only look at the White House and see a black American as President of the United States. If he made it, why can't everyone else?

R. Eugene Spitzer

What is Wrong with Our Colleges?

When I finally got to college, I was around 30 years old. It took me that long because I was in the Navy and could usually be found sailing around the Far East, or wading through the muck of Vietnam. So, having a 30-year old perspective on learning, after going through so many military schools, I was curious as to why it takes so long to graduate. Well, once I began classes, I found out. So much time is wasted in college. During a typical day I would have five or six classes, all focused on different subjects, and none lasted more than two hours. I'd finish one class, then hustle off to the next one. In many of those classes, there were lectures that did not allow interaction with students. Generally, some professor—I use that term loosely—would stand in front, and proceed to bore us on whatever his or her specialty happened to be. We were expected to take lots of notes, keep our mouths shut, and when the class ended, head for the next class. By the time the next class with that professor occurred, I often had to go look at my notes again to figure out where we left off. The most difficult part of going to college, for me, was trying to schedule classes with the "right" professor. That was very competitive. I understand that's still the case today. But I persevered and graduated with a GPA around 3.5 while only attending classes about half the time. I quickly figured out what the important concepts being taught were, and I used a highlighter to mark the text, and then studied those pages before tests. It was pretty easy. In my view, there is no efficiency of effort in college. To me, the college experience is more about the school intentionally dragging out classes so as to maximize the amount of time students had to attend and, thus, maximize tuition costs. Why couldn't they just spend the first four weeks on three or four subjects? You study them all day for a week or two, then take the test and move on. Why make students take five or six classes at the same time, and drag it out for 16 weeks (semester system)? It's as if the college has no desire to innovate and come up with better ways to educate students. The transfer of knowledge and skills is the primary purpose of school, isn't it? School is supposed to transfer knowledge, and teach students HOW to think. I get very uncomfortable when a professor or teacher is telling students WHAT to think. I've read too many stories about that very tactic. This brought me to the conclusion that government schools have become institutions of indoctrination.

When I look at how many students spend five or six years in college trying to graduate, I wonder why it takes so long. I found out. Some students spend a year or two taking remedial classes because they didn't learn enough in high school to prepare themselves for college subjects. Yet colleges keep on charging that tuition, and the parents either pay it or the student gets a loan. By the way, you do know that the current administration took over all student loan programs from private institutions. This is the predicate for the government to decide whether or not to collect those loan payments, or cancel them. That's our money they're loaning out, not theirs.

I read in several papers, on the radio, and on the web that about 50% of graduating students end up moving back in with their parents because they can't get a job. Many of those students now have a college education, no job, and a big student loan to repay which, even if they declared bankruptcy, wouldn't be forgiven. What a deal.

I read an article or two that listed some of the major, prestigious colleges and the size of their respective endowments. One, Harvard I believe, has an endowment of nearly $40 billion, yet their tuition costs never go down. Could Harvard afford to cut tuition costs by about 50% for the next 20 years and still have billions left over? Of course they could. Don't hold your breath.

I recently watched a 20-minute segment on a national TV show about a man named Peter Thiel. Mr Thiel was one of the initial investors in FaceBook, and became a billionaire. He started a program where he pays $100,000 to about 20 students each year to chase their dream. He pays these young people $100,000 to drop out of college and chase their entrepreneurial dream. The final results aren't in on this program, but the kids are chasing their dreams and learning, too.

Why go to college for four years, which could cost you $100,000-250,000 in order to obtain a degree in, say, Latin, French, Gender Studies, Ethnic Studies, Liberal Arts? Where are you going to get a job with that degree except, perhaps, teaching the same subjects in college? But, if mommy and daddy paid the freight, why not go to college, major in something useless, and party hard?

I was sent to over 20 schools in my 20 years in the military. I learned what focused learning is all about. To get my advanced education in electronics, I was sent to a 48-week school. During those 48 weeks we were focused on just about every conceivable electronic concept and circuit, and every transmitter, receiver, and everything else the Navy used for electronic communications at that time. The rules were simple. You were in class for 40 hours, and you had 3-4 hours of outside work every night. Every two weeks you were tested on that module of training. If you passed the test, you moved on. If you failed it, you were allowed one opportunity to repeat the module and test again. If you failed, you were removed from school and made available for assignment to any ship or station in the world. You didn't get a vote. When it was necessary for me to attend a six-month school, at both Army and Navy locations, in order speak, read, and write Vietnamese, the pressure was always on. After the first day of class, no more English was spoken in class by the students or the instructor. Each time you spoke an English word, you paid a dime. By the end of that language training, we had a pile of cash for a heck of a party. We were tested every Friday. Fail three tests, and you're out. Your orders were modified. You would still end up in Vietnam, but your assignment would change to one where you didn't need to speak, read, or write Vietnamese.

In military schools, you will be focused; you will be taught, and you will learn. You are focused on learning a skill, tactics, and not paying attention was very costly. It's analogous, to me anyway, to what college should be about. You're there to learn how to think, and learn skills you'll need to be a productive member of society. You're not really there to drink yourself into a stupor, or to keep changing your major so you can stay there for years and years. Does anyone remember Mario Savio? Mr. Savio was a student at the University of California, Berkeley, California. Mr. Savio's primary focus seemed to be on organizing and leading protests of one sort or another, and he used the college as his base of operations. Mr. Savio attended the University for over seven years until they finally told him it was time to go.

In most colleges it takes 16 weeks to get through a class, with a mid-term, and a final exam. College Freshman can typically be found in an auditorium with 150-200 students, all sitting quietly listening to some pompous blowhard lecturing you on this or that. Far too often you'll be listening to some graduate student aide boring you to death because the "tenured" professor is off writing his or her next paper or book. In the college cocoon, professors must "*publish or perish.*" In the auditorium there is no interaction. I once had a law professor from some Eastern European country whose English was very accented and difficult to understand. This professor created a bell curve for every class. There would be only so many A grades, so many B grades, and so on. There would be no questions until he finished his lecture, which typically left about four minutes. He would not answer any question that he did not believe was worthy of his time. During his lectures, you must have your law book in front of you, opened to the section that he would be lecturing us about, no exceptions.

Another thing to understand about colleges is that more and more students need five and six years to get a degree, if they stick it out. No wonder college costs have quadrupled since 1980.

Over the years I did a lot of volunteer work with foster kids. For four years I was a court-appointed Special Advocate (CASA). I worked for a juvenile court judge. In that role I came into contact with many different child protective service people. Where I live it is required that all case managers working for CPS have a college degree. I had copies of all records and notes written by these case managers. I couldn't count the number of grammatical errors, and the number of meaningless sentences and paragraphs I had to work through. I only worked with one case manager who could write reasonably well. When CPS case managers spoke, I thought I was talking to people who had never finished high school let alone have graduated from college.

Government Schools Are Destroying Education

There are a lot of external forces that shape the minds andbehavior of children. There are differing views on how to mold a person. Some say that you shape the mind, and the behavior will follow. The other view is that you change the behavior and the mind will change over time. I don't know that one method is superior to the other, but in our government school system today, I don't think they work with either theory. For a long, long time it was my understanding that parents were responsible for instilling moral character and values in their children. For the last 20+ years it seems to me that the government school system believes that parents should just drop off their children at school, and the school will shape and mold the children. I'm not particularly keen on that concept given the failure of government schools to even graduate a significant number of students.

Some people believe that the government school system has been around since the Constitution was ratified in 1789. This is not true. Education isn't a part of the Constitution at all. Here's some background on how government schools came into being.

State-sponsored schools were not part of the original makeup of this country. None of the Founders saw providing compulsory, state-sponsored education as a proper function of the central government. The founders were all home-schooled. There were no government schools in any modern sense of that term until the 1840's when Horace Mann's Unitarians started them up in Massachusetts (where else?) as what were then known as common schools. Mann had been to Prussia where he became aware of a far different view of the relationship between central government and its citizens. This was far different than our own tradition which sees

73

the individuals as special both morally and economically. Prussian schools considered children property of the state, and educated them accordingly. This thinking took off, and just look where we are today.

For those of you with children, have you looked at any of the tests your child needs to pass to graduate from, say, the eighth grade? No? Today's tests bear no resemblance to the tests taken by eighth grade students over a century ago. Let's go back and visit the year 1895 right in Salina, Kansas. Here is a set of questions that eighth grade students had to pass in order to graduate to the ninth grade. Are you ready?

8th Grade Final Exam: Salina, KS—1895

Grammar (Time, one hour)

1. Give nine rules for the use of capital letters.
2. Name the parts of speech and define those that have no modifications
3. Define verse, stanza and paragraph.
4. What are the principal parts of a verb? Give principal parts of 'lie', 'play', and 'run'.
5. Define case; illustrate each case.
6 What is punctuation? Give rules for principal marks of punctuation.
7-10. Write a composition of about 150 words and show therein that you understand the practical use of the rules of grammar.

Arithmetic (Time,1 hour 15 minutes)

1. Name and define the Fundamental Rules of Arithmetic.
2. A wagon box is 2 ft. Deep, 10 feet Long, and 3 ft. Wide. How many bushels of wheat will it hold?
3. If a load of wheat weighs 3,942 lbs, what is it worth at 50cts/bushel, deducting 1,050 lbs for tare?
4. District No 33 has a valuation of $35,000. What is the necessary levy to carry on a school seven months at $50 per month, and have $104 for incidentals?
5. Find the cost of 6,720 lbs. Coal at $6.00 per ton.
6. Find the interest of $512.60 for 8 months and 18 days at 7percent per annum.
7. What is the cost of 40 boards 12 inches wide and 16 ft long at $20 per metre?

8. Find bank discount on $300 for 90 days (no grace) at 10 percent.
9. What is the cost of a square farm at $15 per acre, the distance of which is 640 rods?
10. Write a Bank Check, a Promissory Note, and a Receipt.

U.S. History (Time, 45 minutes)

1. Give the epochs into which U.S. History is divided
2. Give an account of the discovery of America by Columbus.
3. Relate the causes and results of the Revolutionary War.
4. Show the territorial growth of the United States.
5. Tell what you can of the history of Kansas.
6. Describe three of the most prominent battles of the Rebellion.
7. Who were the following: Morse, Whitney, Fulton, Bell, Lincoln, Penn, and Howe?
8. Name events connected with the following dates: 1607, 1620, 1800, 1849, 1865.

Orthography (Time, one hour)

1. What is meant by the following: alphabet, phonetic, orthography, etymology, syllabication?
2. What are elementary sounds? How classified?
3. What are the following, and give examples of each: trigraph, subvocals, diphthong, cognate letters, linguals?
4. Give four substitutes for caret 'u'.
5. Give two rules for spelling words with final 'e'. Name two exceptions under each rule.
6. Give two uses of silent letters in spelling. Illustrate each.
7. Define the following prefixes and use in connection with a word: bi, dis, pre, semi, post, non, inter, mono, sup.
8. Mark diacritically and divide into syllables the following, and name the sign that indicates the sound: card, ball, mercy, sir, odd, cell, rise, blood, fare, last.
9. Use the following correctly in sentences: cite, site, sight, fane, fain, feign, vane, vain, vein, raze, raise, rays.
10. Write 10 words frequently mispronounced and indicate pronunciation by use of diacritical marks and by syllabication.

Geography (Time, one hour)

1. What is climate? Upon what does climate depend?
2. How do you account for the extremes of climate in Kansas?
3. Of what use are rivers? Of what use is the ocean?
4. Describe the mountains of North America.
5. Name and describe the following: Monrovia, Odessa, Denver, Manitoba, Hecla, Yukon, St. Helena, Juan Fernandez, Aspinwall and Orinoco.
6. Name and locate the principal trade centers of the U.S.
7. Name all the republics of Europe and give the capital of each.
8. Why is the Atlantic Coast colder than the Pacific in the same latitude?
9. Describe the process by which the water of the ocean returns to the sources of rivers.
10. Describe the movements of the earth. Give the inclination of the earth.

How did you do? I did poorly, too, and I don't recall any of those questions on any test I took while I was in the eighth grade or in college. I challenge any politician to take and pass this test with a 70% score. Does anyone believe they could do it? Me neither. This leads me to this conclusion: American students are being dumbed down. From a central government point of view, I can see their logic. An ignorant population is easily manipulated and controlled. You didn't see any questions in this sample examination dealing with putting condoms on cucumbers, why government handouts are good for the economy, or anything like that.

Some Schools Have Some "Unusual" Electives

According to the New York Times, and many other newspaper reports, schools are coming up with some very unusual electives. There are electives such as:

- Metalsmithing
- Jewelry
- History of rock and roll
- 3D animation
- Woodworking
- SAT Math Preparation (affluent schools have this one)
- Scuba diving
- Kkiteboarding

- Hunting
- Fishing

There have been several books written on why students aren't learning. One of them, "*The Dumbest Generation*," by Michael Graham and Mike Bauernein, does an excellent job of describing why our school students aren't much interested in learning, but are very much consumed with entertainment.

What they surmised, and I agree with them, is that young people are not addicted to learning, but are very much addicted to constant entertainment and amusement. And we can all understand why. Technology has overwhelmed young people. They have more free time, since most don't work part time anymore, have more disposal income—from mom and dad—and the technology provides them with a full day of entertainment. Do students read books today? You must be kidding. If you want to know how dumb some of our young students are today, go to a Florida beach during Spring Break, and interview a few of the students taking a break from their vigorous studies. They will amaze you with how stupid they are. And many of them vote!

So, when you add in MySpace (is that still around?), YouTube, Facebook, Twitter, teen blogs, and other entertainment opportunities, including drugs and alcohol, young people are way too busy for school or learning. Here is a quick test for you. How many books has your child or grandchild read in the past year, for learning or just for entertainment value? If the answer is none, one, or two, you need to get involved, quickly. Take away their X-box, Gameboy, iPhone, iPad, and hand them a book. Actually, I'd allow the iPad to be used if it was for the purpose of downloading and reading a book, preferably a history book.

There is a Major Increase in in the Number of Students Repeating a Grade

Once again the New York Times has stumbled into accidental journalism. According to that newspaper, and others, there are many documented reports showing that government school students in grades K-12 are being held back a grade, especially in grades three through eight, with eighth graders being hit the hardest. The first question that came to my mind when I read some of these stories was, "*How does any child not graduate from the third grade*"? What did the child do, flunk sandbox? The reports out of New York City show that students being held back a grade today is five times greater than just a few years ago. Why is this happening? Gee, could it be that there isn't a lot of teaching going on?

Almost every week you can read stories in our local papers speculating about the solution to education's problems. Invariably, the solution always seems to be to spend more money. No concern about poor teaching ever makes it into print. Over the decades, the demand is always to give schools more money, yet no matter how much money is given to the government school system, it's just never enough to raise the graduation rates and competency of students. In Arizona, 53% of the budget is given to Education, but they want more. In some areas, like Washington, D.C., over $20,000 is spent each year on each child, and yet the student failure rate rises higher and higher. At what point do we have to ask, "Just how much money is enough in order for government schools to graduate students armed with a decent education? And, just to put a cherry on top, will the schools experiencing third-graders failing to be advanced please explain why?

Let's be clear about how much money is given to a school, based on attendance. Just because Washington, D.C. spends $20,000 per year per pupil does not mean that the $20,000 gets to the classroom. Oh, no.

I've attended local school district meetings, spoken with teachers, asked for a balance sheet of how money is spent, and a list of all salaries for all school employees. What I get back is gibberish. The truth is, of all the money given to the school system by us, it'll never be enough because money isn't the problem. The problem rests firmly in the lap of the school administrations and teacher unions (the National Education Association (NEA) and American Federation of Teachers (AFT). Fix those problems, and you'll see a much higher graduation rate for students, for less money invested. And you won't have so many children being held back in any grade as we're seeing today. It's our tax dollars being spent; we need transparency from schools on how it's being spent. Demand it.

Another problem is that teachers cannot be tested for competency, ever. No teacher should be allowed in a classroom unless they fully understand the subject they are teaching, and can teach it using proper English. The teacher unions won't allow it. There have been cases where some teachers were required to teach English, but couldn't speak or write English above an eighth grade level. That teacher couldn't be removed because of teacher union rules. There are incidents where teachers changed the grades of their students to ensure that those students got higher grades, thus making the teacher appear more competent than they actually were. Some were caught. In Atlanta, Georgia many were caught. They're still teaching. Isn't changing a student's grade a crime? I thought so, but evidently teachers are exempt from some laws, courtesy of the teacher's unions.

Most schools don't have enough paper, pencils, pens, or textbooks for their students. The school sends notes home to the parents telling them what they need to buy for their child(ren) in order for their child(ren) to have adequate supplies. Some schools force students to share a textbook. At the same time, school administrators seem to go to endless conferences at bastions of education like Las Vegas, Vail, and Hawaii, using money meant for students. Some school districts make donations to organizations hey like, taking money out of the classroom.

Here's a story to illustrate the point. I worked at a computer hardware/software company in 1981. My sister, a veteran teacher, was teaching at a middle school not far away. We were chatting one day and she was lamenting that she didn't have binders, paper, pencils, or pens for her students. I said I'd see what I could do to help. I asked senior management if they would be willing to donate some of the old binders, some pads of paper, pens, and anything else that would help out a school, and they agreed. My sister had fellow teachers come to our offices one afternoon, and we loaded up a large pickup truck with a lot of what they needed. You'd have thought I was a rock star. The teachers were so grateful that my company would donate these supplies to help the kids. If the company hadn't offered to help, several hundred students would have had no supplies since the school provided nothing. The administration at that school was living large on their inflated salaries. This was not a school in a high income neighborhood. This was a low income neighborhood. For parents to had to buy these supplies would have really hurt them in their pocketbook. The question I have is, just what is the priority for these government schools? It doesn't appear that students are very high on the pecking order.

If you want to get an idea of who is doing well at your kid's school, drive to the school parking lot in the morning or afternoon. Find the reserved spots for senior administration folks. Then count the number of Lexus, BMWs, Cadillac cars parked in those slots. Then go look at the parking area for the teachers, and see how many very old cars you see there. That gives you a perspective on where the money is going.

If you can get access to the information in your child's school, find out how many of those schools provide school supplies for the children. Find out how much the layers of administration make in salaries and benefits. Find out what janitors are paid. Ask for a list of all non-teaching employees at your child's school. If you can get that information, you'll see where the money is spent.

Why, when a local area has the opportunity to send some students to a charter school through a voucher, does a raffle have to be held? It's because there may be 200 seats open at a charter school, and 5,000 parents want to take advantage of the opportunity to get their children out of "failing" government schools. And the leftists don't like this at all.

In New York city, a teacher who has committed acts so egregious that even the teacher's union won't let him or her be in a classroom, is still protected. There's a building in New York called the "*rubber room.*" John Stossel did an excellent one-hour show on just this subject. Reports indicate that it can take up to ten years to fire an incompetent or dangerous teacher in New York, thanks to the teacher's unions. The offending teacher is sent to the rubber room. They spend their days reading, accessing the Internet, napping, whatever they want to do. They draw full pay and receive full benefits, all thanks to the teacher's union. If you ever saw the Rube Goldberg-like flowchart showing the steps necessary to fire a teacher, you'd fall down laughing. This is just another example of the power of teacher unions.

For those several hundred non-teaching teachers in a local school system, what do you think it costs taxpayers? This would be funny if it weren't so tragic. So, students are failing, being set back a year, and yet a teacher can't be fired for incompetence. And the teacher's unions say, "Give us more money." It's a tragedy, and we're letting it happen.

There is also the factor of free speech and political correctness in schools. For example, some schools, from New York to California, have various lists of banned words in tests. Here are just a few.

- Birthdays
- Celebrities
- Cigarettes
- Crime
- Divorce
- Evolution
- Politics

- Sex
- Religion
- Poverty
- Expensive car names
- Alcohol
- Death
- Disease

There are many, many more, but you get the point. Our schools are deciding what words can be used in tests in a futile attempt to "protect" children and their feelings. Protect children from what, real life? How many of these mutants in education today went through school without seeing or hearing any of these words, and how did they turn out? Wait a minute; forget that. We know how they turned out.

Are you outraged over this? You should be. This kind of thing goes on in government schools all over America. Take a visit to any charter or private school, and see if they have a forbidden words list for test questions. They don't. What these bureaucrats in the New York school system are doing borders on criminal to me. It's well beyond stupid. I was always under this silly assumption that schools existed in order to teach children how to think, not what to think, and prepare them for the real world? Do these teacher unions and leftist politicians really believe that they're preparing the students for real life, or do they even care? When these bureaucrats or teacher union folks were in school, did they have a forbidden words list? Were they offended—terrible word—by words used on tests? Of course they weren't. It's as if the government school system is just a large petri dish where only the most virulent strains of ignorance emerge.

Just how do you test students on U.S. History if you can't include the word slavery in the test question? How do the test writers phrase the question? I've got it; call it the "*unpaid servitude*" era in American history. That should do it.

How do the testers write questions for examinations that do not use any of the words in the list? Please, somebody, explain this to me.

Teacher unions are supportive of Democrat politicians at all levels, in great numbers. Polling and surveys have proven this. Why? Teacher unions discovered a long time ago that if they contribute piles of cash to Democrat candidates—I call them bribes—the unions can rely on the Democrats to keep the status quo for education, and support teacher unions. Democrat politicians ensure that the kingdom of government schools stays in place. If you don't believe me, take a look at how many bills have been brought up in Congress to open up "school choice" and "school vouchers," and see how many have received Democrat support. None. Democrats can be counted on to fight against charter schools and vouchers, the children's needs be damned.

Look online for the American Federation of Teachers and the National Teacher's Association respective home pages. Read what they're all about, the focus of their agenda. Those agendas do not focus on the children but, rather, on power, and they have a lot of it. The Democrat party is beholden to teacher unions because of the money. Do some basic research and find out how many children of Washington politicians, Democrat and Republican, attend government schools. I'll save you some time, less than 50% of the children of Washington politicians send their children to government schools. Over half of their children attend private schools. It's great for them, but not for the working class.

I remember when I was in high school. It wasn't a large school by today's standards, but there were about 1,300-1,400 students. You could walk into the Administration office, and count all of the employees in about ten seconds. There was a Principal, a Vice-Principal, a nurse's aide, and some office staff. That was it. The various sports teams each had a coach and one assistant. There were, I think, three janitors that worked at night, and another janitor on hand during the day. The total number of employees was less than 25. Some of the sports coaches were also classroom teachers.

Now take a look at how many employees work at any given high school today. Anyone want to bet that there are over 75, maybe 100 employees in a high school of comparable size? When I was in high school, there were maybe five school buses. They were used primarily to transport sports teams or the band to some event. Most kids walked to school, rode a bike, or drove a car (those pesky rich kids). Me? I walked to school, a distance of about two or two and a half miles—and no, it wasn't through 10-foot high snow drifts. Now look at how many school buses there are at any given high school. For each school district there is a fleet of buses. A fleet. How many janitors, union employees, do the schools have on the payroll now? Do the schools need all of these employees? Of course not. The teacher unions force schools to create and fill these positions, and that's more money not reaching the classroom.

Within the school administration itself, there are literally legions of employees. Many schools have teachers who never see a classroom. I learned this in conversations with teachers from several schools. There are teachers on the payroll to teach classroom teachers how to teach, and around here they make over $60,000 per year. You might want to read that sentence a couple of times. I thought teachers were qualified to teach when they were hired. Evidently that's not the case. Perhaps the classes needed for a teaching credential might include several intern assignments, practice teaching assignments, and situations they might encounter, and how to handle them. This teacher's teacher is no doubt a union-driven position, costing you and me a lot of money. There are all kinds of counselors on the payroll, too. The coaching for the various sports in high schools is more like a college staff. There are coaches and numerous assistants for each sport. How much money is diverted from the classroom for all of this peripheral nonsense? Oh, I've got it. It's not their money; it's ours.

Many years ago, when I was retiring from the military, I talked to my sister about perhaps getting my teaching credential and becoming a school teacher. I'd been a certified Naval Instructor and really enjoyed it. My sister told me in no uncertain terms that I was nuts. She said that I'd already taken one vow of poverty in the military; why would I want to take another vow of poverty as a teacher? This conversation occurred in 1978, when teachers weren't paid all that well, and still aren't when compared to school administrators. She also told me that I wouldn't last as a teacher because she knew how I worked as an instructor for the Navy. I had a curriculum and an instructor's guide, but often I'd improvise in order to make sure my students understood. I wanted to make sure that I saw "*the light go on in their eyes.*" I was told by a military instructor with many years of experience that, "*If your students didn't learn it, you didn't teach it.*" And that became my mantra. I don't believe that government schools even know what that mantra means. The other thing my sister told me was that in government schools you teach what they tell you, and you teach it the way they tell you. If you deviate and become creative, you won't last long. So, I passed on becoming a teacher.

The government school policy on sex, from my observations, is that kids are going to have sex anyway, so give them condoms for free, in middle schools as well as in high schools. Back in the 1990's we had a Surgeon General of the United States that said exactly that. Well, just as an aside, you and I pay for those free condoms. What's next regarding sex among school children, providing a couple of rooms, complete with a nice bed, nightstand, a shower, maybe a pack of cigarettes, and a refrigerator stocked some beer? Why do government schools endorse children having sex without consequences? For that matter, why are government schools getting involved in a social issue such as this in the first place? If school kids are getting the message from their school that they're going to have sex anyway, why not just go have sex? And if you didn't pick up your free condom, and the girl doesn't insist on you using one, what happens? Does this government school attitude contribute to the number of young girls getting pregnant? Gosh, ya think? And what about all of the sexually transmitted diseases (STD) connected to sex today?

On the up side, kids can't bring an aspirin to school or they'll get busted for drug possession. But, on the down side, kids can do drug deals on campus, and probably never get caught. Government school officials just don't want to get that involved in that.

School kids can and do wear clothes that border on the obscene. I was driving past a middle school one afternoon, in the spring, and I thought for a minute that I was driving the streets where hookers ply their trade. 10, 11, 12-year old girls in mini-skirts, low cut blouses, bra straps hanging out, wearing high heels, piercings, and makeup all over them. I really thought they were trolling for some action, not going to school, but maybe that's the same thing. The school doesn't seem to care what kids wear-freedom of speech you know. Some of the boys are wearing pants about six sizes too big, without a belt, holding them up with one hand as they shuffle along, and this is cool? Showing your underwear seems to be another cool thing, too. I wonder if that's related to the old story we're all heard, that we're always supposed to wear clean underwear in case we're in an accident. No, that can't be it. Maybe those pants were on sale, and they couldn't afford a belt. Yeah, that has to be it. I wonder how parents could let their daughters leave for school and not notice that they are dressed like whores. Fathers, if there is one in the picture, look at their son with his baggy pants, no belt, and say, "wow, you look great."

What's causing all of this to happen? There isn't enough paper to write all of the reasons down. One reason has surfaced. The destruction of the family unit has torn a big hole in the fabric of America. And it has been the Communist Democrats that have pursued this destruction. The lack of a loving, stable home, with a father and a mother dedicated to being involved in the lives of their children has cost our children dearly. Parents can provide them with accountability, responsibility, and guide them to their dream of reaching as high as they can. Once the nuclear family is torn apart, anything can happen, and none of it is good. We have more and more children having children. Government schools don't much care what kids wear, or don't wear, or care much about what goes on inside the walls of the school. Government schools are just education mills, going through the motions, at an exorbitant cost.

Some in political power want the nuclear family redefined. No longer should it be mom, dad, and the kids. No, no, no. Government believes that it is now a part of the family. Some of our leaders also believe that the dad is no longer necessary. Look at how many of these so-called female Hollywood stars have children but no husband or father in the picture. There are homosexual women who adopt children and they, and their wife or husband—I'm confused as to which role the other woman plays—raise these children with no male presence or role model influence. And two homosexual men will adopt children, with no female nurturing or influence. Government thinks this is just fine. At the same time, kids are exposed to the peer pressure of drug use, and many succumb. Kids suffer more depressions, and many more commit suicide. The number of single-parent families is rising dramatically. The government does not seem concerned about the destruction of the family.

Is this the America we want for our kids and grandkids? They may have two mothers, no father. They may have two fathers, no mother. They may have a mother, but no father. They may have a father and no mother. They look around and see that other kids have a mom and a dad, and wonder what's wrong with them. To be fair, there is no scientific data to absolutely show that these types of "families" have more or less instances of kids gone bad than the traditional family. What I fail to understand is why some believe that the original nuclear family had to be destroyed. Is it intentional so as to break down families into some meaningless structure that can be redefined to include homosexual unions to be as normal as any other "marriage." Being able to get "married" is the *Holy Grail* for homosexuals, despite the fact that the vast majority of Americans oppose it. Government schools are facilitating the destruction of the family as are most government entities.

Any government school that would dare to defy the government mandates or the teacher unions will pay dearly. Government schools suffer from the heavy hand of teacher unions dictating the bureaucracy of education. Government schools are forced to adopt a promiscuous attitude with child sex. One of the most important things to understand about government schools is the lack of parental involvement. Too many parents seem to think of government schools as day care centers, and don't care what happens there. If their son or daughter were to act up, cause trouble, have a fight, and the school has to suspend little Joey or Sally, then the parents come alive. It's all the fault of the teacher or the school; it's never the fault of their precious little miscreant. Some parents literally attack a teacher or school if their child becomes a monster, but never care enough to get involved in their child's education. Most parents just want their kids to disappear to school each day, and be home when the parents arrive. Other than that, they don't care. I believe that this is the more important problem because these government schools couldn't get away with half of the stuff they do if the parents gave a damn.

Some kids cheat in school; parents don't seem to care. Some kids download term papers from the Internet; parents don't seem to care. Kids get multiple tattoos; parents don't seem to care. Kids get their ears pierced, their noses pierced, their eyebrows pierced, their lips pierced, get their tongues pierced, their bellybutton pierced, their genitalia pierced, and parents don't seem to care. I wonder just who is paying for all this body work? Their little Johnny looks like a billboard for a tattoo parlor; and parents don't seem to care. Kids demand and get the latest iPod, iPhone, iPad, and parents just keep shelling out the money, or use the credit card. Kids send nude photos of themselves through their cell phones, and parents don't seem to care. Kids refuse to clean their room, refuse to come home on time, stay up half the night playing video games (bought for them by their parents), won't get up and get to school on time; won't do homework; fail test after test; and the parents don't seem to care. That's what the government schools are facing each and every year. Some parents believe that their role is to become their child's best friend, not parent them. They're wrong. The job of a parent is to prepare their children for real life, not indulge their every whim.

There are some schools in this country that don't give grades in high school. They want these children to feel good about themselves, build self-esteem. Oh my goodness, isn't that sweet? What happens if one of those children wants to go to college? What do they tell the college administrators—we didn't have grades, but I really feel good about myself? Good luck with that one. How about when those children have to interview for a job? What happens when ten people interview for one job opening, which means nine of them don't get the job? They are told no, you don't get the job. Go feel good about yourself someplace else. How are these children supposed to cope and deal with this rejection? They've never been taught by their parents or the school that there are winners, and there are losers in life. Here's what the parents of these children should do.

Ask those teachers and the school administrators where no grades are assigned if they got grades in high school. They'll have to answer yes. Ask them if they got grades when they went to college. They'll have to answer yes. Ask them if they had to take and pass tests to get their respective teaching credentials. They'll have to answer yes. Now, ask them how any of these students who are not receiving grades in high school will be able to get into college if they have no grades. The answer just has to be a riot. What was good for the teachers and administrators then isn't good for your children now. What they're doing is preparing those children for is no useful education and unemployment. Is that what America's government schools should be doing, preparing children to be on welfare forever?

In many schools, there is no physical education period. That's right, no physical exercise period at school. The schools then complain that students are too fat. Duh. I can't speak for girls, but for boys, getting outside and running around is a good thing. Pent up energy is released, playing games is good for them. But no, some schools just think PE is bad for kids and at the same time complain that too many kids are becoming obese, and many boys are unruly in class.

Some schools do not allow any touching between students. In the halls, classroom, or outside, there is to be no touching. So, young boys can't shake hands or slap each other on the back. The same applies to the girls. Girls can't hold hands and can't give each other a hug. No, no, no.

Your Tax Dollars Are Paying for Food Wagons in Government Schools

It has now become commonplace in schools across the country to feed children, paying for it with our tax dollars. Some are fed breakfast, some are fed breakfast and lunch, and others are being fed three meals a day. Aren't we generous and compassionate? Yes, your tax dollars are used to a) hire extra school staff to set up and feed the children one, two, or three meals a day. The federal government actually solicits families to sign up their children for the "free" meals. Isn't it amazing that the government has so much "free" money to spend when the nation is $16 Trillion in debt? I'm just asking. What does it take to get a child enrolled for free meals? Sign a form. There is no investigation into the finances of the family signing up their child(ren) for free meals. There are even plans to implement free meals on days when there is no school (like summer vacation). Isn't that just swell? This is yet another responsibility taken off the table for parents. Let the government feed your children. Where in the Constitution does it say that the government has the authority to spend tax dollars on meals for children in school? It's not there.

There have been several investigative reports done, and published in local papers—without any government cooperation—showing that over 75% of the food served at those "free" meals is tossed into the garbage can, uneaten. It seems that some children want food that fits their cultural tastes, or isn't what they would eat at home. Like the Guantanamo prison for terrorists, many of these kids want culturally acceptable food. How many of the children being fed at these schools are here illegally? No one knows for sure since schools are forbidden from determining if a child is an illegal alien during enrollment. It just wouldn't be nice to intrude into their lives that way. But, we will feed them so as not to trouble the parents with actually cooking for their children. Just open your wallet and pay and pay and pay. Is this the kind of America we want, where the government takes over the feeding of our children and grandchildren? Is the government inventing another entitlement, which is another way of saying that the government is "bribing" voters with handouts?

Do some of you remember a book that came out some years back, called "*It Takes a Village?*" This was a book that Hillary Clinton took credit for writing though some informed sources said it was written by someone else (a ghost writer), and Hillary just put her name on it. The point of the book is to imply, no, declare, that parents can't raise their children alone. It requires government programs, government schools, all kinds of government intervention in order for a child to be raised properly, whatever that means. Since it's Hillary Clinton writing it, sort of, it means that if you choose not to abort your child, the baby should be turned over to the government once you've weaned and toilet trained him or her. The government can and should raise that child, not the parents.

Here are some classes that absolutely should be taught in government high schools, not that they ever will.

- Checking accounts and Checkbooks 101. Introduce what a checkbook is, how the whole process of a checking account works. Demonstrate and have students perform exercises on depositing money into their bank's account. Learn how to read a bank statement on how much money you have.
- Savings Accounts 101. Introduce the concept of saving money in a bank savings account, and how to do it. Teach and demonstrate how to open a savings account, how

to add money to your savings account, and how to read a bank statement on the value of the savings account.

- Credit Cards 101. Introduce the concept of credit to students. Demonstrate how what they charge on a credit card means that the student has now acquired a debt. Those things a child buys on credit. Teach and demonstrate the concept of interest charges on credit card balances. Teach and demonstrate how to pay off a credit card balance, and what happens when they don't.

- Interviewing for a Job 101. This could and probably should be taught in colleges as well as high schools. Teach and demonstrate the process of applying and interviewing for a job. Teach the concept of competition for a job, and how to deal with the rejection of not getting the job. Teach and have role play job interview sessions. Teach and demonstrate how to dress for a job interview. Introduce and demonstrate how to create a resume. Teach and demonstrate the process of looking for a job.

- How Personal Appearance Affects Job Interviews 101. Teach and demonstrate the effects of personal dress and grooming affect the impression a job candidate has on the hiring manager. Teach and demonstrate how facial piercings and large numbers of tattoos that are easily seen can negatively affect the impression job seekers have on hiring managers. Teach students that there is no hiring manager who must hire you, and the resume, appearance, and ability to communicate all directly affect how you are perceived during a job interview.

- Having Children While in School 101. Teach students the ramifications of having children before being able to support them. Provide an objective list of the costs of prenatal care, giving birth in the hospital, and purchasing all the supplies needed to take care of the baby. Present the implications of where to live with the baby, and the costs borne by the grandparents of the child. Provide portrayals of a young woman, without a husband or father, trying to raise and care for a baby while trying to complete studies in school. Always include a presentation on the moral and financial responsibility on the father of the baby, and whether the father is willing to help raise and care for the child, or leave that responsibility up to the mother.

Perhaps if the government schools would provide these classes, and I'm sure you could think of several others, the students would be better served.

Do We Need a Pesky Congress Any Longer?

The short answer is, of course we do. First of all, our Constitution calls for a Congress, and sets forth how it will be comprised, but it's no secret that the current President has no use for such a body unless they'll do what he tells them to do. This President would like to do away with Congress and issue laws and orders, and spend money he doesn't have, as he sees fit. When you look at this list of Czars below, and couple them with the cabinet secretaries, you've got a politburo suitable for Communist Russia. And this President selected and appointed these czars. What is a politburo? Let me tell you. Here's the top definition: "The supreme policy-making authority in most Communist countries."

Well then, what is a Czar. Again, let me tell you. "An autocratic ruler or leader."

The President has said on more than one occasion that he wished the Congress would do what he wanted to have them do, but he wasn't going to let that stop him from doing what he believes is best for the country. And what he thinks is best is to "*transform*" America into a Communist country. Those are my words, not his, but I think the implication of his words is clear.

Look at the titles of these "Czars." Some of their titles seem to mirror committee titles in the Congress. Look at the similarity of views between these Czars. They are almost uniformly against the Second Amendment, wanting no citizen to own a weapon. They are in agreement in their support of abortion. They are uniformly opposed to private sector businesses. They are very much pro-United Nations. See the section on Agenda 21, and you'll have no doubt as to why the Czars favor the United Nations.

If this president manages to get reelected, he will have nothing to stop him from trampling the Constitution, ignoring Congress completely, daring anyone to stop him as he rushes to get his agenda completed. From all of the signs, the people he has surrounded himself with, and his actions thus far, and the conclusion is easy to reach; he is a Communist, and must be removed from office. What do you think? Is this the America you want to pass on to your kids and grandkids?

Richard Holbrooke—Afghanistan Czar—This guy is an ultrak-liberal, anti-gun former Governor Of New Mexico. Holbrooke is pro-abortion, favors drug legalization, and would like to get rid of the Second Amendment to the Constitution. Sure, and I'd like to send him to live in Cuba.

Ed Montgomery—Auto recovery Czar—This fellow is a known anti-business and black American activist. He strongly supports Affirmative Action (reverse discrimination) and Job Preference for black Americans. As the University of Maryland, Dean of the Business School, he teaches that U.S. business has caused world poverty. He is also a board member of ACORN, and a member of the Communist DuBois Club.

Jeffrey Crowley—AIDS Czar—Mr. Crowley is a radical homosexual and homosexual rights activist. He believes in and supports homosexual marriage and wants a special status designation for homosexuals only, which includes free healthcare.

Alan Bersin—Border Czar—He is an ultra-liberal friend of Hillary Clinton. He served as the Border Czar under our old friend, Janet Reno—his orders were to keep the borders open, and keep the federal government away from any involvement.

David J. Hayes—California Water Czar—He is a senior fellow with the radical environmentalist group "Progress Policy". He has no education, background, or experience in water management.

Ron Bloom—Car Czar—He was an auto union worker. He is known to be anti-business and anti-nuclear power. He worked hard to force the United States auto makers out of business. He sits on the Board of Chrysler which is now Union-owned. I wonder what he's doing to get GM to repay the $35-40 billion they still owe the taxpayers.

Dennis Ross—Central Region Czar—He believes and supports *U.S.* policy is the cause of war in the Middle East. He is one of the President's apologists to the world. He is very anti-gun and very much favors abortion.

Lynn Rosenthal—Domestic Violence Czar—She is the director of the National Network to End Domestic Violence. She has a reputation as a vicious anti-male feminist. She even supports male castration. Ouch. Just a quick question—if you're in charge of domestic violence, does that mean you're in charge of causing more domestic violence, or confining the domestic violence so it only applies to hurting men? Just asking.

Gil Kerlikowske—Drug Czar—He is a devoted lobbyist for every restrictive gun law proposal you can find, and is the former Chief of Police in liberal Seattle WA. He believes that no American should own a firearm, and very much supports the legalization of all drugs.

Carol Browner—Energy and Environment Czar—She is known as a political radical. She is the former head of the EPA. She is also known for her anti-business activism. She favors total gun ban in the U.S. Isn't she now, more or less, still in charge of the EPA?

Joshua DuBois—Faith-based Czar—He is a very political black activist. He has a degree in Black Nationalism. He is a lobbyist to stop all gun ownership by citizens. Just what does a Faith-based Czar actually do?

Cameron Davis—Great Lakes Czar—he is a Chicago-based radical anti-business environmentalist. He has said that he blames George Bush for "Poisoning the water that minorities have to drink." He has no experience or training in water management whatsoever, but he is a former ACORN board member so I guess that counts.

Van Jones—Green Jobs Czar—(since resigned). He is a black activist with strong anti-white views. He is a member of the American Communist Party and San Francisco Communist Party. He once stated that George Bush caused the 9/11 attacks and wanted Bush investigated by the World Court for war crimes. At least he admitted he was a proud Communist.

Daniel Fried—Guantanamo Closure Czar—He is a human rights activist for foreign terrorists. He has stated that he believes America has caused the Global War on Terrorism. He believes that terrorists have rights above and beyond the rights of Americans.

Nancy-Ann DeParle—Health Czar—She is the former head of Medicare / Medicaid. She is a strong proponent of Healthcare Rationing (i.e. "Death Panels"). She is married to a reporter for the New York Times.

Vivek Kundra—Information Czar—He was born in New Delhi, India. He controls all public information, including labels and news releases. He also has the ability to monitor all private Internet emails.

Todd Stern—International Climate Czar—He has a reputation of being very anti-business, and is the former White House Chief of Staff. He is a strong supporter of the Kyoto Accord. He is also pushing hard for Cap and Trade legislation. To round our his credentials, he blames U.S. business for Global Warming, and opposes prosperity for U.S. businesses.

Dennis Blair—Intelligence Czar—He is retired from the U.S. Navy. In his position, he stopped the U.S. guided missile program because he believed it to be "provocative." He is the Chairman of the ultra-Liberal "Council on Foreign Relations" which blames American organizations for regional wars. It should be noted, however, that many Republican political leaders are members of the CFR.

George Mitchell—Mideast Peace Czar—He is the former Senator from Maine. He is considered to be a leftist radical. He has said that Israel should be split up into "2 or 3" smaller, more manageable plots" He sincerely opposes nuclear energy, very much against citizen gun ownership, and is a pro homosexual "rights" advocate.

Kenneth Feinberg—Pay Czar—He was the Chief of Staff to Ted Kennedy. He is a lawyer who was involved in the payoffs to victim families as a result of the 9/11 attack, from which he made a small fortune.

Cass Sunstein—Regulatory Czar—He is an avowed liberal activist judge who believes free speech needs to be limited for the "common good." He essentially opposes the First Amendment. He has ruled against personal freedoms many times on private gun ownership and right to free speech cases.

John Holdren—Science Czar—He is a fierce ideological environmentalist, and a Sierra Club anti-business activist. He believes that U.S. business has caused world poverty. He has no Science training.

Earl Devaney—Stimulus Accountability Czar—He spent career trying to take guns away from American citizens. He believes in Open Borders with Mexico. He has authored a statement that blames U.S. gun stores for drug war in Mexico.

J. Scott Gration—Sudan Czar—He is a native of Democratic Republic of the Congo. He believes the U.S. does little to help Third World countries. He is a member of the CFR, asking for higher U.S. taxes to support the United Nations.

Herb Allison—TARP Czar—He is or was the CEO of Fannie Mae. He was one of the people primarily responsible for the U.S. recession by used real estate mortgages to back up the U.S. stock market. The result of this action was that millions of people lost their homes.

John Brennan—Terrorism Czar—He's now one of the security and anti-terrorism cabal. This is a man who is an anti-CIA activist. He has absolutely no training, education, or experience in diplomatic or government affairs. He also believes in an open border with Mexico, and proposes that we have a dialogue with terrorists. He has also suggested to the president that the United States disband its military.

Aneesh Chopra—Technology Czar—This is another czar with no technology training. He worked for the Advisory Board Company, a healthcare think tank for hospitals. He in an anti-doctor activist. He is a supporter of healthcare rationing (death panels). He wants all doctors to work exclusively for the government Healthcare plan.

Adolfo Carrion Jr.—Urban Affairs Czar—He is a Puerto Rico-born anti-American activist and a member of a Latin America leftist organization. He is also a slum lord millionaire in the Bronx, New York. He personally owns several lavish homes and condominiums which he got from "sweetheart" deals with labor unions. He is an advocate of higher taxes on the middle class to pay for minority housing and healthcare.

Ashton Carter—Weapons Czar—He is a devout leftist who wants all private weapons in the U.S. destroyed. He supports a United nations ban on firearms ownership in America.

Gary Samore—WMD Policy Czar—He is a former member of the Communist Party of America. He has advocated for the destruction of all weapons of mass destruction in the United States, including nuclear, as a show of good faith.

The Czars have changed over the past couple of years. Look at their associations and relationships. With this bunch surrounding the President, it's no wonder he doesn't pay any attention to the Congress. Show this list to your leftist friends and ask them to defend the views of this bunch.

I believe that the President intends to do what he wants and dare someone, or somebody, to stop him.

There is NO Such Thing as a Hate Crime

Let me give you a hypothetical situation. A burglar, a white man, breaks into a house in the middle of the night, believing that no one is home. While in the process of filling his bag with silverware, jewelry, and other valuables, in the dark, he is confronted by a man coming down the stairs, yelling out. The burglar is armed. The man coming down the stairs starts rushing into the room where the burglar is located. The burglar fires his gun and kills the man, then runs away. He is caught a few days later. He is charged with assorted crimes, plus one additional charge—a hate crime. It turns out the man he shot was a black American. It doesn't matter that the burglar didn't know the home owner was a black American, it only matters that he was. In America today, that's a hate crime. If you are convicted of a hate crime, extra years are added to your sentence as an additional penalty. So, instead of getting, say, 25 years in prison, the burglar could receive an additional 10-15 years because of the hate crime enhancement.

Here are some other situations. Can you determine which are hate crimes, and which are not?

Two women, both white, get in a fight outside a bar. Neither woman identifies herself as a homosexual. One woman stabs the other, and kills her. Is this a hate crime? Answer: No.

Two men, both black Americans, get in a fight, and one shoots the other, and the man dies. Is this a hate crime? Answer: No.

Two men, both homosexual, beat up a third man, also a homosexual, rob him, stab him, and he dies. Is this a hate crime? Answer: No.

A white man gets into a drunken brawl with another man, who is a black American, and that man dies. Is this a hate crime? Answer: Yes.

A Latino woman, in the course of a robbery, shoots and kills a white man who is working in the store. Is this a hate crime? Answer: No.

Two black men carjack a vehicle, and in the process, kill the car owner, who is white. Is this a hate crime? Answer: No.

At a football game, two men get into a fight that spills out into the parking lot. As a result, one man kills the other with a knife. The man who committed the crime is a heterosexual white man. The man killed is a white homosexual man, though neither knew the sexual persuasion of the other. Is this a hate crime? Answer: Yes.

Are you noticing a pattern here? If two white men have a years-long squabble, have had several fights before, and one man finally gets so mad he gets a gun and shoots the other man, that's not a hate crime because neither man is a member of a "*protected*" class of Americans.

It breaks down like this. Many politicians, with willing support from judges, decided that the justice system has the amazing power to see into the minds of accused criminals, especially those who commit crimes against helpless members of protected classes of Americans. These protected classes include homosexuals of either gender, black Americans of either gender, Latino Americans of either gender and, perhaps, Asians of either gender. This is all stacked against white men and women. They are not members of a protected class.

What is so silly about this is that there is no definitive way of determining what a hate crime is, especially if it is confined to victims who are members of a protected class of people.

If I was a member of one of these protected classes, I'd wonder why the government, and judges, believes that they know what was in the heart and mind of the perpetrator. The truth is that they don't. That's not the intent of this manufactured legislation. The sole purpose of the hate crime legislation is to toss a pandering bone to certain classes of people to get their vote and support. Any member of the President's administration or of Congress who actually believes there is such a thing as a hate crime is nuts. Any judge who enforces a hate crime enhancement doesn't deserve to be on the bench. Any lawyer who charges someone with a hate crime should lose their law license. There are more than enough laws in existence to deal with criminal acts. There are penalties for breaking those laws. Now we have legislators and courts deciding that they know what's in the mind of a law breaker. It's stupid on its face. We have to penalize some people more than others for the same crime. Why? Hate is a state of mind, or an attitude; it's not a behavior, and it has nothing to do with committing a crime. Hate crime enhancements are also very discriminatory, and maybe that's the point. In this country we punish bad behavior; we don't punish thought.

Get U.S. Out of United Nations, Now

Over the years I've come to the conclusion that the United Nations is a criminal organization intent on ruling the world, and our political leaders seem to be fine with that. The U.N. has no standing military. They get other countries to send their military to operate under U.N. control. Say what? It's very clear in our military that no member of our armed forces will ever take orders from anyone not a member of the U.S. military. One serviceman was court martialed and tossed out of the military because he refused to wear the beret of the U.N. and take orders from some foreign commander. The U.N. has no money, produces nothing, and sells nothing. The U.N. has no power to tax, though they're working on that. I think it would be a great idea to tell the U.N. to move its building to Zambia, Russia, or France. Let those countries put up with this horde of freeloaders. Wait, I have a better idea. Move the U.N. building to Greece. It would give some employment to Greeks, and some income for restaurants and massage parlors. While we're at it, let's reduce our contribution to the U.N. to 1/197th of the total bill. Every country should pay its "fair share" to be in the U.N. If any of the 197 countries just said, "We aren't paying," what would the U.N. do about that—send them a bill? What if all 197 countries said, "We're not paying." Would the U.N. just go away? I'll vote for that. Given that America is about $16 Trillion in debt, maybe cutting off the U.N. would help a little bit. The U.N. is constantly pushing its agenda, its treaties, trying to get countries to sign on. There's Agenda 21 which few people in the America even know about. There's the world wide arms treaty, designed to disarm every country that is a member of the U.N.—our Secretary of State, Hillary Clinton, has been quoted as being supportive of that treaty. The Law of the Sea Treaty (LOST) is another brainchild of this brain dead organization. LOST is intended to take control of all of the oceans. If the U.N. gains control of the oceans, the U.S. will suffer greatly, and there is nothing to stop the U.N. from taxing Americans for use of the oceans without having to go through the U.S. Congress. The U.N. seems determined to turn the United States into a third world cesspool, destroying our Constitution, and controlling all of us. We need to get out of the U.N., and toss them off our soil, sooner rather than later.

Within the United Nations there is a Security Council. When this council votes, not very often, any country with a member in the Security Council can vote No on an issue, and it is not approved. All of the member countries must vote Yes for any proposal to be approved. The five permanent members of the U.N. Security Council are the United States, Russia, France, United Kingdom, and China. France? Would anyone care to make a bet on whether Russia or China will ever support the U.S. on the Security Council? Me neither. There are also ten non-permanent members of the Security Council, and those members serve a limited term. Currently, those ten countries are Columbia, Germany, Guatemala, South Africa, Togo, Portugal, Pakistan, Morocco, India, and Azerbaijan. Now many of those countries like America? The funding of the United Nations is "shared" by the member countries based on their "ability" to pay. Really? The United States pays about 22% of the total U.N. budget, which is about $1.1 billion per year. This information is readily available from many sources. We're a country that is more than $16 Trillion in debt, with an economy that has been going nowhere for over four years, and very high unemployment. But the United States pays 22% of the budget for the United Nations?

The deliberative process in the United Nations reminds me of a scene from one of the *Star Wars* movies where the "galaxy or universe council" has to have one committee, then another committee, and yet more committees study a problem, for months, maybe years, without actually doing anything to resolve the problem. That scene reminds me a lot of how the United Nations operates. One thing the United Nations likes to do is come up with treaties, lots of treaties, and none of those treaties, in my view, are in the best interests of the United States. According to the United Nations' own web site, there are over 500 treaties deposited with the Secretary-General of the United Nations. You also need to understand that if any treaty is presented to the United States, the President may or may not sign that treaty. If the President signs that treaty, it goes before the U.S. Senate for ratification. If that treaty is ratified by the U.S. Senate, it supersedes any conflict with our U.S. Constitution. Ratified treaties are the new law, the U.S. Constitution is subordinate. There is one thing to be thankful for regarding United Nations treaties. The United Nations doesn't hide treaties from view. You can access their web site and find them all. Let's look at just a few of them.

Law of the Sea Treaty (LOST)'

At least this treaty is appropriately named. This treaty has been under construction since the mid 1940's. The LOST gives the United Nations vast control over the use and exploitation of the sea's' resources. Although in November, 1993 the treaty gained the number of ratifications needed to take effect on November 16, 1994, the United States should still refrain from signing and ratifying it.

The LOST establishes rules for such matters as resource jurisdiction, navigation, and seabed mining. Although proponents of the treaty say that an internationally recognized system of rules is important, commerce and transportation have proceeded unhampered without the treaty, and other mechanisms exist for resolving international disputes. Moreover, the treaty's objectionable provisions on seabed mining, if they become effective, will harm both the West and the developing world. The LOST's mandates will increase costs and depress productivity.

The U.N. itself won't be enforcing these "guidelines." They have a few enforcement organizations already in place. These organizations, such as the International Maritime Organization, the International Whaling Organization, and the International Seabed Authority would have United Nations authority to investigate, and stop any activity that violates the treaty. Fines or direct taxation on American citizens would then be imposed. That is from the Law of the Sea Treaty Information Center. The LOST calls for technology transfers and wealth transfers from developed to undeveloped nations. It also <u>requires</u> parties to the treaty to <u>adopt regulations and laws</u> in order to control pollution of the marine environment. Such provisions were among the reasons President Ronald Reagan rejected the treaty in 1982. As Edwin Meese, U.S. Attorney General under President Reagan, explained some years ago, ". . . it was out of step with the concepts of economic liberty and free enterprise that Ronald Reagan wants to inspire throughout the world."

In addition to the economic provisions, the treaty also establishes specific jurisdictional limits on the ocean area that countries may claim, including a 12-mile territorial sea limit and a 200-mile exclusive economic zone limit.

Some proponents of the treaty believe that the treaty establishes a system of property rights for mineral extraction in deep sea beds, making the investment in such ventures more attractive.

LOST very well may confer upon the U.N, for the first time, the ability to <u>tax Americans directly, without congressional approval</u>.

Notwithstanding concerns raised about the Law of the Sea Treaty—and there have been many—the U.S. Senate Foreign Relations Committee recommended U.S. accession to the treaty in a unanimous vote in March 2004 (during President Bush's Presidency). As of now a vote of the entire U.S. Senate has yet to be scheduled. However, some releases say that the current President intends to sign on to the treaty, and has now called on the Senate to ratify this treaty this year. To me this is a treasonous act.

If this treaty were signed and ratified, our U.S. Navy ships would have to inform the U.N. before it leaves port, reporting its destination and route. Wouldn't our enemies love to know where our submarines are going, and how they'll get there? These ships could not dump anything into the ocean that would be a "polluting agent." You know, like dumping human waste overboard on a six-month cruise, or dumping garbage overboard. That would be polluting, and that's a no no. If a U.S. airliner, commercial or military, traveling over an ocean, had to dump fuel before landing for safety's sake, that would be polluting the ocean, and a huge fine would be imposed by the U.N. If U.S. citizens wanted to explore the ocean bottom for precious gems, shipwrecks, or anything else, permission would have to be obtained from the U.N. and a "fee" paid. In addition, anything recovered would be subject to a tax by the U.N. This sure sounds like "One World Order" stuff to me. Why would any U.S. President sign such a treaty, and why would any U.S. Senator vote to ratify it?

Agenda 21

The United Nations Conference on Environment and Development (UNCED), also called the Earth Summit—those two words always scare me—took place in Rio de Janeiro, Brazil, in June, 1992. This largest-ever world meeting brought Heads of State and government officials together with international organizations and representatives of non-government organizations (NGOs) from around the world.

A 700-page global plan of action called Agenda 21 was produced as a result of the Earth Summit: it represents the consensus—another scary word—reached by 178 States (countries) on how all of those countries, under the auspices of the United Nations, can secure OUR future. Agenda 21 is like a blueprint (or maybe we should call it a *"greenprint"*!) for global partnership aiming at a high quality environment and a healthy economy for all peoples of the planet.

Agenda 21 addresses the critical issues they say that we face as a *global community*—an even more scary term—continuing damage to ecosystems, the worsening of poverty, hunger and ill health, increasing world population and illiteracy. Agenda 21 is composed of 40 chapters that identify each challenge and propose simple, realistic solutions towards sustainable development which is: meeting the needs of the present without compromising the ability of future generations to meet their own needs.

Around the world, governments, businesses, non-governmental and other organizations are already putting the ideas from Agenda 21 to work. It is crucial to maintain the momentum of the Rio process and implement the agreements that were reached. This task will require not only the leadership and funding of governments and business, but also the vision, cooperation, and work of every citizen (voluntarily?). Sustainable development cannot be achieved without all sectors of society working together.

I extracted this description from the United Nations web site, but added some commentary. This whole concept scares the dickens out of me. Is this part of that so-called One World Order we've all heard about? It sure looks like it. There are hundreds of web sites devoted to the subject if you want to learn more. From articles I've read in local papers, messages that I've received from other people, my own research, portions of Agenda 21 are being implemented in the United States. You don't believe me? Ouch, that hurts. But take a look at this note and associated links from a friend of mine who tracks information on Agenda 21 on a daily basis.

"I just completed a trip to the West rim of The Grand Canyon and, while there, discovered that the rim is part of the United Nations? Portions of the West Rim are now under *"Sustainable Development."* You can look up "World Heritage Sites" for yourself and follow the links provided. You can obtain a lengthy list of American sites that are under the control of the United Nations today, right here in the good old USA. If this doesn't take your breath away, what would? From what I can surmise, these lands will become off limits to humans by about the year 2035? Maybe you won't be here then, but your children and grandchildren will be. Is this what we are going to leave them?

http://en.wikipedia.org/wiki/World_Heritage_Site or http://whc.unesco.org/en/list

R. Eugene Spitzer

U.N. Control of the Internet

In late May the U.S. House of Representatives met to consider an international proposal to give the United Nations more control over the Internet. Thankfully, the House said No to this proposal, for now. The proposal is backed by China, Russia, Brazil, India, and several other U.N. member countries. This proposal would give the U.N.'s International Telecommunication Union (ITU) more control over the governance of the Internet. The hearing was expected to bring more attention in the U.S. to the measure, which would give the U.N. more control over cybersecurity, data privacy, technical standards, and the Web's address system. It would also allow foreign government-owned Internet providers to charge extra for international traffic and allow for more price controls. My main question of the U.S. House at the time was, "What the hell are you thinking?" Why would the United States even consider such a proposal by the U.N.? This is insane.

Fortunately, enough intelligent minds brought sanity to the hearing and, as the Washington Times reported, the U.S. told the United Nations to take a hike. Here's a short summary of what happened: "United States officials, lawmakers, and technology leaders offered a resounding "no" a proposal to bring the Internet under United Nations' control and said they would lead efforts to stop the move. Some nations, including Russia and China, say the Internet is still controlled by the United States and that a U.N.effort would give a greater voice to the developing world. But many in the United States believe that a U.N.-governed Internet would give authoritarian nations the power to throttle free speech, and allow others to impose tariff or other restrictions."

What really chaps my hide is that the United States would even listen to a proposal such as this. I'm thankful that some officials still remember what country that live in. We can all see what the intent of this proposal was, redistribution of wealth from the United States to other countries with the U.N. taking its cut.

There are other treaties floating around, but the two mentioned here are, in my opinion, the most egregious as they relate to the United States.

The U.S. State Department (AKA the Department of Bribes)

I'm sorry folks, but the more I learn about how the State department works, the less I like it. Let's start by trying to figure out why we have as our Secretary of Bribes a female, all in the interest of diversity and sexual equality no doubt, but dumb. Our government leaders have done this before, but I don't understand why. And it has nothing to do with whether a woman can do the job of bribing other countries as well as a man.

Those countries run by Muslims really aren't allowed to touch any woman that is not their wife. So, when our Secretary of Bribes waddles off the plane in her new, custom-fitted pants suit, and thrusts her hand out, the Muslim leaders have this look of horror on their face. You can see them, in their minds, "How much Purell will it take to cleanse me, and will Allah give me a break for breaking one of his laws?" That's the first thing. If we're so interested in not offending leaders of Muslim countries, shouldn't we know that Muslims don't deal with women, don't respect women, and consider women as less a person than a man? Or are we saying we just don't give a damn what their religion says about women? Couldn't the administration send a senior male representative to meet with these leaders? I'm all for having the best qualified person serve as Secretary of Bribes, which then begs the question, what qualifies Hillary Clinton for the job? Oh, I forgot. She ran against Obama for President, and this was a payoff to her. Yep, that must be it. Brilliant, just brilliant.

Now, let's deal with this farce called diplomacy. Having spent 20 years in the military, being stationed in various countries, and traveling to others for extended periods, I believe I have a pretty good feel for what passes as business and government functions in those countries. I found that in a large number of countries, bribery is a part of any transaction; it's a cultural thing. They don't call it bribery; they call it a cost of doing business. If you deal with the government of these countries, and you're working on a diplomatic matter, better tack on about 20% in fees to the prime minister, president, tyrant-in-charge, pick your favorite title. That's the cost of doing business, and we do it all the time. No doubt, bags of cash are delivered to the head of state as our way of saying how much we care about him or her. Yeah, right.

Now, if you factor in Muslims in charge of running, ruling, or dictating to a country, you have a whole new paradigm which, evidently, our Department of Bribes doesn't understand. And just to add a "kicker" to the equation, anyone who has read the Qu'ran will notice that lying is a legitimate means to an end to followers of Islam. I thought only the leftists followed that policy, but they evidently learned it from the followers of Islam.

Look at North Korea. How many treaties have we signed with North Korea that were violated within days or weeks? You guessed it; every one of them. Why? North Korea knows that we will give them money, food, almost anything they want if they just sign a piece of paper and do the requisite photo op. After we leave they go back to building nuclear weapons, starving their people, and we send them money and food. Somehow, the money ends up in a Swiss bank account in Kim Jung (mentally) Ill's account until he assumed room temperature, and now his 28-year old son gets it. You can bet the farm that the starving citizens of North Korea don't see any of that money. The food gets siphoned off to feed the military, and the people continue to starve. Have you ever seen a view of North and South Korea from above, at night? South Korea is lit up like a Christmas tree, and North Korea has practically no lights. The people continue to starve, and North Korea guards its borders with a vengeance, to keep the people in, not to keep others out. They like it when some idiots wander into North Korea. They capture them, and then sell them back to their country of origin for a princely sum. But you and I give our tax dollars so our Department of Bribes can keep giving chunks of it to North Korea in return for, essentially, nothing. What a country. For over 50 years, administrations tout each treaty as a major step forward in our relations with North Korea. The North Korean government has a good laugh, and goes back to business as usual.

Let's now look at Iran. For how many years have we been saying that we would never allow Iran to build and possess nuclear weapons? Answer. Nearly 20 years. What has the U.S. accomplished in its relations with Iran during that time? Answer? Nothing. What has the U.N. done? Answer? Nothing. Iran know we won't do anything. We think that *"sanctions"* will do the trick. How's that working out so far, Department of Bribes? To Iran's leadership, we're a paper tiger.

There comes a time when our babies in government needs to understand a few things. First of all, we are the light of the world. The U.S. is the country that all other countries turn to for help wherever tragedy strikes. The U.S. has the greatest military in the history of the world. We are currently the lone superpower in the world. We need to act like it. When some rogue nation starts rattling its sabers, we need to have a serious meeting with them, and let them know that they need to knock it off or else. Diplomacy used to work, many decades ago. Diplomacy today consists of America giving money to despotic countries to try and get them to like us. It has never worked. The American taxpayer is being robbed by their government. We could have ended Vietnam in about six months if we'd just gone in there and won it. We took out Hussein in Iraq, and his killer relatives and cronies in less than three weeks, and we should have gone home. We can stop Iran from getting nuclear weapons if we really want to do it. But our spineless government, led by a very spineless Department of Bribes always thinks some piece of paper and a few meetings will solve everything. It has never solved anything.

If you look at our relations with the countries of the world, let's add up the score, shall we? Israel no longer trusts us. The U.S. seems to be content for Israel to be blown off the map by Iran while giving lip service of support. Syria's leaders are busy killing their citizens while the U.S. says, "Uh, that's really bad, but we're talking to them all the time." Yeah, that'll stop the genocide. And in Pakistan, you know, the country with all those nuclear weapons? Well, we did go in there and put a few well-placed rounds through that mutt, Bin Laden, and they got testy about it. They were just hiding the architect of mass murder around the world, but he was really a nice guy. So, Pakistan is in turmoil, and how is our diplomacy working out there? Well, well, not so much. Then there is Iraq. With Congressional approval—but no declaration of war—the U.S. invaded Iraq and pretty much wiped the bad guys out in a few weeks. Then, for some reason, the U.S. decided to stick around and try to turn a tribal culture into a central government-run democracy. Iraq isn't Germany or Japan, folks. To be fair, you and I didn't decide to do that. No, President Bush and Congress decided to do that. Now we've decided to leave. Did we win? Is Iraq now a democracy? No? Oh, well. In Afghanistan, the "right" war according to our current President, we've been there for about a decade, chasing bad guys that we don't recognize because they look like the good guys, losing combat warriors along the way, but now we've set a date to leave and come home? Did we win? No? Oh, well. In Libya, that Khadafi fellow finally went totally nuts, and the people wanted him out—well, they actually wanted him dead—but he didn't want to go. So he started killing citizens by the hundreds. It evidently wasn't important enough for the U.S.—the police force of the world—to step in and remove the tin pot dictator. Did we win? We didn't go there. Oh, well. Then there's Rowanda where genocide has been going on for decades, and we just wring our hands and say, tsk, tsk. It's evidently not important enough for the U.S. to go in and kill the bad guys. How about our relations with China? They love us or, rather, they love our money, and our technology secrets, the ones they hack in and steal. We keep buying their crap, we keep borrowing money from them, and human rights abuses, well, what can we do? We owe them so much money, and we evidently love buying all of their crap, like Nike shoes and iPads. Where's our Department of

Bribes in our dealings with China. China devalues its currency to create an even bigger trade imbalance, and America does nothing.

We keep hearing about what a bang up job Hillary Clinton has done as Secretary of Bribes, but just what has she done? More countries than ever hate us today, and Russia and China are plotting our demise as a world power. Hey, Hillary, make sure all of this gets in your resume when you make that run for President. Just as an aside, I wouldn't be surprised at all if she replaces Job Biden on the Obama reelection ticket as preparation for a presidential run in 2016. There are still a lot of people who, for some unfathomable reason, think she would be a great President. Really? What has she ever accomplished?

You can look around the globe and see this same stupid behavior by our government going on day after day, week after week, month after month, and year after year. The truth is, our administration, and those that came before them, know nothing about how to deal with people that only understand power and force. Government administrations also don't know how to deal with power and force. Here's what our Secretary of State should do to actually make some progress.

Let's settle the North Korean problem in one day. We arrange for talks with North Korea on whatever pretext necessary. We send someone like former Ambassador John Bolton to speak on behalf of the President. Mr. Bolton arrives in North Korea, meets with the top officials, maybe even the top dictator himself. The meeting is short. It goes something like this:

"Good afternoon, thanks for meeting with me. This won't take long. This is what's going to happen. First, we have placed gro-synchronous satellites over your country; we're watching everything that goes on. You're going to dismantle and destroy all of your nuclear weapons manufacturing facilities within seven days, and then destroy all of your nuclear weapons. Yes, destroy all of them. You will also cease all thoughts of selling nuclear weapons or technology to anyone. In return, we won't destroy every one of your presidential palaces and those huge homes that you all live in, and every military base you have. After you finish that task, you will start feeding your people, using all of that hidden wealth you have stashed away. You will do this. Deviate from this process, and boom, you're gone. Have a nice day. No need to get up; I'll find my own way out."

The North Korean dictators understand power and force. They won't test our resolve. If they do, blow up all of those buildings and homes. Case closed. We let China know what we have done, and tell them to remain calm or we'll stop paying back our debt, and put an embargo on all of that crap they sell us. We keep monitoring them, and the same rules apply. Once they comply on a regular basis, we can help them with water, power, crops, and improving the quality of life for the North Korean people, under our supervision of course.

Hey, that was fun. Let's go visit Iran, have a little sit down. Have a similar discussion. Let the Mullah's know that we're not playing nice-nice diplomacy anymore, because they don't understand or respect it. So, if they doubt that we're serious, blow up a few weapons factories, put those satellites up there, watch their every move, and let them know that they will stop all nuclear arms development, and do it now. They will dismantle all weapons they have constructed, and any attempt to transfer or transport nuclear materials out of the country will be met with force. After North Korea, the Iranian leaders won't test us. Problem solved. China and Russia won't be happy, and we shouldn't much care. Again, Russia and China understand power and force. Ronald Reagan made that clear back in the 1980's.

If you recall, once the U.S. invaded Iraq, Libya's Gaddafi couldn't disarm fast enough. Power and force work with these little despots.

While we're at it, let's knock off all this nation-building nonsense. It's a joke and, more importantly, it's none of our business. The nation building practices of the 1940's don't work today, and we shouldn't persist in doing attempting them. Countries are free to function in any form of government the people want so long as their behavior does not threaten our national security.

But our Department of Bribes is always wanting to do diplomatic things with leaders of countries that don't a) understand diplomatic things, and b) do not understand or want this thing we call a "nation." We shouldn't care. So long as they pose no threat to our national security, leave them alone.

Endangered Species List

We read about or hear about these various species of animals, mammals, fish, and fungi that are "endangered." Have you ever wondered just how many species are actually endangered according to—some federal government is involved. We've all read stories about a farmer who can't till his land because he might kill a Kangaroo rat, an endangered animal. That farmer should have seen the little sign around the Kangaroo rat's neck saying, "*Can't Touch me, I'm Protected from Humans*." That incident occurred in California, and we all know how nuts they are in that state. I was always curious about endangered species so I decided to do a little research. Wow, what a shock. Protecting endangered species is an expensive proposition. The federal and state governments spent nearly $1.6 billion of our tax dollars on conserving threatened and endangered species in 2007, plus another $127 million in land purchases for habitat preservation, according to a new report from the U.S. Fish & Wildlife Service (FWS).

The Endangered Species Act (ESA for short) was enacted by Congress in 1973 while Nixon was still President. Much of this information is publicly available, and came from the *Atlantic Monthly* and *Fish and Wildlife* publications, and their respective web sites. You can visit their web sites, or buy a copy of the magazine if you want to know more. This information is not someone's opinion, or an article written by an advocate or proponent of the ESA. It's a government program. Understanding that, here are the mandates under which the ESA has the responsibility to protect:

- **Endangered Species**—species that are <u>likely to become</u> extinct throughout all or a large portion of their range (our land).
- **Threatened Species**—species that are <u>likely to become</u> endangered in the near future.
- **Critical habitat**—vital to the survival of endangered or threatened species.

Under the Endangered Species Act, the U.S. Fish and Wildlife Service oversees the listing and protection of all terrestrial animals—they haven't figured out how to deal with extraterrestrial animals and plants yet—and plants as well as freshwater fish. The National Marine Fisheries Service oversees marine fish and wildlife.

Just how does a species get on that endangered species list anyway? When the U.S. Fish and Wildlife Service or the National Marine Fisheries Service is investigating the health of a species, they look at scientific data collected by local, state and national scientists.

In order to be listed as a candidate, a species has to be found to qualify for protected status under the Endangered Species Act.

Whether or not a species is listed as endangered or threatened then depends on a number of factors, including the urgency and whether adequate protections exist through other means.

When deciding whether a species should be added to the Endangered Species List, the following criteria are evaluated:

- Has a large percentage of the species vital habitat been degraded or destroyed—even if its habitat is your land?
- Has the species been over consumed by commercial, recreational, scientific or educational uses?
- Is the species threatened by disease or predation? I guess that means if a coyote is catching and eating too many of a certain frog, those coyotes need a stern lecture on leaving those poor frogs alone.
- Do current regulations or legislations inadequately protect the species or does the government need to write even more of those regulations?
- Are there other manmade factors that threaten the long-term survival of the species? Evidently there's a new rule in the government—no species is allowed to go extinct. I wonder if that applies to German cockroaches, too. How about fire ants? How about mosquitos?

If scientific research reveals that the answer to one or more of the above questions is yes, the species can be listed under the Endangered Species Act. To come to the conclusion that a species is endangered, does that mean than hundreds of thousands of government Fish and Wildlife employee go out looking for crimes against the latest species? Maybe they just sneak onto farms and watch the farmers, and nail them if some new protected species is spotted.

If a species is endangered or threatened, just what does that mean? Once a species becomes listed as "endangered" or "threatened," it receives special protections by the federal government. Animals are protected from "take" and being traded or sold. A listed plant is protected if on federal property or if federal actions are involved, such as the issuing of a federal permit on private land. This means that your land really isn't your land. The land belongs to the animals; you're just allowed to live there, and pay for everything, so long as you don't bother the protected species. That's our government in action. I wonder if any species has formed a union with ACLU support.

The term "take" is used in the Endangered Species Act to include, "harass, harm, pursue, hunt, shoot, wound, kill, trap, capture, or collect, or to attempt to engage in any such conduct." The law also protects against interfering in vital breeding and behavioral activities or degrading critical habitat. This last part is where they really get you. You could decide to take down a half-dozen trees in order to plant a garden. But before you proceed you need an ESA official to inspect your land, inspect your trees, and decide whether or not you'll be able to plant your garden. If some species inhabits those trees, you won't receive the permit. This takes us another step closer to ending private property rights.

The primary goal of the Endangered Species Act is to make species' populations healthy and vital so they can be delisted from the Endangered Species Act. At least that's what they say. The U.S. Fish and Wildlife Service and the National Marine Fisheries Service actively invest time and resources to bringing endangered or threatened species back from the brink of extinction. I wonder just how far "back" from extinction is the goal. If there used to be a thousand of some species, and they do a count, and find there are only 400 of them now in existence, do they help that species to get back to 1,000 or more, or is 600 enough? Who decides? And just who is counting them?

In the 2010 update by the International Union for the conservation of nature's list of threatened species, 17,315 were listed as vulnerable, endangered, or critically endangered. This is worldwide. Within the U.S. there are about 1,750 protected species. And just for the record, the human species will never make that list although I think we're more endangered than a lot of those species on the list.

From that endless list, here are just a few of the endangered species. Abe's Salamander, Aberdare Mole Shrew, opatrika Madagascar Frog. Abor Bug-eyed Frog. Abra Acanacu Marsupial Frog, Abra Malaga Toad, Adelaide Pigmy Blue-tongue Skink, Adriatic Salmon, Adriatic Sturgeon, African Blind Barb Fish, African Butter Catfish, African Egg Frog, Andaman Scops-owl, Andaman Serpent-eagle, Andaman Spiny Shrew, Andaman Treepie, Andaman White-toothed Shrew, Andaman Wood-pigeon, Andaman Woodpecker, Andean Bear, Andean Caenolestid, Andean Cat, Zorro Bubble-nest Frog, *Zospeum biscaiense, Zubovskia banatica,* Zug's Robber Frog, Zulia Toad Headed Sideneck, Zullich's Blue, Zululand Black Millipede, Yemen Thrush, Yemen Warbler, Yenyuan Stream Salamander, Yetla False Brook Salamander, Yinggeling Flying Frog, Yinnietharra Rock Dragon, Yiwu Salamander, and don't forget the Yonenaga's Atlantic Spiny-rat. Do they have contests to come up with names for each of these creatures, plants, or fungi? Do the members of a protected species know what their name is? Inquiring minds would like to know. This borders on insanity, folks.

I believe that if these people had been around back in the day of the dinosaurs, the T-Rex would have been put on the endangered species list, and we would all have been eaten. That's how stupid this is. No one wants to see all the elephants or lions or tigers killed, but some common sense is needed. These endangered species folks have, as governments always do, abused the whole concept. Why this out of control emphasis on protecting rats, toads, and certain fungus?

You can do an easy Internet search and see the whole list if you have lots of free time. I scrolled through the list to get the examples above, but the more I looked at the list, the more irate I got over what the government has done, and continues to do.

Just a short story you may have read or heard about. In New York there was an attempt by the animal-over-human folks to force people who were experiencing a massive rat problem in their homes, to have the rats removed, but not killed. No, the rats were to be humanely trapped, along with all their siblings and parents, and transported out of state. Yes, it's true. The city of New York wanted vermin trappers to somehow identify a rat's family members and capture them all, humanely, then turn them loose in an adjoining state. Fortunately, governors in those adjoining states found out about this new requirement and warned New York City that they better drop those plans immediately or face serious consequences. Mayor Bloomberg quickly and quietly backed down. Have you ever seen the size of the rats in New York City? Some are big enough for a saddle! Some government official actually came up with this idea, and it took other states to put a stop to it.

Does America Still Have Religious Freedom?

There are two major reasons the United States has been known as the place to live. They are freedom, and especially freedom of religion. If you look at Middle Eastern countries, there is typically only one faith permitted, Islam. Christian churches have been burned down; Christians have been beaten and driven from several countries. Other countries essentially have no religion at all, though any faith is welcome.

But in America you are free to pursue your religion without fear, or you were until recent years. Our founders even included that freedom in the U.S. Constitution, in the First Amendment. That Amendment says, in part, "Congress shall make no law respecting an establishment of religion, or prohibiting the free exercise thereof."

This amendment, a part of the Bill of Rights, was written specifically to stop the religious persecution many citizens were subjected to in England with its Church of England, which was the only religion allowed. The founders never wanted that to happen in America. The meaning of that statement in the First Amendment is clear; the government cannot establish a religtioin to the exclusion of all other religions, but every citizen is free to practice their faith as they see fit. When you read that portion of the First Amendment, there are two very important components. The first is that the state (government) cannot establish a religion to the exclusion of all others. The second part of that portion of the First Amendment makes it clear that the people of America are free to worship their faith without interference from the government. That worked well for America for a long time. However, in the past 30-40 years, assaults on the Christian faith have become more pronounced and more strident. To some extent, the followers of Islam have also suffered persecution in celebrating their faith in America.

But when a government school tells its students that they cannot bring a Christian Bible to school to read on their lunch break, that is a clear violation of the First Amendment. I would encourage every parent whose child has suffered this Constitutional assault to file complaints with the school teacher, the school principal, the school district, the State Superintendent of Public Education, and with the County Attorney. These schools do it again and again, and dare the parents to try and stop the prohibition. When students at government schools are told that the Christmas holiday period is no longer Christmas, but a Winter Break, that's also a violation of the First Amendment in two ways. The first is the right of free speech, and the second is the freedom to express your faith. When students are told that they cannot wear Christmas-colored clothing during the Christmas season—what is that? Students must wear other colored clothing during the Christmas season. This is another violation of the First Amendment as well. Students who write essays that contain any Christian reference are told to go write about something else. Students are not allowed to sing Christmas songs in pageants or school plays. Government Schools seem intent on removing anything that even hints at Christianity, paying no attention to the U.S. Constitution. Individual government school employees are making these decisions, and parents are not fighting back. The government is counting on the reluctance of citizens to fight against unconstitutional actions.

Why do some schools either ban the Pledge of Allegiance, or ban the speaking of the words, "Under God" in that pledge, this is also an infringement on the First Amendment. When a student says the words, "under God" in the pledge, God can mean the Christian God, the Jewish God, the Islamic God, and so on. If I had children in school, I'd encourage them to say the pledge, and include the words, Under God, in that pledge. But, to be honest, the words Under God didn't come into legitimate, national use in the pledge until 1954 when President Eisenhower signed the legislation. I was finishing Junior High School that year, but I recited the pledge in all its glory from that point on.

During the Christmas holiday, many employees have been told to remove symbols of Christmas from their desks because they might "offend" non-Christians. I'm sorry, but if someone wants to say that they're offended by a Christian symbol on my desk, that's their problem, not mine. The "free exercise of religion" is my right. It doesn't say, ". . . . the free exercise thereof unless someone is offended." If followers of Islam are given time off five or six times a day to go to a private place, put down a prayer rug, and pray, I can put a Christian cross on my desk.

There have been some notable incidents that have garnered media attention that make some of us scratch our heads in disbelief. The first was a group of taxi drivers in a Northeastern city who demanded that they have the right to refuse to accept any passenger who had a guide dog with them, and anyone who was carrying any form of liquor, even if it was in a bag, because of their faith. The law mattered not a bit to them. And taxi also drivers demanded that the airports they served install private foot baths so they could wash their feet as their religion required. I have a suggestion for those folks; wash your feet before you go to work. If you don't want to carry passengers who have a guide dog or have a bottle of liquor in their possession, go get another job. It's not our responsibility to accommodate your demands. It's your responsibility to assimilate into our society.

Then there were Muslim students at a college in the northeast that demanded that they have their own dormitory, separate from the other students. They wanted segregation so they wouldn't have to live in the same living quarters as non-Muslims. This kind of nonsense is occurring more and more as one religion is demanding accommodation from society, regardless of our laws. What do you think would happen if all Christian students at a college demanded that they have separate dormitory accommodations so they wouldn't have to be exposed to students of other faiths? They'd be laughed out of the Dean's office.

But the attacks are just as bad outside of school and the workplace. There was an excellent article published at a great web site, WallBuilders.com, authored by David Barton, published a chronology of the attacks on Christianity in just the past few years by the current President.

- April 2008—During his campaign to become President, the current occupant of the White House speaks disrespectfully of Christians, saying they "cling to their guns and religion" and have an "antipathy towards people who aren't like them.

- February 2009—The President announces plans to revoke conscience protection for health workers who refuse to participate in medical activities that go against their beliefs, and fully implements the plan in February 2011.

- April 2009—When speaking at Georgetown University, the President orders that a monogram symbolizing Jesus' name be covered when he is making his speech.

- May 2009—The President declines to host services for the National Prayer Day (a day established by federal law) at the White House.

- April 2009—In a deliberate act of disrespect, the President nominated three pro-abortion ambassadors to the Vatican; of course, the pro-life Vatican rejected all three.

- October 19, 2010—The President begins deliberately omitting the phrase about "the Creator" when quoting the Declaration of Independence—an omission he has made on no less than seven occasions.

- November 2010—The President misquotes the National Motto, saying it is "E pluribus unum" rather than "In God We Trust" as established by federal law.

- January 2011—After a federal law was passed to transfer a WWI Memorial in the Mojave Desert to private ownership, the U. S. Supreme Court ruled that the cross in the memorial could continue to stand, but the President's administration refused to allow the land to be transferred as required by law, and refused to allow the cross to be re-erected as ordered by the Court.

- February 2011—Although he filled posts in the State Department, for more than two years the President did not fill the post of religious freedom ambassador, an official that works against religious persecution across the world; he filled it only after heavy pressure from the public and from Congress.

- April 2011—For the first time in American history, the President urges passage of a non-discrimination law that does not contain hiring protections for religious groups, forcing religious organizations to hire according to federal mandates without regard to the dictates of their own faith, thus eliminating conscience protection in hiring.

- August 2011—The President's administration releases its new health care rules that override religious conscience protections for medical workers in the areas of abortion and contraception.
- November 2011—the President opposes inclusion of President Franklin Roosevelt's famous D-Day Prayer in the WWII Memorial.
- November 2011—Unlike previous presidents, this President studiously avoids any religious references in his Thanksgiving speech.
- December 2011—The President's administration denigrates other countries' religious beliefs as an obstacle to radical homosexual rights.
- January 2012—The President's administration argues that the First Amendment provides no protection for churches and synagogues in hiring their pastors and rabbis.
- February 2012—The President's administration forgives student loans in exchange for public service, but announces it will no longer forgive student loans if the public service is related to religion.

Acts of hostility from the President-led military toward people of Biblical faith:

- August 2011—The Air Force stops teaching the Just War theory to officers in California because the course is taught by chaplains and is based on a philosophy introduced by St. Augustine in the third century AD—a theory long taught by civilized nations across the world (except America).
- September 2011—Air Force Chief of Staff prohibits commanders from notifying airmen of programs and services available to them from chaplains.
- September 2011—The Army issues guidelines for Walter Reed Medical Center stipulating that "No religious items (i.e. Bibles, reading materials and/or facts) are allowed to be given away or used during a visit."
- November 2011—The Air Force Academy rescinds support for Operation Christmas Child, a program to send holiday gifts to impoverished children across the world, because the program is run by a Christian charity.
- November 2011—The Air Force Academy pays $80,000 to add a Stonehenge-like worship center for pagans, druids, witches, and Wiccans.
- February 2012—The U. S. Military Academy at West Point disinvites three star Army general and decorated war hero Lieutenant General William G. ("Jerry") Boykin (retired) from speaking at an event because he is an outspoken Christian.

- February 2012—The Air Force removes "God" from the patch of Rapid Capabilities Office (the word on the patch was in Latin: Dei).
- February 2012—The Army orders Catholic chaplains not to read a letter to parishioners that their archbishop asked them to read.

Acts of hostility toward Biblical values:

- January 2009—The President lifts restrictions on U.S. government funding for groups that provide abortion services or counseling abroad, forcing taxpayers to fund pro-abortion groups that either promote or perform abortions in other nations.
- January 2009—The President's nominee for deputy secretary of state asserts that American taxpayers are required to pay for abortions and that limits on abortion funding are unconstitutional.
- 'March 2009—The President's administration shut out pro-life groups from attending a White House-sponsored health care summit.
- March 2009—The President orders taxpayer funding of embryonic stem cell research.
- March 2009—The President's administration gave $50 million for the UNFPA, the UN population agency that promotes abortion and works closely with Chinese population control officials who use forced abortions and involuntary sterilizations.
- May 2009—The White House budget eliminates all funding for abstinence-only education and replaces it with "comprehensive" sexual education, repeatedly proven to increase teen pregnancies and abortions. The President continues the deletion in subsequent budgets.
- May 2009—The President's officials assemble a terrorism dictionary calling pro-life advocates violent and charging that they use racism in their "criminal" activities.
- July 2009—The President's administration illegally extends federal benefits to same-sex partners of Foreign Service and Executive Branch employees, in direction violation of the federal Defense of Marriage Act.
- September 16, 2009—The President's administration appoints as EEOC Commissioner Chai Feldblum, who asserts that society should "not tolerate" any "private beliefs," including religious beliefs, if they may negatively affect homosexual "equality."
- July 2010—The President's administration uses federal funds in violation of federal law to get Kenya to change its constitution to include abortion.

- August 2010—The President's administration cuts funding for 176 abstinence education programs.
- September 2010—The President's administration tells researchers to ignore a judge's decision striking down federal funding for embryonic stem cell research.
- February 2011—The President directs the Justice Department to stop defending the federal Defense of Marriage Act.
- March 2011—The President's administration refuses to investigate videos showing Planned Parenthood helping alleged sex traffickers get abortions for victimized underage girls.
- July 2011—The President allows homosexuals to serve openly in the military, reversing a policy originally instituted by George Washington in March 1778, and reinforced by former President Bill Clinton.
- September 2011—The Pentagon directs that military chaplains may perform same-sex marriages at military facilities in violation of the federal Defense of Marriage Act.
- October 2011—The President's administration eliminates federal grants to the U.S. Conference of Catholic Bishops for their extensive programs that aid victims of human trafficking because the Catholic Church is anti-abortion.

Acts of preferentialism for Islam:

- May 2009—While the President does not host any National Day of Prayer event at the White House, he does host White House Iftar dinners in honor of Ramadan.
- April 2010—Christian leader Franklin Graham is disinvited from the Pentagon's National Day of Prayer Event because of complaints from the Muslim community.
- April 2010—The President's administration requires rewriting of government documents and a change in administration vocabulary to remove terms that are deemed offensive to Muslims, including jihad, jihadists, terrorists, radical Islamic, etc.
- August 2010—The President speaks with great praise of Islam and condescendingly of Christianity.
- August 2010—The President went to great lengths to speak out on multiple occasions on behalf of building an Islamic mosque at Ground Zero, while at the same time he was silent about a Christian church being denied permission to rebuild their church that was destroyed on 9/11, at that location.
- 2010—While every White House traditionally issues hundreds of official proclamations and statements on numerous occasions, this White House avoids traditional Biblical

holidays and events but regularly recognizes major Muslim holidays, as evidenced by its 2010 statements on Ramadan, Eid-ul-Fitr, Hajj, and Eid-ul-Adha.

- October 2011—The President's Muslim advisers block Middle Eastern Christians' access to the White House.
- February 2012—The President's administration makes effusive apologies for Korans being burned by the U. S. military, but when Bibles were burned by the military, numerous reasons were offered as to why it was the right thing to do.

I am not a rocket scientist, and I don't play one on television, but it seems obvious to me that there is a bias against one religion, Christianity, and a favoritism expressed towards another faith, Islam, by the President of the United States. Much of what you read above were clear violations of federal law or the U.S. Constitution, yet these actions have gone unchallenged. I do not understand why the Congress has not stepped in and at least tried to undo some of the damage done by this President. I understand, to some extent, the reluctance of senior military officers not taking a stand against these outrageous acts regarding the treatment of Christian military warriors. If they speak up, their careers are over. Military Chaplains are another matter. They have an obligation to resign and speak out against these egregious acts.

There was an incident in Dearborn, Michigan in 2011 where Christians were arrested and taken to jail for the night for "disturbing the peace." That doesn't sound unusual, but read on. These Christians were standing outside on a public street where an Arab International Festival was being held. They were handing out copies of the Gospel of John, written in English and Arabic, to people leaving or entering the festival. Within three minutes of their arrival, about nine police officers arrived and surrounded the men. They forced the person with the video camera to turn it off, and then confiscated it. They were also told that they cannot be on a public street outside the festival, but would have to stay at least five blocks away from entrance. The good news is that though they were charged, a jury threw the case out, except for one man, a former Muslim, who converted to Christianity. He was charged with failure to obey a law enforcement order.

You have to understand that under the Muslim faith, many followers operate under a code called *Sharia Law*. I have two friends who have made careers in the study of the Middle East and, more specifically, the Islamic faith. They have written extensively about Islam, and given many speeches on Islam. I interviewed the two of them on my now defunct web radio show. They cited the Qu'ran in describing the laws under which followers of Islam must behave.

Sharia Law is not a part of the Qu'ran; it is a separate document. Under Sharia Law, a Muslim cannot speak with anyone of another faith, and cannot convert from Islam to some other faith, under penalty of death. In the earlier incident, the operators of the festival said that the attendees felt intimidated with Christians outside the entrance, so the police were called, and dutifully arrested those pesky Christians even though no laws were broken.

There are several stories that have appeared in the media that speak of the number of Muslims who have moved to Dearborn. Those stories also include statements from Muslims that make clear what their intentions are for this city. They intend to take over Dearborn politically, and elect Muslims to all of the offices, and the police will follow the laws of Sharia in this town. This is a clear violation of the Constitution, but obviously they don't care all that much because their allegiance does not align with America, but with their faith. Again, this has a lot to do with America becoming a stew pot rather than the melting pot it was for over two centuries. There are several video clips of the incident in Dearborn, as well as several articles that have appeared in print.

In the United Kingdom and in France, the Muslims are making similar attempts to take over sections of cities, or whole cities, and impose Sharia law on the citizens.

There is this rather large, relatively speaking, organization called CAIR. CAIR is the Council on American-Islamic Relations. To me it's nothing but a front group for Islam. They have very effective spokesmen for their council—no women, of course—but they've lied so often it's hard to find any nuggets of truth in anything they say. In the Middle East Quarterly, one of their headlines is: CAIR: Islamists Fooling the Establishment, and give example after example of how CAIR exists as a propaganda arm of the takeover of America ambitions of Islam. And CAIR does a pretty good job considering that we have so many fools in Washington and in the media. They'll fall for just about anything unless it's conservative or Christian.

So, do we really have freedom of religion? I think that if you're a Muslim, you pretty much can do what you want regarding your faith. But if you're Christian, you better watch out. The federal government, under current management, is doing all it can to diminish God in this great nation, and CAIR is enjoying every minute of it. I hope you'll think about all of this religious infighting, and the effect it can and will have on your kids and grandkids. America's biggest asset, envied by the world, is freedom. I want my kids and grandkids to have the freedom intended by our founders, and our Constitution. How about your kids and grandkids?

The Man Made Global Warming Myth

From the Friends of Science website, friendsofscience.org, here are some common myths and facts about global warming. Al Gore's protests notwithstanding, human-caused climate change or whatever new name has been invented is another whopper. It should be noted that many of the "scientists" supposedly supporting this lie are the same ones who were telling us that we were entering an ice age back in the 1970's. I guess some scientists will change their findings if there's enough money involved.

MYTH 1: Global temperatures are rising at a rapid, unprecedented rate.

FACT: Accurate satellite, balloon, and mountain top observations made over the last three decades have not shown any significant change in the long term rate of increase in global temperatures. Average ground station readings do show a mild warming of 0.6 to 0.8C over the last 100 years, which is well within the natural variations recorded in the last millennium. The ground station network suffers from an uneven distribution across the globe; the stations are preferentially located in growing urban and industrial areas ("heat islands"), which show substantially higher readings than adjacent rural areas ("land use effects").

There has been no catastrophic warming recorded.

MYTH 2: The "hockey stick" graph proves that the earth has experienced a steady, very gradual temperature increase for 1,000 years, then recently began a sudden increase.

FACT: Significant changes in climate have continually occurred throughout geologic time. For instance, the Medieval Warm Period, from around 1000 to1200 AD (when the Vikings farmed on Greenland) was followed by a period known as the Little Ice Age. Since the end of the 17th Century the "average global temperature" has been rising at the low steady rate mentioned above; although from 1940-1970 temperatures actually dropped, leading to a Global Cooling scare.

The "hockey stick", a poster boy of both the U.N.s IPCC and Canada's Environment Department, ignores historical recorded climatic swings, and has now also been proven to be flawed and statistically unreliable as well. It is a computer construct and a faulty one at that.

MYTH 3: Human produced carbon dioxide has increased over the last 100 years, adding to the Greenhouse effect, thus warming the earth.

FACT: Carbon dioxide levels have indeed changed for various reasons, human and otherwise, just as they have throughout geologic time. Since the beginning of the industrial revolution, the CO_2 content of the atmosphere has increased. The RATE of growth during this period has also increased from about 0.2% per year to the present rate of about 0.4% per year, which growth rate has now been constant for the past 25 years. However, there is no proof that CO_2 is the main driver of global warming. As measured in ice cores dated over many thousands of years, CO_2 levels move up and down AFTER the temperature has done so, and thus are the RESULT OF, NOT THE CAUSE of warming. Geological field work in recent sediments confirms this causal relationship. There is solid evidence that, as temperatures move up and down naturally and cyclically through solar radiation, orbital and galactic influences, the warming surface layers of the earth's oceans expel more CO_2 as a result.

MYTH 4: CO2 is the most common greenhouse gas.

FACT: Greenhouse gases form about 3% of the atmosphere by volume. They consist of varying amounts, (about 97%) of water vapor and clouds, with the remainder being gases like CO_2, CH_4, Ozone, and N_2O, of which carbon dioxide is the largest amount. Hence, CO_2 constitutes about 0.037% of the atmosphere. While the minor gases are more effective as "greenhouse agents" than water vapor and clouds, the latter are overwhelming the effect by their sheer volume and—in the end—are thought to be responsible for 60% of the "Greenhouse effect".

Those attributing climate change to CO_2 rarely mention this important fact.

MYTH 5: Computer models verify that CO2 increases will cause significant global warming.

FACT: Computer models can be made to "verify" anything by changing some of the 5 million input parameters or any of a multitude of negative and positive feedbacks in the program used. They do not "prove" anything. Also, computer models predicting global warming are incapable of properly including the effects of the sun, cosmic rays and the clouds. The sun is a major cause of temperature variation on the earth surface as its received radiation changes all the time, This happens largely in cyclical fashion. The number and the lengths in time of sunspots can be correlated very closely with average temperatures on earth, e.g. the Little Ice

Age and the Medieval Warm Period. Varying intensity of solar heat radiation affects the surface temperature of the oceans and the currents. Warmer ocean water expels gases, some of which are CO_2. Solar radiation interferes with the cosmic ray flux, thus influencing the amount ionized nuclei which control cloud cover.

MYTH 6: The U.N. proved that man-made CO2 causes global warming.

FACT: In a 1996 report by the U.N. on global warming, two statements were deleted from the final draft. Here they are:

1) "None of the studies cited above has shown clear evidence that we can attribute the observed climate changes to increases in greenhouse gases."
2) "No study to date has positively attributed all or part of the climate change to man-made causes"

To the present day there is still no scientific proof that man-made CO2 causes significant global warming.

MYTH 7: CO2 is a pollutant.

FACT: This is absolutely not true. Nitrogen forms 80% of our atmosphere. We could not live in 100% nitrogen either. Carbon dioxide is no more a pollutant than nitrogen. CO2 is essential to life on earth. It is necessary for plant growth since increased CO2 intake as a result of increased atmospheric concentration causes many trees and other plants to grow more vigorously. Unfortunately, the Canadian Government has included CO2 with a number of truly toxic and noxious substances listed by the Environmental Protection Act, only as their means to politically control it.

MYTH 8: Global warming will cause more storms and other weather extremes.

FACT: There is no scientific or statistical evidence whatsoever that supports such claims on a global scale. Regional variations may occur. Growing insurance and infrastructure repair costs, particularly in coastal areas, are sometimes claimed to be the result of increasing frequency and severity of storms, whereas in reality they are a function of increasing population density, escalating development value, and ever more media reporting.

MYTH 9: Receding glaciers and the calving of ice shelves are proof of global warming.

FACT: Glaciers have been receding and growing cyclically for hundreds of years. Recent glacier melting is a consequence of coming out of the very cool period of the Little Ice Age. Ice shelves have been breaking off for centuries. Scientists know of at least 33 periods of glaciers growing and then retreating. It's normal. Besides, glacier's health is dependent as much on precipitation as on temperature.

MYTH 10: The earth's poles are warming; polar ice caps are breaking up and melting, and the sea level rising.

FACT: The earth is variable. The western Arctic may be getting somewhat warmer, due to unrelated cyclic events in the Pacific Ocean, but the Eastern Arctic and Greenland are getting colder. The small Palmer Peninsula of Antarctica is getting warmer, while the main Antarctic continent is actually cooling. Ice thicknesses are increasing both on Greenland and in Antarctica.

Sea level monitoring in the Pacific (Tuvalu) and Indian Oceans (Maldives) has shown no sign of any sea level rise.

Here's a little more truth about the Global Warming Scam. Princeton University physicist Dr. Will Happer, who says he was fired by Vice President Al Gore for failing to adhere to Gore's views on global warming, has now declared that man-made warming fears are "mistaken."

Happer, who served as the Director of Energy Research at the Department of Energy from 1990 to 1993, said, "I had the privilege of being fired by Al Gore when I refused to go along with his alarmism. I did not need the job that badly."

He said in 1993, "I was told that science was not going to intrude on policy."

Now, Happer has asked to join the more than 650 international scientists who have spoken out against man-made global warming fears and are cited in the 2008 U.S. Senate Minority Report from Environmental and Public Works Committee ranking member James Inhofe, R-Okla.

"I am convinced that the current alarm over carbon dioxide is mistaken," Happer told the committee on Dec. 22 of that year.

Before inauguration, our current President chose as his top science adviser, Harvard University professor John Holdren. Holdren is a staunch believer in the dangers of man-made global warming and advised Gore on his documentary *"An Inconvenient Truth."* I actually think it should have been called *"The Inconvenient Lie,"* but that's just me.

Dr. Happer has published over 200 scientific papers, and is a Fellow of the American Physical Society, The American Association for the Advancement of Science, and the National Academy of Sciences.

Sen. Inhofe said that the statements of prominent scientists like Happer who are willing to publicly dissent from climate fears strike a blow to the United Nations, Gore, and the media's claims about global warming.

"The endless claims of a 'consensus' about man-made global warming grow less and less credible every day," Inhofe said.

Happer declared, "I have spent a long research career studying physics that is closely related to the greenhouse effect—for example, absorption and emission of visible and infrared radiation, and fluid flow. Fears about man-made global warming are unwarranted and are not based on good science. The earth's climate is changing now, as it always has. There is no evidence that the changes differ in any qualitative way from those of the past . . .

"Computer models used to generate frightening scenarios from increasing levels of carbon dioxide have scant credibility."

OK, Mr. President, Mr. Gore, and the rest of the Global Warming worshippers, let's hear your response. Every time Gore says that "there is consensus among the scientific community on man-made climate change," he is lying, and we know he is lying. Many people know that Gore set up a carbon credit company where, for a large fee, a company could emit more "pollution" into the air provided they bought carbon credits from Mr. Gore's company, thus enriching Gore using a hoax. I find that disgusting.

Are We At War with Mexico?'

I didn't think so, but events and some statements make me wonder if I missed yet another memo. There's this little problem with our border being so porous that drug and human smugglers seem to come and go as they please. Our Border Patrol works very hard, but because the federal government refuses to complete the double-layered fence that was approved years ago, there are vast reaches of open ground along our border. Then we had, and continue to have, illegal alien smugglers on this side of the border fighting the County Sheriff's deputies, with one being killed. Why are illegal aliens coming into Arizona and having gun battles with U.S. law enforcement? Is this the opening salvo of an invasion? There have been over 10,000 murders in border city areas just South of our border, in Texas and Arizona, and now they've spilled over into our country. The federal government seems content with some Americans dying because of this porous border, and I keep asking myself why our government won't complete the dang fence, put down some ground sensors, and stop the invasion. Every time I read about how many illegal aliens come across the border into the United States I ask myself, how many of those illegal aliens were from the Middle East? Does anyone believe that only people fro Mexico and points south sneak into our country? Don't you think that the terrorists have figured out by now that getting into America to do their terrorist acts is very easy, if they'd just come up through Mexico they'd be home free. Yet Homeland Security keeps saying that the borders have never been more secure. It makes me wonder.

In June the President issued an order, instruction, or suggestion to Homeland Security, which runs ICE, to leave illegal aliens alone if they are between 15-30 and have never been arrested. OK, let's go with that. First of all, how do illegal aliens prove a) they're between 15-30, b) they've been here for five consecutive years and, c) have never been arrested or in trouble with the law? And, what happens to illegal aliens under the age of 15? Don't worry, though, you know that ICE will do a fantastic job of verifying the legitimacy of these 800,000-1,000,000 illegal aliens. What about the other 15-20 million illegal aliens who have invaded our country? Let's say that a plan is developed to allow the 15-20 million illegal aliens to get a resident card that allows them to stay in the country, but not acquire citizenship. I don't think it will happen, but it could. I would bet serious money that within two years there would be a push from Washington saying, "Since these good people are legally in this country, and contributing to our society, they should have the right to vote." You can see this coming, can't you? For those of the leftist persuasion, they see this as a huge voting bloc, and will do anything to get them the vote because they believe they'll vote for the left. You add 15-20 million people who aren't citizens to the voting rolls, and you have added 15-20 million votes for the leftists. And don't forget, most of them have no education, and no job skills. Welfare rolls will skyrocket, costing you and me billions.

People reading the rest of this topic need to understand one thing. Law enforcement supporters, like me, and the vast majority of Americans, believe in the rule of law. We want to know who is coming into our country. We don't hate Latinos, we don't hate Europeans, or Africans, or anyone else. What we are so exercised about is the behavior of people that cross our borders illegally, and then they demand all sorts of things from the American taxpayers. That drives us nuts. But get over this word "hate" as it pertains to illegal immigration. We hate the behavior, but we have nothing against any person as a human being.

Over the past two or three years the largest city in Arizona, Phoenix, has had numerous marches through the downtown streets by illegal aliens and open border supporters, carrying flags of Mexico, demanding their rights. There was a demonstration at the state capitol where the protesters put an American flag on the ground and then trampled it, laughing. Can you imagine what would happen if people from another country entered Mexico, went to their state capitol, put a flag of Mexico on the ground, and trampled it? I can guarantee you that the people who did it would still be in a prison somewhere in Mexico.

Thus far I haven't figured out what those rights are. They have certain rights under OUR Constitution if they are arrested or jailed, the right to be treated the same as others who are incarcerated. They have the right to emergency medical care if they become injured within our borders. They have no right to be here or to stay here, demanding that they be given jobs, receive welfare and food stamps, free housing, and demanding free education for any children they brought with them when they broke the law and snuck into our country. So, what rights are they demanding?

I then started seeing statements in the press or on television from supporters of illegal aliens, and this really alarmed me. Here are just a few.

<u>Augustin Cebada, B</u>rown Berets: "Go back to Boston! Go back to Plymouth Rock, Pilgrims! Get out! We are the future. You are old and tired. Go on. We have beaten you. Leave like beaten rats. You old white people. It is your duty to die. Through love of having children, we are going to take over.

Richard Alatorre, Los Angeles City Council: "They're afraid we're going to take over the governmental institutions and other institutions. They're right. We will take them over . . . We are here to stay."

Excelsior, the national newspaper of Mexico: "The American Southwest seems to be slowly returning to the jurisdiction of Mexico without firing a single shot."

Professor Jose Angel Gutierrez, University of Texas; "We have an aging white America . . . They are not making babies. They are dying. The explosion is in our population . . . I love it. They are shitting in their pants with fear. I love it."

Art Torres, Chairman of the California Democratic Party: "Remember 187-proposition to deny taxpayer funds for services to non-citizens—was the last gasp of white America in California . . ."

Gloria Molina, Los Angeles County Supervisor: "We are politicizing every single one of these new citizens that are becoming citizens of this country . . . . I gotta tell you that a lot of people are saying, 'I'm going to go out there and vote because I want to pay them back.'"

Mario Obledo, California Coalition of Hispanic Organizations and California State Secretary of Health, Education and Welfare under Governor Jerry Brown, also awarded the Presidential Medal of Freedom by President Bill Clinton: "California is going to be a Hispanic state. Anyone who doesn't like it should leave."

Jose Pescador Osuna, Mexican Consul General: "We are practicing 'La Reconquista' in California . . ."

Professor Fernando Guerra, Loyola Marymount University: "We need to avoid a white backlash by using codes understood by Latinos . . . ."

Did you know that immigrants from Mexico and other non-European countries can come to this country and get preferences in jobs, education, and government contracts? It's called affirmative action or racial privilege. The Emperor of Japan or the President of Mexico could migrate here and immediately be eligible for special rights unavailable for Americans of European descent. Not too long ago a vote was taken in the U.S. Congress to end this practice.

It was defeated. Every single Democratic senator except Ernest Hollings voted to maintain special privileges for Hispanic, Asian, and African immigrants. They were joined by thirteen Republicans. Bill Clinton and Al Gore have repeatedly stated that they believe that massive immigration from countries like Mexico is good. They have also backed special privileges for these immigrants.

After reading these quotes, is it fair to assume that, with all of the illegal aliens already in this country, and more coming every day, we are experiencing some sort of undeclared war with Mexico? Both political parties in Congress, in large and small numbers, appear to support some kind of special privileges for these illegal alien invaders. I do not understand this attitude. Are we a nation of laws for all, or a nation of some laws for us, and different laws for others?

No one has the "right" to come into our country without going through the legal immigration system. The federal government has no right to put its citizens in harm's way because of their inaction, and refusal to enforce existing law. I've read, as have you no doubt, that the Attorney General has said that they are only going to pursue deportation of those illegal aliens who commit crimes. He appears to have no interest in stopping the invasion by illegal aliens, whether they are from Mexico or some other country.

As an American, I find this totally unacceptable. We have MS-13 gangs setting up shop all over this country—the stories are on the news all the time. Ninety percent of those MS-13 gang members are here illegally, from Mexico and South American countries. The police can't, or won't round them up and either imprison or deport them. We have had murders in Arizona caused by illegal aliens. We have had illegal aliens who have been deported five, six, seven times who have snuck back into Arizona again. Nothing happens to them. It's become a merry-go-round. There was a recent incident where an illegal alien snuck back across the border, for the sixth time, got drunk, was driving a car with no license, and mowed down and killed innocent American citizens. Our emergency rooms are overrun with illegal aliens demanding health care, yet never willing to pay for any of it. In Southern Arizona there have been several hospitals that had to shut down. They couldn't stay open because over 80% of the patients were illegal aliens, and none of them had insurance, or paid for any treatment. Is this good for America? When are more Americans, like you, going to put increasing pressure on your state governments to stop the invasion? And please don't get me started on the insanity that is the Dream Act. This is an outrage to Americans. America is giving away admissions to colleges to the children of illegal aliens thus denying admission to our sons and daughters.

Someone please explain the logic of that to me. It's unconscionable. Is this the America you want for your kids and grandkids. I sure hope not. But if citizens don't hold public officials accountable, nothing is going to get better for us.

Why Are Taxpayers Helping to Fund Planned Parenthood?

The whole issue of abortion is being fought seemingly forever. There are those that favor abortion at any time during a pregnancy for whatever reason the pregnant mother chooses. There are those that favor abortion up until the 20th week, and then don't want a baby killed after that. There are still others, over half of the country that believe that life begins at conception—count me among them—that believe that a pregnancy should go to term unless the life of the mother is at stake. When the baby is born, the child can be put up for adoption, and the mother can go on with her life. There are agencies, Planned Parenthood notably among them, that perform large numbers of abortions. Recent statistics on the abortions performed by Planned Parenthood put the number at about 340,000 per year. The taxpayers pay Planned Parenthood about $500 million each year to support these abortions. Why? If, as many shriek, Planned Parenthood is such a valuable medical facility, why can't they compete in the marketplace like other businesses? Why do taxpayers have to pay $500 million each year to keep them in business? Why am I forced to pay some of my tax dollars?

Recently, the following was sent around in an E-mail to thousands of recipients. It speaks volumes about Planned Parenthood, and you need to know about it.

Planned Parenthood is creating a brave new world for us all. As revealed in a shocking new video release by Lila Rose and the Live Action team, Planned Parenthood is advising young women that they can terminate their pregnancy if they're unhappy with the gender of the child. Imagine that you find out that you're having a girl, but you wanted to have a boy. If you go to Planned Parenthood, they have, and will advise you that you can just abort—murder—that unborn child and try again. Sex-selection is nothing more than social engineering. Tragically, sex-selection abortions are not just happening in China; they are happing right here in America!

Planned Parenthood is playing God by steering parents towards a decision as to whether their baby is good enough to live, or not the right gender and, therefore, should die. Have we finally reached a point where life has such little value? Has pregnancy been degraded to an experience similar to deciding on which fruit to buy at the supermarket? "This one is too ripe, another too soft, this one has a blemish. These eyes are not blue enough, the hair is black and not blond, it's the wrong color, or it's a boy and not a girl." It's never been more important that we draw the line in the sand and stop Planned Parenthood from supporting a truly evil practice that has no place in our society than right now.

Sincerely,
Marjorie Dannenfeiser,
President, Susan B. Anthony List

I've seen two videos showing Planned Parenthood employees giving this exact advice, yet spokespeople say it was taken out of context. Really? The conversation was pretty clear and unedited, as far as I could tell. You and I are giving some of our tax dollars to support abortions and now gender selection abortions. Is that what America has become?

Some years ago I watched a video on television. It was a sonogram of a baby in a mother's womb at the age of six weeks. That sonogram showed the full form of a human, complete with arms, legs, torso, and head. It was not a collection of cells as the pro-abortionists would have us believe. What I found strange about that video was that it disappeared from view after about two weeks, never to be seen again. I wonder what pressure was brought to bear to get that video killed.

The abortionists call themselves pro-life. I refer to them as pro-death. I would hope that more and more people would speak out, stand up, and fight against the infanticide promoted as a woman's right to choose. A woman has the right to choose whether or not to have sex. That woman has the right to choose whether to wear protection or insist that her partner use protection. A woman has the right to take birth control pills. With all that, the pro-abortionists say a woman gets another right to choose, and she can choose death for her unborn child. Did anyone ask the unborn baby if he or she would choose to be murdered before it has a chance to draw a breath? Is that the country you want your kids and grandkids to inherit? I hope not.

Isn't RAP Music an Oxymoron?

RAP music has "stars" with such names as Snoop Dogg, Fitty-Cent, Dr. Dre, Run D.M.C., A Tribe Called Quest, Afrika Bambaataa, Notorious B.I.G., Puff Daddy, Lil Wayne, Ludicrus—at least that one is appropriate—LL Cool J, Ice-T, Ice Cube, EPMD, and Emnem. Are they so ashamed of what they do that they don't want their real names revealed? That must be it. What's even more hilarious is that when two of these RAP "artists" got into movies and TV, they have to keep their monikers or people won't know who they are (Ice-T and L L Cool J). Is this what American music has come to today? Is this what you want your kids listening to and imitating?

Some of their song titles are quite catchy, too. Songs named "Get Ur Freak On," "You Gots to Chill," "Big Poppa," "Nuthin But a "G" Thang," "Juicy," "Mama said knock you out," and many other classics.

I think I've learned a major rule that must be followed to get the full effects of RAP music. If you're in your car, you have to roll the windows down, even if it's snowing, and turn the volume all the way up, then fire up that RAP. It's even classier if you've paid a few thousand dollars and added 15 or 20 speakers to your car so everyone within 100 yards can share the joy of the music with you. I'm not sure why. Maybe it has something to do with getting the music into your soul, or maybe RAP music is a scheme perpetrated by hearing-aid companies. Now, if you're home, you must open your windows, and your front door to get the full effects of RAP music.

I also learned that most RAP music is based on a kind of poetry, centered on killing police officers, and degrading women, with all kinds of obscene, rhyming lyrics. That has to be hard work, don't you think?

I'm not sure, maybe it's just me, but it appears that you're not supposed to really understand the words in a RAP "song," or "poem." No, you are supposed to focus on the beat, and try to dance to it in some form or fashion.

I remember seeing Snoop Dogg on a television show one night. I'm not sure why he was there, but he wasn't singing RAP, carrying a gun or smoking dope, so how dangerous could he be? He was challenging someone to a debate about something, and challenged that person to come on down to his home in the "hood," and debate. Then I found out that he lives in a mansion in Hollywood, and I thought to myself, that's not a bad "hood" to be hanging out in.

It turns out that most RAP stars are black Americans, except for that Emnem character. When I've had to listen to some RAP music, because the car next to me at a stop light was blasting it out all over the neighborhood, I noticed that "hood," and "my posse," or "my boys" were included in the lyrics (at least I think they were lyrics). I must be getting my groove on. I'm not sure some of us stupid old guys could get away with shouting lyrics like that. Not unless we wore dark glasses, lots of bling, and a baseball hat turned sideways.

I've also discovered that many RAP stars get arrested for drug possession and use. and a number of them get shot. I'm not sure why they were shot. Maybe it was because the shooter had listened to some RAP music and it drove him crazy, but I could be wrong. They also have an award ceremony, just like the Oscars or the Grammy's, but at their awards show, they have fighting and shouting, and all out brawls, just to keep that tough guy image alive.

On a more serious note, I just don't consider RAP to be music. I believe that Hip-Hop is also in the non-musical genre. Genre, I like that word. I know that record company moguls will yell and scream that I'm out of my mind, that RAP is a wonderful form of musical expression. I guess if I was hauling in tens of millions of dollars peddling this stuff, I'd defend it, too.

RAP seems to be a means by which really angry guys and gals can get up on stage and threaten everyone, talk about carrying guns—being strapped—getting stoned, and slapping around some of their "ho's." People pay them to do it. After their show, they get into their chauffer driven limousine. and head for their 4-star hotel room, or chartered jet.

Primarily, RAP is a big joke on young people who have succumbed to peer pressure. and have been indoctrinated into thinking that it's real music. It's for the rebel in those young folks who shell out their dollars—or their parent's dollars—to go to concerts, buy those RAP albums. and feel oh so relevant and rebellious. Meanwhile, these RAP stars and the music moguls laugh all the way to the bank. RAP has infected a lot of the youth around the world. Sometimes I wish it were legal to just take a baseball bat to the stereo in those cars that blast that gibberish at full volume.

Is it Decorating or Desecrating Your Body?

First of all, I have to ask a question, and it's only related to the topic in a tangential way. I wore a baseball hat for many years, mostly while playing baseball, and later, while playing golf. I never thought about turning it sideways or turning it around backwards. It never occurred to me that I need to use that hat to protect my neck from the sun. I always thought the baseball hat was for keeping the sun out of my eyes. Baseball players still use it for that purpose, as do millions of golfers. Everywhere I look I see these guys with their baseball hats on sideways or backwards. Did I miss the announcement on the new and improved use of baseball hats? Someone better tell all those golfers, too. I know, I know, this had nothing to do with decorating your body, but it's been bothering me.

My early recollections of people with tattoos were of sailors and convicts. That was it. If you saw a guy with tattoos—I never saw a woman with tattoos as a youngster, a sheltered life, I guess—I knew that he was or had been a sailor, or he was an ex-convict. When I went into the Navy, I saw tattoos on at least half the sailors I ran into. It was a tradition. I have to admit that, back when I was a young sailor, a bunch of us went to town, drank way too much, and then we all went to a tattoo parlor where we all got a Navy anchor with the letters U.S.N. underneath. I wasn't proud of it when I sobered up, but there it was. Fortunately, even in my stupor, I was smart enough to get the tattoo high up on my left arm so no one could see it unless I took off my shift. I do remember that it hurt like the dickens when I got it. And then, to display my continuing stupidity, I got another small tattoo on my upper right arm, a cobra snake, after another night of celebratory drinking. Don't ask me why I got the tattoos. I have absolutely no clue. It could have been Navy peer pressure, I suppose. I think that'll be my story and I'll stick to it. I wish I hadn't done it, but in those days, once you got the tattoo, you had that tattoo, and you couldn't get rid of it. So, I've acknowledged that I'm criticizing others for doing something I did. It kind of exposes my hypocrisy in this area, but what can I say?

Today, it seems as though more and more young people have tattoos, and they're right out there, in your face, all over. We've all seen some of these kids around. They have tattoos all over their arms, a few on their neck, on their legs, maybe one or two on their face, maybe some in other places that, fortunately, we can't see. They may have four or five earrings in each ear, a ring in their nose, a couple in their eyebrows, and perhaps a few in their upper or lower lip, or tongue. If this is just youthful rebellion, I think they've gone just a bit too far, don't you? And I have to ask myself, "Did this kid's parents agree to this "decoration?" I just can't picture a parent saying to little Joey, "Yes, son, you have bare places on your arms. You need to fill those spots in with a few more "tats." Maybe the parents have tattoos and think that it's just a cool thing to do. There is, evidently, little thought given to what this child will face when he enters the workforce.

If you were a business owner and needed to hire a cashier, clerk, or anyone who would be dealing with the public, would you consider hiring someone who had all those tattoos and piercings? Would you want someone with that appearance greeting your customers? I didn't think so. The only potential employer for young men adorned in this manner would be a tattoo parlor. I knew a young man when I worked at a small business. This guy was a crackerjack telephone salesman; he could close sales better than any of the outside sales force. When he asked to be promoted to outside sales, so he could make more money on commissions, the company president told him, "You're great at what you do, but I can't have you meeting our customers and prospects looking like that. Even if you wore a long sleeve short, there are still all those things on your face and neck. I don't want my company image represented with that." She was right. It's up to those kids if they want to decorate (desecrate?) their body, have a great time with it. But, when that young man can't get a decent job, what then? Don't blame it on society. When his working life is confined to low paying, menial jobs, away from customers, don't blame society. These kids could start by asking why their parents didn't stop them from making these decisions regarding tattoos and piercings. Before getting those decorations, perhaps ask themselves, why did they get them in the first place, giving absolutely no thought to the future when they enter the workplace.

I am also confused by some adult men who, for some reason I don't understand, like to wear just one earring, in their left ear or their right ear. There are some men who wear earrings in both ears. I see some sports stars doing it, some of those Hollywood movie "stars" doing it, but I've never been able to figure out why. Is there some secret message given when a grown man has an earring in his left ear? How about if it's in his right ear? What if he has earrings in both ears? Does that signify something I don't know about? Inquiring minds want to know. I've heard that some years back, homosexual men would wear an earring in one of their ears to signal other homosexual men that they were available, but I'm not sure that was ever true. I hope someone writes a column to explain why grown men feel the urge to stick earrings in their ears.

Let's not leave out the young girls. You've seen them, too. A lot of these girls have the "tramp" stamp tattoo on their lower back, and they make sure to wear short shirts so we can all see it. I didn't make that name up; it's what most people call a tattoo on a girl's lower back, just above her butt, a "tramp" stamp. What it's supposed to imply, I don't know, but for many people the name given to it seems appropriate to the person who displays it. There are girls with other tattoos on their ankles or calves, the easier to be seen I suppose. Again, what parent tells their daughter that it's just the coolest thing to put tattoos on your body? What's the message they want to send? Then we have girls who have a stud implanted in their tongue. Their tongue! Are you kidding me? That has to hurt. I'm not going to get one to find out, but my tongue hurts just thinking about it. I had no clue what that stud in the tongue was for until a girl in our office told me. I'll let you figure it out; it's not for mixed company. Then there are the studs in the nose, pierced eyebrows, multiple earrings, and they do this because, because, because? Some women have had piercings in their sexual area because, because, because? Oh, now I get it. Ouch, that had to hurt, too. A nice tattoo above one or both breasts also seems to be popular. Let me ask the guys; why would you want to date a girl decorated like this, unless it was for some particular reason. Is this a girl you'd take home to meet the family? I didn't think so.

I've been in grocery stores around here in the summer when it's very warm, to put it mildly. I see middle-aged and older women who got tattoos in their youth walking around the store, two or three kids in tow, with tattoos on their arms, their lower back—it's well exposed—and on their ankles and calves. They look ridiculous to me, and I think that it imparts an image of them that isn't flattering. I'd bet that if you asked them about the tattoos, and they were honest, they'd tell you they regret getting them. However, if you do ask one of those women, I'd suggest being a few feet away because they might just decide to kick your butt for asking. I'm just saying.

I've seen convicts in prison with prison 'tats' all over their bodies—I was a volunteer, not an inmate, in Arizona state prisons and in a federal prison, and to some extent, I understood. In many cases these are men who are criminals, don't know how to be anything but criminals, and understand that they will spend most of their lives in prison. So, they get illegal tattoos everywhere—it's a violation to be caught with tattooing paraphernalia in prison, though an awful lot of convicts find a way to get their tattoos. What are you going to do to a convict who is serving 50 years or life without parole, give him a timeout? With some of the gangs, the gang tattoo is required to be on their body in a specific location; all the rest are just to relieve boredom.

But I believe that today, too many of our kids are defacing—decorating—their bodies for no other reason than peer peer pressure and parental neglect. What really bothers me is that the parents of these kids let them do it, without giving much thought to how this will affect their child's life in five or ten years. Parents are making shameful decisions.

Hopefully, in the not too distant future, some technology will be developed so that people can remove these tattoos inexpensively. There are some procedures available today, but they take quite a long time, and are costly.

As for me, I'd support passing a law that says if a child gets a tattoo or a body piercing, the parents have to get the same tattoos or piercings. Wouldn't that spice up the office?

The Internet—A Blessing and a Curse

With the passage of time, the Internet has gotten bigger and bigger, and truly has become the World Wide Web. I use the Internet every day. I use it for research, to verify something I've been sent, or something I want to learn more about. I also write articles for web sites. You can go just about anywhere on the Internet. My wife uses a new tool called Skype®, to see and talk to her sister in another country, for free. That's a wonderful use of the Internet, and reduces our phone bill dramatically. But you know that a medium, such as the Internet, is going to be invaded by all kinds of people who are up to no good. The federal government reports that there are hundreds, sometimes thousands of attempts to break into government networks each day.

Credit card companies report attempts to hack into their computer systems, and some of them have been successful. Google, Yahoo, and other Internet companies have been hacked, and customer data stolen. Many large businesses also report attempts, and some successes, in hacking into their company's web site in order to steal customer data.

There are the hackers who will use the Internet to try and gain access to your computer in order to steal your contact list. They implant a Trojan horse virus, then originate outgoing e-mails containing viruses using your name as the originator, and your contact list for addressees. Hackers will also steal the user names and passwords you use on various web sites. There have been many successful attempts to hack "smart" phones in order to steal photos, such as those nude photos of yourself you took after a particularly drunken party. Those photos then end up on the Internet. There are also people that want to send you SPAM. If you don't have some serious anti-virus software on your computer, you're a victim in waiting. If you've ever had your own web site, there are perils galore. First of all, your site could be hacked by people with evil intent. If your site host doesn't have very good firewall protection, and if you don't have a good administrative ID and password, the hackers can get into your site and literally take it over. They can post obscene material, insert links to take visitors to other sites that are pornographic, or just shut the site down. I've experienced it. It went on for several weeks before the host administrator could fix the problems in their firewall and bring it to a halt. With another host site, the hackers couldn't get through, but that didn't bother them. These people were just enemies of free speech. Some person or persons found my site, didn't like what I was posting—a column on the stupidity of medical marijuana—and got several of their friends to file complaints with search engine companies, such as Bing®, Mozilla®, Google®, and Microsoft®. All they had to do was send a complaint to these companies stating that my site was full of viruses that infected their computers. It wasn't true; the site was clean. Several of those search engine companies immediately blacklisted my site, and attempts to get to it were blocked, with big warning messages that my site could contain viruses. It took my "webmaster" a long time to convince these companies that the site had been tested six ways from Sunday and there were no viruses on the site, before the blocks were removed. No doubt they'll try again.

I get at least 3-4 e-mail messages each day, claiming to have originated with some bank or another or other on-line companies I use. They all claim one of two things, they're updating their site and need me to click on a link and update my account information, or they have noticed that my account with them has been accessed by different computers so I need to click on a link and update my account information. I forward them to my Internet Service Provider (ISP) as spam or identity theft attempts, but they keep coming. I'm sure you've gotten them, too. These are one of the new breed of thieves, cyber-thieves. Don't fall for it. And never respond to any e-mail message that pretends to be from any governmental agency threatening you with this or that action if you don't respond immediately. The government never sends these kinds of e-mail messages. The government has your address and phone number. Any official communication will come by letter, usually registered. Banks and credit card companies also don't send these "urgent" e-mail message telling you to click on the link and update your account information. I am concerned that so many people fall for this stuff.

There are people who build web sites designed to look like legitimate sites, mimicking a department store, for example. If you slightly mistype the address (URL) of the store, you could well end up on a site that looks like the one you wanted to access, but it isn't. You create an account, do some shopping, and then you provide them your personal information AND your credit card data. That's exactly what they want. You'll never receive what you ordered, but your credit card will be drained within hours. There are also a lot of people who use the Internet in order to sell sex. As I mentioned elsewhere, there are over 340 million pornography web sites today, and the number is growing. Many of them charge a fee in order to see "the really good stuff," but they'll show you some porn for free in order to entice you. With all of the pornography on the Internet, you'd think the women involved in fighting the degradation of their gender would be screaming for something to be done, but I hear nothing but silence. Ninety-nine percent of the pornography shows women being used as sex objects, in every imaginable way. No, I haven't personally watched this stuff, but there are all kinds of data available on the subject. There are, of course, homosexual sites, for males and females. There are bestiality sites for the animal "lovers." Anything you can think of that involves some sort of sexual perversion has at least a few hundred Internet sites from which to choose. There are also several "hook up" sites for people who want to meet other people for a little sex. There is now a site for married people who just want a little excitement—sex—without their spouse knowing about it.

There are software products you can buy and install on your home computer, especially if it's used by one of the children. These software programs will allow users to block access to sites you don't want your kids to access. Just as a question for discussion, if a child is able to access pornography for several years, does it shape their opinion of women? I'm just asking.

There are a lot of news sites on the Internet, and a lot of newspapers as well. You can cancel your newspaper subscription if you wish because, in many cases, you can read the newspaper in your town on the Internet, for free. It's not quite the same as having those paper pages in your hand, along with your morning cup of coffee, but it's not bad. This is one of the reasons that so many print publications are going the way of the dinosaur. In Arizona, most people are happy that the primary newspaper, The Arizona Republic, is in huge financial trouble for this and other reasons.

The Internet is also full of blogs and so-called "News" sites. Many of the blogs are good. Many of the news sites are good as well. I had a blog site, and I thought it was great. But remember, if someone has a blog site, you're reading their opinion, not necessarily objective facts. Many news sites provide up-to-the-minute news releases, something newspapers can't match. There are some sites, such as Media Matters for America, that make no pretense of presenting the news in an objective manner. They are a leftist site. and take everything they get and manipulate it to fit their agenda. There have been several stories about this organization, most of them stating that Media Matters for America has weekly meetings with the White House staff to get their talking points for the following week. Then there's the Daily Kos site. Though much less prominent than it once was, I find it a repulsive site because of all the slanderous things they put up there. There's the famous, infamous, MoveOn.Org. This site, with major funding from Socialist George Soros, is all about attacking all things conservative, Christian, and Republican. It doesn't appear that folks that work at these sites want to have a debate on ideas; they're more interested in the politics of personal destruction. Many people go to those sites, but I can only hope those same folks also go to other, more legitimate, news sites to get some balance.

WorldNetDaily is a conservative site. It's been accused of being a conspiracy site since one of the principal writers, Jerome Corsi, has published several books on the current President that are not flattering. They present stories that are devoted primarily to support of conservative positions and exposing leftist or Democrat stories. But they also put stories there that the "lame stream" media wouldn't touch. So, in the aggregate, the Internet is a major example of free speech. With few exceptions, no one can violate the right of free speech. You'll find people tweeting hateful things, too. So long as no law has been broken, such as an overt threat to harm or kill someone, the water's fine, come on in. These sites exist, and have every right to exist. I remember a line from the movie, "The Godfather" in which a father advised his sons to "*Keep your friends close and your enemies close*r." I look at many of the sites to either find out what the radical left is lying about that day, or find out the real story. The Internet is a wonderful invention, and, as technology moves forward, the Internet gets better and better in many ways. You just have to beware of all of the criminals that attempt to use the Internet to scam you, and they're all over the world.

I am on Facebook, but only under duress. I have a presence but I never visit it. I have no vicarious interest in knowing what everyone I ever knew is doing these days. If I want to communicate with them I'll drop them an e-mail or give them a call. And no, I don't care what they had for breakfast, but hundreds of millions of people do. Good for them; leave me out of it. And I don't "tweet,' either. To me that's another useless piece of technology. But I know there are an awful lot of people that like to brag about how many followers they have on Twitter, as if it's some form of bragging right. I have zero followers because I'm not there!

Can We Really Move To Alternative Energy Now?

We've been listening to all this blather from politicians and environmentalists for years. We have to reduce our dependence on foreign oil. I agree, don't you? The best way to do that is to drill our own oil, right here in America. Back in 1977 former President Jimmy Carter created the Department of Energy. The number one objective of this department was, wait for it, to reduce our dependence on foreign sources of oil. After 35 years how has that worked out for us? It's laughable. But the objective of creating still another government bureaucracy was certainly achieved, as you read earlier. Here in this country, permits for drilling on federal land and under the waters for oil are way down—actually, almost non-existent—and we continue to be dependent on other countries, many of them in the Middle East, for our oil imports. But the conversation seems to be centered on gasoline. Yes, gasoline is one refined product that begins its life as crude oil. But, there are many other products that are refined from oil. Here are a few.

- Refined oil, for lubrication of automobiles, trucks, aircraft, windmills, and machinery of all kinds,
- Paraffin used in all kinds of produces, car wax for example,
- Asphalt, the stuff used for most highway and road surfacing all over the country, as well as shingles for buildings and home,
- Industrial fuel oil,
- Home heating oil,
- Diesel fuel that is burned to create heat, create steam for turbines, generate electricity for trucks and cars,
- Kersosene,
- Washers, grommets, fan belts, hoses of all kinds,
- Polystyrene
- Automobile, truck, aircraft, tractor tires, construction vehicle tires,
- Latex used in gloves and several hundred other products,
- Polyethylene resin,
- Plastics used in thousands of different products; just look around your kitchen,
- Kevlar vests to protect law enforcement officers.

This is by no means an all-inclusive list. But if you look at just these products, all derived from crude oil, you have to stop and think for a minute. How can having less oil in the United

States, or switching to other forms of "energy" to replace oil possibly work for us? When you think of solar power, windmill power, algae power, do you see any of those energy sources being able to provide the products that we absolutely must have for our country? Me neither.

It's unfortunate but we have a relatively large group of people, of all ages, and walks of life, lobbying to reduce oil drilling, and oil acquisition within the United States. Don't drill for oil anywhere within our country, or in the waters off our coasts, but give government loans to, say, Brazil, so they can drill for oil, and then we'll buy the oil they produce. We give money to Brazil so they can drill for oil, then we give more money to Brazil to buy their oil. Does that make any sense to you at all? Me neither.

The fact is there is no energy source, naturally occurring or otherwise, that can replace oil now, and those who say otherwise are either lying or ignorant. We need to wake up and understand our situation, then get the attention of our elected representatives, and educate them. It would also be a good idea to educate the public as well. Too many citizens fall for the no-drilling mantra. We have more than enough oil under our ground, or under the waters of America, to last us well over 100 years. This would give private sector companies time to develop the technology and products that can eventually replace oil. To force us to keep buying oil from countries, many of whom don't like us, while our oil sits untapped, is well beyond silly.

Wars, Conflicts, and Interventions

Some of you may not know this, but the U.S. has not had a declared war since WWII, which was the last war won by the United States military. It was a two-front war, in Europe and fighting against Japan. These were declared wars, though Germany never attacked us. Japan, however, did attack us. On both fronts the U. S. fought and forced the enemy to surrender. Korea was not a declared war; Vietnam was not a declared war; Iraq was not a declared war; Afghanistan is not a declared war. Somalia was not a declared war, and neither was Grenada. As one Marine put it, "Grenada was two days of fighting and two weeks of surfing." But the point is that America has not declared a war since WWII, and has not "won" a war since WWII.

The United States will never win a war again. First of all, the nature of war has changed dramatically. Back in WWII, nations wore uniforms, fought under the flag of their country, and fighting necessitated the use of large numbers of men with rifles, tanks, and aircraft. Today, wars can be fought with drone aircraft, missiles, high altitude bombing and, hopefully not, nuclear weapons. If you recall, there was talk of coming home with pride when we abandoned Vietnam. With the Korean "conflict," the term victory was never used. It wasn't used in Vietnam, either. We won't have victory because when the United States gets its military involved now—for other than "Meals on wheels" duties—victory is no longer defined. It's almost as if, "We're going to send a bunch of America's young warriors with guns over to that country and shoot some people, and some of our warriors will die, too; then we'll come home." If there is no clear objective, then any cessation of hostilities will do.

In South Korea, we went there because the South Koreans feared that North Korea was going to attack and conquer them. So, we sent troops and, evidently, forgot they were there. Victory was never defined. Actually, the end game was never defined. There was no victory because North Korea never surrendered. We've kept thousands of our troops in South Korea for over 60 years, still guarding that 38th parallel in case those North Koreans decide to come swarming in. Sixty years, are you kidding me? Get us out of South Korea. North Korea has nuclear weapons. They can't seem to figure out how to mount them on the warhead of a missile yet, but you know they're working on it. They don't need to march south, they just need to launch a half-dozen nuclear warheads and South Korea is vaporized. There won't be any need for ground troops, except for mop up duty. So, just what are a few thousand U.S. military personnel on the border going to do to prevent a nuclear attack? Nothing. Secondly, South Korea has a fully functioning military, and they can guard their border with the North quite nicely, thank you very much.

In Vietnam it was much the same thing. North Vietnam didn't declare war on us. The South Vietnamese government asked us to send our troops over there to die so those nasty North Vietnamese wouldn't take over South Vietnam. It started by sending a few military "advisors" to help the South Vietnamese learn how to fight, but quickly escalated un Kennedy, and then Johnson. Could we have won that undeclared war? Yes, quite easily, with practically no loss of life. But we sent hundreds of thousands of our warriors there, and over 55,000 of them died. After all those years, and all those lives lost, we put our tail between our legs and scurried home. Today, if I'm not mistaken, North Vietnam and South Vietnam are one country under the control of North Vietnam. What a terrible waste of life.

We sent troops to Somalia to track down some warlords. I have no idea why the President thought this was a good idea—a few Navy SEALS inserted into that cesspool could have taken out those warlords in about 24 hours. Was Somalia a threat to our national security? No. But troops and helicopters were sent to Somalia, but not before the news cameras and reporters arrived, so they could be set up on the beach as our troops came ashore. Wow, a real life made for TV military movie. Yeah, right. Anyone see the movie, *"Black Hawk Down"*? That was Somalia. We got trashed by a bunch of disorganized, low technology thugs. Again, I was wondering just how we would define victory. In this case, we didn't have to worry about it because we fled the country, and some of our warriors were killed.

After 9/11, it was determined that the mastermind of the attack, Osama Bin Laden, had orchestrated it from Afghanistan. What to do? I know, let's invade Iraq. That makes perfect sense, right? There were five different countries that sent us their intelligence report that said crazy ole Saddam Hussein had weapons of mass destruction, and was trying to build nuclear weapons. Just what that had to do with the attacks of 9/11 is unclear. The intelligence reports were good enough for our President. And off we went. Well, not exactly. It took us six months to get our troops to the border of Iraq, get the logistics set up, get the aircraft into the area. And then off we go. During that period, satellite photos showed huge convoys of trucks leaving Iraq, heading for Pakistan and Syria. Gee, I wonder what was in those trucks? Oh, never mind; off we go. We did that little Shock and Awe Fourth of July celebration with real bombs, and then we invaded. The President did his "Mission Accomplished" on the deck of an aircraft carrier signaling the success of the air campaign, which the "lame stream" media reinterpreted to mean the war was over. We took Bagdad in about four hours, and then hunted down most of the real bad guys, and either killed them or captured them, turning them over to Iraqi authorities for trial. We pulled Saddam out of his hidey hole after a while, and the Iraqi people hung him after a short trial. OK, let's go home. Remember, all of this time the U.S. knew that Bin Laden was not in Iraq, and had not been in Iraq. Bring out troops home from Iraq. Well, not so fast. What? We won, didn't we? We were victorious; let's go home. Hold on a minute. Look, we really busted up this place—which typically happens when you drop bombs all over the place, so we have to rebuild it. Why? But, the good news is that the Iraqi government, the new group of thugs that will run the country, will pay us with Iraqi oil. Well, not so fast. We never got the oil, but we stayed anyway, for about nine years, spent hundreds of billions of dollars, and lost more of our warriors. We chased those Al Qaeda all over the place, and killed a bunch of them. We rebuilt their electrical grid, rebuilt their water system, and did all sorts of great work. Now can we go home? Sure, let's go home. Is there any chance of Iraq becoming a threat to our national security? Well, it turned out that they weren't a threat before, so I'd say it's safe to assume they won't be a threat anytime soon. But, the braintrust in Washington decided to stay in Iraq to teach a tribal culture how to live under a central government. Oh yeah, that'll work. At the same time it was decided, not by you and me, that we just had to ramp up the invasion of Afghanistan. Now we have a nation building operation in Iraq, with still more of our warriors being killed, while increasing our presence in Afghanistan, the "good" war.

Afghanistan is like your worst nightmare for a place to go hiking, multiplied by about 4,000. I also wouldn't recommend it if you're looking for a nice resort hotel with tennis and golf. It's a dusty, dirty, barren place with mountains all around, steep mountains, caves everywhere in those mountains, and little villages scattered about, with few cities of any major size. We would probably call those cities small towns over here, badly in need of electricity, clean water, and flush toilets. But, we had to go punish them for allowing Bin Laden to hatch his plot to attack America and look for those Taliban folks. That Bin Laden was probably not in Afghanistan any longer seemed not to matter. This is the war we should fight, said our current President. So, we fought and then we surged. Many of our military personnel were killed, many more seriously wounded, some with IEDs provided by Iran, but darn it, that Bin Laden guy couldn't be found. There had been reports that Bin Laden was hiding in a cave in Tora Bora, a particularly difficult mountain range with literally thousands of caves throughout. The locals weren't very helpful, and all efforts to find Bin Laden failed. Then, reports said he was gone. Hell, he could have been hiding in any one of the two or three thousand caves and we'd have never found him. But, as of today, we still have a presence there, even though Bin Laden assumed room temperature well over a year ago in Pakistan. We've liberated the Afghan people; they're free. They love us so much they only kill a few of our warriors each month in appreciation. And, there are still those pesky Taliban lurking around. How do we know when we've won in Afghanistan? We're there trying to democratize Afghanistan, showing them how to switch from a tribal culture to a central form of governance. Does this sound familiar?

We've gotten into undeclared wars that weren't wars. We went into these "conflicts" with no exit strategy or a means to determine if or when we've achieved the objective (won), but we spend billions of our tax dollars to help countries rebuild after we've leveled them, and they thank us by trying to kill our military warriors. Is that pretty much it for our strategy?

What is the Cost for a Free Society?

Here are some Child Protective Services incidents. We've all read horror stories about babies being born to drug-addicted mothers. These poor children start out life addicted to drugs, and had no choice in the matter. Some recent statistics put the number at about 300,000 babies born, each year, addicted to drugs. For four years I volunteered to work with foster children, representing them in court as the juvenile court judge's advocate. During that time I encountered children, some as young as six-months of age, fighting for life through a methamphetamine addiction, compliments of the child's mother. The mother had never been married, and had three other children by different men. None of these men paid child support, and only one of the men acknowledged that he was the parent of one of the children. Child Protective Services had not found the other fathers, and didn't appear to be looking for them very hard, even when the mother identified them. In some cases, the mother wasn't sure who the father was because she was under the influence at several parties, and had unprotected sex with many men.

The grandmother lived in her own home with her boyfriend. The grandmother allowed her daughter to drop out of school in the 8th grade, and run the streets, getting into trouble, getting into drugs and, eventually, giving birth to four children, none of whom she could afford to raise. The daughter is now about 30, still addicted to drugs, and lives with various men. This is just one cost in a free society. In a country like China, that mother would have had her babies aborted, and she may well have been sterilized and, possibly, been jailed for drug use. We, as a society, bear the cost of our freedom. Would you want to change society so as to be more like China? Me neither. Freedom isn't free.

But in the case of this mother, Child Protective Services (CPS) doesn't worry about finding the fathers and making them pay child support. Why? Because CPS lives on our tax dollars, and they just consume those tax dollars to pay for the care of the children and the mother. The grandmother has not been held culpable, either. She allowed her daughter to become the woman she is today through very bad parenting, but she walks free. Only we the taxpayers pay for this kind of behavior. The children are the victims.

The problem of illegitimate children is growing every year. Just in case you don't remember, the Reverend Jesse Jackson calls his illegitimate child a "love" child. Some recent statistics reveal that approximately 70% of children born to black American women are born without a father. For Latinos, it's about 50%, and for white Americans it's about 35%. We can ignore the problem. We can turn our backs on it, but it's getting worse, not better. What should be done? What kind of a future do you think these children have? Who are their role models? What is society's responsibility to these children? What are their chances of growing up loved and having a chance at a normal, productive life? How about a baby, born addicted to methamphetamine? Where are Jesse Jackson and Al Sharpton? Why aren't they in the black communities, telling the citizens what is going on, that a single mother with multiple children, living on welare, is condemning those children to poverty?

This is just one example of life in America today, and what your kids and grandkids have to look forward to in the future. If CPS takes parental rights away from a parent, or takes custody of those children, where do those children end up? Some end up in foster homes, some end up in foster group homes, some end up in crisis centers for children. There are not enough foster homes to house all of the children that have been taken away from their parents. In group homes there are often 8-14 children living in one house, with a group home manager and some assistants. A child might spend years in that group home until they reach age 18, at which time they have "aged out" of CPS custody and care, and are on their own, literally. As a free society, how do we deal with this massive problem? I don't know that there is an easy answer, but the problem is getting bigger and bigger.

Look at our Second Amendment which says, in part, ". . . . .the right of the people to keep and bear arms shall not be infringed." In a free society, living under a Constitution such as ours, that freedom does pose some risks. The founders believed that every man, woman, and child had the right to keep and bear arms, so the Second Amendment was added. Some documents from that period reveal that the founders believed that the people should have the means to resist a tyrannical government. Almost every administration in the past 100 years has tried to find a way to get around the Second Amendment, believing that a disarmed population is more easily controlled, should it be necessary. That's the basic argument. Do some people violate the law by using their firearms to do evil things? Yes, absolutely they do. But the reaction to that act is not overturning the Second Amendment but, rather, to punish the offender for breaking the law. No person can violate the Constitution, but they can violate a law that is established to deal with people using a right improperly. Do we want a country where there is a police officer on every corner, a video camera placed every quarter mile on every street, a video camera or three in every business, every home, every store, and in every bathroom? In a free society some people break the law, and there are punishments for those people. The solution is not to get rid of this or that amendment, although too many people in government would like to do just that. Despite what some cities have done in making gun ownership difficult or impossible, we all have the right to keep and bear arms, with some exceptions, such as being mentally unstable or being an ex-felon. Unfortunately, the bar has been raised very high on confining mentally ill or unstable people for fear of violating their civil rights.

In many cases, the crime committed with a firearm could have been prevented if the people who knew that the purchaser of the firearm was unstable or acting in an unstable manner. If you look at the case in Arizona where a member of the U.S. House of Representatives was shot, along with several others, it could have been prevented. The alleged shooter was tossed out of college because of his irrational, threatening behavior towards other students, but the school did not contact law enforcement ostensibly because they didn't want to get involved. In fact, the school did nothing. When the alleged shooter went into a gun store and bought the weapon, the required background check was performed. The result was a clean report and the sale was completed. Is that the gun store's fault? If you saw someone you recognized as an ex-felon in the parking lot of a gun show, and that person was buying a gun from someone else outside the show, do you have a responsibility to call the police? Ethically and morally you do, but most people don't want to get involved. Should the gun seller have insisted on doing a background check before selling the weapon? Yes. The background check would have come back with a warning that the buyer was an ex-felon, and, therefore, no sale could be made. The person selling the gun out of the trunk of his or her car was probably doing so because the gun was a stolen weapon, or they didn't want to pay the fee to set up a table inside the gun show. There's a case where the law could be written to prevent such sales. Then, that law could be used to arrest both the buyer and the seller. What if I have an old shotgun that is no longer being used, and I decide to sell it. Do I have a legal responsibility to ensure that the buyer can pass a background check? You bet I do. But how many sales of weapons happen without any background check? Way too many. But this has nothing to do with getting rid of the Second Amendment; it has to do with setting up laws and enforcing laws for how guns are bought and sold. But the right to legally purchase a firearm cannot be infringed so long as the law is not broken.

There are those who believe that law enforcement's job it to protect the people and that makes sense. The problem is that the police are a reactive organization not a pro-active organization. A good example is a home invasion, or a rape of a woman in her home. If a home invasion happens, and the occupants are unarmed, they may get beaten, tied up, and the house emptied of all valuables. After the home invaders are gone, one of the occupants gets loose, and calls

911. The police are dispatched, but the crime has already been committed, and the criminals are long gone. What if that home owner had a firearm at hand, and was able to defend him or herself against the invaders at the time? What if you're a woman at home, alone, and in the middle of the night, you hear someone in your house, but you're unarmed. The intruder can overpower you and do whatever they want, including killing you, and there won't be any police around. If you've been killed it may be a long time before someone finds your body, and then calls the police. That doesn't do you any good, does it? Even if you had time to dial 911 before the intruder pounced, you may still end up dead. What if you kept a small handgun at your bedside and, when that intruder entered the room, you were able to fire a shot to ward him off, or shot him and ended the threat? Now you can call 911 and tell them to bring a body bag for the criminal. You get the idea. As the book title of some years back stated quite clearly, "*More Guns, Less Crime.*" And it's Constitutional. If you don't like guns, don't want a gun around, or don't even like seeing a gun, fine. But don't start demanding that the Constitution be changed so no one can own a firearm.

In a free society a woman can have as many babies as she wants. In a free society a man can father as many children as he wants. But, as a free society we have to decide what, if anything, can or should be done to try and stem the tide of unwanted or unloved children.

In a free society the right to free speech should never infringed, even if we don't like what is said. The whole intent of the First Amendment was to encourage the free exchange of ideas and opinions without fear of censorship. Free speech has been defined and redefined several times, but the principle remains. I'm free to say or write what I want without fear of reprisal by government or by others. Free speech has now been defined so as to include campaign contributions to political candidates. I'm free to contribute money to the candidate of my choice within legal limits. Free speech has now come to include money given to others for causes and candidates. That's a good thing. Free speech does not include someone threatening to kill another person, or libeling or slandering another person.

There are some college campuses that have implemented speech codes to stifle any speech that "might" offend anyone. Yes, you read that correctly. No matter what anyone says or writes, someone may well say that they're offended. Such speech codes as these are intended to stifle free speech, on college campus, no less. This is *Cultural Marxism* writ large. That's insane. Our kids and grandkids are in college to learn "how" to think, not "what" to think. People say or write things that tick me off all the time, but they have the right to say or write them. and I have the right to rebut or ignore them. I know people who never watch a certain TV channel or listen to a certain radio station because they don't like what they're seeing or hearing. I'm just the opposite. I watch TV stations and listen to radio stations where I don't agree with much of anything that is said, but I watch or listen to them so I know what the "other" side is saying. I often contact a show or station to rebut what was said. I have a conservative web site. I get all kinds of hate e-mail from people who visit my site because they don't want me writing the columns I post there. They're entitled to send me hate mail, express their venom, it doesn't bother me. What would bother me and cause me to take action is if someone threatened me or my family with physical violence because that's against the law. In those instances, if they occur, I will file a complaint with law enforcement. There is a town in Massachusetts that has passed a law where if you swear in public you can receive a ticket and have to pay a $20 fine. Is that a good thing? If it is, can you imagine how many fines would be levied at a pro football game or a pro hockey game? Wow, that's a money maker. How about if a professional golfer swears after hitting a bad shot, and the TV camera catches it, as well as 100 or so fans standing nearby? Should that be a $20 fine, too? What is a swear word, anyway? Is "damn a swear word? How about the word, s**t? Is that a swear word, too? Who decides what constitutes a swear word, the government? If I referred to a puppy born of a female dog, can I call that dog a "son of a b***h?" See what a slippery slope this is for us?

When I've been out with my wife, usually on a golf course, some young man lets loose with a string of obscenities. I ask the man to please refrain from the swearing because women are present—typical male thinking that it's OK for men to swear around each other, but not when women are around. Sometimes it works, sometimes it doesn't, but at least he knows that his behavior is bothering people. Often, the friends of the offender tell him to shut up. If I don't want to listen to that language any longer, I can remove myself from the situation. I'm not bound by some "man thing" law to confront the man doing the swearing. The incidents of road rage would drop dramatically if more people would just quit believing that they have to confront the offender. Nothing good ever comes from it.

Should it be a violation of law to swear? It's sad that people can't express themselves without the need to swear, but do we want anti-swearing laws? As a former military man, I can tell you that it took me some time in civilian life to clean up my speech.

In a European town where my wife's family lives, there is a city ordinance that requires homeowners to be responsible for not only the upkeep of their homes and yards, but also to keep their "half" of the street in front of their house clean. This saves the city money for street sweepers. Is this a good thing? When I'm out in front of my home, if I see a paper cup, a piece of newspaper, or similar kinds of trash, I go pick it up and put it in my garbage can. It's not that terrible a task, and it helps keep the neighborhood looking better. My neighbors do the same. I'd like to think that most homeowners have a pride of ownership sufficient to keep their property looking as nice as possible, and if they see some trash, they pick it up. But Americans don't need a law. Where I think some ordinance or law could be written is for the owners of foreclosed properties. During this recession, millions of homes sit vacant, some sitting for years. The yards look like jungles; windows are broken, shrubs and plants have died, and the homes look terrible. I believe that the owners of those vacant properties have a responsibility to keep them clean and looking decent. I don't care if it's a large bank or some absentee owner; they need to clean their properties up. But we live in a free society so how many laws do we need for these situations?

Have you ever been a participant in a march or a rally to fight for or against some issue? Even if you haven't, you've no doubt seen the news coverage. In a free society, the First Amendment gives people the right to peacefully assemble and petition their grievances. They can carry signs, they can give speeches, or just have a party, but once that march or rally takes the form of assaults on other people or the destruction of property, the law has been broken, and those who commit those assaults or damage property must be arrested, tried, and put in jail, along with a fine sufficient to restore the property or pay any and all medical costs for injured people. When a rally or march turns violent, it becomes nothing but an assembly of thugs. That should be stopped by law enforcement. Peaceful petition of grievances doesn't include clubbing someone over the head because they disagree with you. Just look at the Zuccotti Park in New York. This was the first incident involving the Occupy Wall Street thugs. During the weeks they occupied that park, no one else could use it, business property was damaged, drugs were sold and used, women were raped, and the park was so filthy when they left that New York spent tens of thousands of dollars cleaning it up. Only the most egregious violators were arrested. The taxpayers shelled out the money to clean up the mess. Where was law enforcement? What if one of our kids or grandkids got caught in or close to that park? Is that what you want them subjected to by this bunch of anarchist thugs? What can you do to put a stop to it? Was this the exercise of free speech, or the assembly of a mob? What about the people operating under the banner of the Occupy Wall Street thugs, practically destroyed downtown Oakland, California. Again, very few arrests were made. It's as if law enforcement and government were afraid of the thugs. That needs to stop.

In a free society, do we all have the right to drive a vehicle? No, we don't. A driver's license is not a right, it's a privilege. To obtain a driver's license you must earn it by passing a written examination and a driving test. If you pass, you must pay a fee before the license is issued. No one has the right to drive while impaired, regardless of whether that impairment is physical or mental. Someone who is high on drugs does not have the right to drive, even though they have a license. If the impaired driver causes a loss of life or destruction of property, the law has severe penalties. Drunk drivers deserve no sympathy. As far as I'm concerned, if you drive drunk you intend to hurt or kill someone, and should be locked up for a long, long time. A free society doesn't entitle anyone to operate a 4,000 pound vehicle with no ability to control it or exercise good judgment. Lock them up.

In a free society, do you have a right to fly on a commercial airplane? Up to a point. You have the right to buy a ticket. If you show a proper photo ID and no banned items in your luggage, you'll get through security. Happy flying. Once on the aircraft, do you have a right to get drunk and bother people? Of course not. If you are flying on an aircraft and make a nuisance of yourself, you can be turned over to law enforcement unpon arrival at your destination, and charges can be brought against you.

In a free society, does everyone have a right to an education? Yes. But, does everyone have a right to a free education? Absolutely not. First of all, please take a look through the Constitution. See if you can find anything in that document that even mentions education. You won't find it. Our states have always provided K-12 education without tuition, the cost being borne through property taxes and other levies administered by the various governors. When it comes to college, there is no right to free education, either. There never has been a right to a free college education. People keep coming up with new "rights," but they exist only in their minds. If parents and kids are upset with how much it costs to go to college, they need to address those concerns with the college and the government. Student loans have become big business, and the federal government controls almost all of them. There are scholarships available at most colleges for academic and athletic performers of high caliber. If your child or grandchild, however, decides to just limp through high school, chances are they won't be admitted to some of the better schools for academic or athletic reasons. If they apply and are admitted, they're going to need a student loan if his or her parents won't pa the bill.

By contrast, in most Communist countries there is no right to education. The government decides who goes to school and who gets trained as a factory worker or farmer, engineer or scientist, or to be trained as a leader. If the government does pick a child for college, they'll be studying for a degree in whatever the government needs. So, for all those kids in America today that think they deserve free education, get over yourselves; it's not going to happen. The best thing that could be done, regarding education, is if the federal government got out of the education business, and let the states run their own education systems.

In our free society, do we have a right to privacy? Absolutely. Our right to privacy is contained in the Fourth Amendment to the U.S. Constitution. This issue has come to the fore recently because of the federal government and state government use of drone aircraft to "spy" on citizens without a warrant showing probable cause. These drones can fly over your house and take pictures of you or family members playing in the yard, swimming in the pool, or getting a nude sun tan. The technology on these drones can also use heat sensors to monitor activity within your home. They also can use their cameras to look inside your windows to see what you're doing in your own home. My first question is, why? Why would state or federal government agencies want to have drones taking video or still photographs of just anyone? It makes no sense. This is very much a Big Brother assault on citizens. I understand the use of drones to follow a fleeing suspect or spotting people coming over the border from Mexico. In those circumstances they're being used for law enforcement purposes. It's against the law for me to shoot at them; they're up too high, anyway. But, if for any reason. I was arrested for a crime, real or imagined, because of pictures taken by a drone aircraft, while I was in my home, there would be a major lawsuit over violation of my Fourth Amendment rights.

In a free society does anyone have a right to a job? You're kidding, right? We live in a competitive society in America. When a business is hiring an employee, there are usually many applicants for that job, you are only one of them. You must compete for that job. If you have no education, no experience, no set of skills matching what the employer wants, you won't get the job, and no law has been broken. If you went to college, went to graduate school, and now have a string of letters after your name, you still have no right to a job. That right doesn't exist, and it should never exist. Businesses hire, or should hire, the best possible candidate for a job so they get the best value for the money they spend. Well, that was before race baiters like Jesse Jackson started extorting businesses for not hiring enough black Americans. But those hires would be made under duress and fear, not because those hired were the best candidates. If you don't want to compete for a job, you're going to be unemployed for a long, long time. Get over it. Get your education, learn some good work habits, and quit demanding that people give you what you want. It's not going to happen.

In our free society, do we have a right to free healthcare? No. The U.S. Constitution says nothing about the government or any other entity providing healthcare for anyone. Back when I was a youngster we didn't have health insurance. When my parents took me to the doctor for whatever reason, I received treatment, and the doctor's office sent my parents the bill. My parents wrote them a check. It was called fee for service. The government wasn't involved, and neither were health insurance companies. Life was simpler then. Over the years some of the larger companies, in an effort to keep employees, started providing a basic healthcare benefit through an insurance company. By bundling several employees together, the insurance company issued the coverage knowing that some employees wouldn't need much if any care, and thus the cost to care for the others would not lose money. The employee paid a share, the company paid the rest. But the federal government was not involved, which is always a good thing. Over time the number of benefits, the number of insurance companies involved, the number of specialties practiced, and advances in technology took over, leading us to where we are today. Now we have employees demanding that their health insurance "benefits" include free this, free that, and they don't want their co-payment to increase. They want the insurance company to pay for it. There was this sham testimony given by a woman, who claimed that it was costing her female college friends—she didn't mention having any male college friends—over $3,000 for contraceptives while they're in college. She wanted "free" contraceptives for all college women. First of all, you can buy a one-month supply of birth control pills at a drug store for about $10. That makes the total cost about $480 for four years in college. If that's too much, find your local free clinic or Planned Parenthood office; they provide birth control pills for free (well, free to the patient, a cost to us taxpayers). But no, this woman wanted "free" birth control pills. That's where some people are when it comes to healthcare. Now we have the "no pre-existing condition" scenario where a person can wait until they get a serious medical problem, and then go to an insurance company and demand a policy. First of all, that's not health insurance. This is a form of discount medical care at the expense of the insurance company. This type of policy is a sham. The new policy-holder pays a monthly premium of some dollar amount, and perhaps get $1-2 million in medical treatment. One guess as to who pays for all that medical treatment. The other policy-holders will pay in the form of higher premiums. There is no right to free healthcare insurance or free healthcare, with the exception of an emergency or life-threatening situation. In that situation the paramedics will come and get you and take you to a hospital that will treat you. If you can't pay, you can't pay. We have so many people now, believing that they are entitled to free services, and a government that wants to pander to them by coming up with more and more government programs to get them free stuff. There is no "free" stuff. Someone is paying the bills. For the entitled class, they don't care so long as it isn't them. I call these people parasites.

Sexual Predators

Consider all of the sex crimes occurring today. I've had several discussions about sexual predators with people. Most of the discussions seem to revolve around predators that stalk and assault children. When did this start becoming such a major problem? It certainly wasn't anything like that when I was young. My friends and I could walk the streets, play in the park, or on the playground, and never feared anyone attempting to kidnap us, rape us, or rape and kill us. For the past two or three decades, the problem has escalated. The number of sexual predators that prey on children has continued to grow. Just look at the number of men, and women, who have been convicted of sexual assaults on children. Then, I wonder, how many child predators haven't been caught, and continue assaulting our kids and grandkids. You've all read the stories or seen them on television, where a school teacher, male or female, has had sexual relations with their students.

If the teacher commits this act of statutory rape, and is caught, that behavior is, or should be, a major felony. I think it is much more traumatic for a young girl to be sexually assaulted by her male teacher. The girl may well feel so ashamed that she wouldn't tell anyone, but it will certainly affect her life forever. These teachers need to be arrested, tried and, if found guilty, given the same sentence as any other child rapist.

What makes a child sex predator? What are the factors that influence some man—almost always it's men—to think about, fantasize about, and act on some desire to kidnap a child that is five, six, or seven years old, have sex with them and, in many cases, kill them and toss them away like a bag of trash? Could this have been caused by the decline in moral values caused by television shows, pornography on the Internet, or reading salacious stories in the newspapers? Could it be caused by a terrible childhood, where the predator was the victim of child sexual abuse when they were young? But, we all have to wonder just how does some man make the decision to kidnap, rape, sodomize, and kill a child for personal gratification. Is that person insane? If caught and found guilty, should that man ever be let out of prison? I've seen many studies on the subject, and the consensus seems to be that a child predator cannot be rehabilitated. If released from prison, that child predator will re-offend over 70% of the time. Other than physical or chemical castration, c an our society be assured that this predator will not re-offend? Can society make that decision and force the law to be changed? Can the law be changed so that child predators are sentenced to life in prison without parole? What do you think? If a child sexual predator is released and moves into a house three doors down the street from you and your kids, is that OK? Do you want your kids and grandkids to be targets of a child predator whom has served their sentence and is now back on the street? Should the law be changed to require chemical castration of any convicted child predator? Would you support such laws? Are there some criminals who should never be allowed back on the street? Yes, there are. Many criminals commit crimes so heinous that they receive a life sentence without parole. What's more heinous than the rape and murder of a child? What do you think? We, the citizens of American, have an opinion, too. Don't leave it up to the psycho-babblers to create even more excuses for horrendous behavior, with promises of a cure. Our children need protection from child predators. Let's knock off this registering them as sex offenders, or putting ankle bracelets on them so the police can track them, after the fact. By the time law enforcement reacts, another child may well have suffered a horrible death. Enough is enough.

The Mainstream (Lame Stream) Media

You may have seen it, heard about it, or discussed it. The "it" I'm talking about is the media. More specifically, how the media goes about reporting the news. From what I've seen, read, and heard, I think it's fair to say that the so-called mainstream media has an agenda in its reporting. To clarify, by "*Lame Stream*" media I mean the major TV news networks, ABC, CBS, and NBC. I also include the cable channels CNBC, CNN, and MSNBC. I didn't include FoxNews, cable edition, because they do a good job of having guests from all perspectives on their shows to debate issues. Then, I include major newspapers, such as the Los Angeles Times, New York Times, San Francisco Chronicle, Arizona Republic, Boston Globe, Chicago Sun-Times, and many more.

Some polling done about 8 years ago—you can look it up—showed that at least 85% of reporters for newspapers, and hosts of TV news and political shows, voted Democrat. That's a pretty fair indictment of the media from where I sit. For example, take the New York Times. This newspaper is the source of stories for many, many other newspapers. The New York Times runs a story, and dozens of other newspapers pick it up and run it, too. TV networks also pick up New York Times stores, and use them as topics, but never disagreeing with the agenda of the stories. The New York times often skip stories that favor conservatives, Christians, or Republicans, focusing instead on extolling the virtues of Democrat or liberal folks. I believe that most of these organizations manufacture polls, the results of which fit their agenda. Polls are all about a) who you poll, b) the questions you ask, and c) how you frame the question. Any good pollster can give just about any desired result.

Dating the 1990's, there were attempts to censor or shut down some TV and radio shows, which very unethical, not that ethics enters the picture for most leftist media. People vote with their remote and their wallets. Some historians may remember the name, Joseph Goebbels. Goebbels was the minister of propaganda for Hitler's Nazi Germany. Goebbels was responsible for ensuring that all "news" was controlled by Hitler's regime, to ensure that only the news they wanted published got into the media. Goebbels was very good at his job. When Germany was suffering big losses, Goebbels made sure that German citizens read all about German triumphs and major victories for the homeland. Hitler was also portrayed as almost a deity. Ring any bells for you?

I read that Goebbels died decades ago, but I'm not so sure. If you look at many of the nation's newspapers, most of which are losing readers by the thousands, you'll see that, in general, only stories favorable to the left (Democrats) are published, while stories favorable to the right (Republicans) are distorted, taken out of context, or not reported. In instance after instance, the newspapers don't even cover events that are not favorable to the Democrats, especially the current President. They just ignore them. They have been known (the New York Times) to leak confidential information, fed to them by a Democrat in Congress, even after the administration pleads with them not to publish it because lives would be lost. They didn't care, and off to the printer it went. They were proud of doing it. This is the same newspaper that has fired all kinds of employees, lagging sales, but still continues to publish false stories, manufactured facts and, generally, attempts to create news not report it. But for some reason, there is a core of people, most of them politicians, who read it every day. Most other newspapers read the New York Times as well, looking for stories to run because they're too lazy to do any real reporting. It's just easier to repeat the sludge from the New York Times, and newswires, such as the Associated Press. The television media isn't any better. There's one cable channel in particular, MSNBC fortunately, few people watch, that gets many of its stories from an organization called Media Matters for America, a leftist organization—with a lot of funding help from George Soros—that focuses on finding dirt on conservatives, then feeding it to television stations for airing. And it works. You see, the hosts and hostettes at MSNBC, not being particularly bright, love having their stories handed to them. They seem to practice raising and lowering their eyebrows, looking serious, and regurgitating what they've been given. Oh, it's marvelous.

One of the hosts, Chris Matthews, is totally in the tank for all things Democrat, and even gets chills up his leg when the President gives speeches (his words). Evidently, he's easily aroused. Another one, Rachel Maddow, doesn't appear to have had an original thought since puberty. She just spits out what she's told, tries to make it sound intelligent—give her a 4 out of 10 on that one—and just rails for women's rights—to contraceptives for free, abortion on demand, equal pay, and all things radical. Ed Schultz, the angry man, is always ranting about all things conservative. He once referred to a female radio talk show host as "*a right wing radio slut.*" He's such a classy guy. Schultz wants the government to give away (spend) more money on the poor. Just a note—the average "wage" for the non-working folks on welfare is about $32,000 per year. Who wouldn't want that? No sense going back to work; just vote Democrat and keep on getting that "free" money. Might need a new plasma TV, or the latest iPad or iPod; always things you need for your free housing. NBC TV was recently caught editing a 911 call from George Zimmerman, the man who shot Trayvon Martin in Florida in. Zimmerman claims self-defense. The 911 call was edited so as to make it appear that Zimmerman was a racist, when in fact the 911 operator had asked him if the person he was watching appeared to be black, Hispanic, or white. Only then did Zimmerman respond that the man looked black. The 911 operator question was edited out of the call. Ooops. Then there was the Dan Rather major fraud where documents purporting to prove George W. Bush was AWOL during his National Guard service. The documents were proven, by hundreds of people, to have been fraudulently produced. One reason they were proven fraudulent was because the print type used on those documents hadn't been invented at the time those documents were supposedly created. The documents also were printed on a laser printer, which also had yet to be invented. Oooops. In some recent primary elections, the major networks reported, as soon as the polls closed, that the Democrat looked like a winner, only to be proven totally wrong. However, in the Wisconsin governor recall election, they reported that the race was too close to call even though the governor was over seven points ahead. It's that kind of reporting that makes most people very suspicious of the "lame stream" media.

On a local level, there are stations that report a "breaking" story about allegations against, usually, our county Sheriff. The story typically consists of two or three people giving their version of the allegation, with no response from the Sheriff's office. Local Channel 5 is probably the worst offended. They seem to delight in airing any story that supports illegal aliens, and disparages the law, and especially the county Sheriff. In many instances, those people interviewed end up being proven to be liars, and the breaking news becomes garbage paper, but you'll never hear an apology from the TV station. It's unfortunate that so many people think they're getting unbiased news from the newspaper or from television.

R. Eugene Spitzer

Drug Use in Society

Think back to when you were a kid in school. I've done some reflection, too. What I remember from my youth was, primarily, there were no drugs to speak of except, you guessed it, alcohol. In high school it was "cool" for some kids to drink. Being one of the stupid kids at the time, I drank beer, and sometimes some cheap wine—Yuch. Marijuana was a drug we knew about, but didn't have a clue on how to get it, and probably didn't have the money to pay for it, anyway. But, we could get beer pretty easily. Most small, community liquor stores would sell beer to me because, at 15 or 16, I looked like I was in my 20's, and they weren't much interested in "carding" me if doing so would cost them a sale. One of our other tricks was to get a mayonnaise jar, clean it well, then pour a little bit from each liquor bottle in my parents stash. I'd then add some water to the bottles so they wouldn't notice. My mayonnaise jar would have four or five kinds of liquor, but I was too stupid to care. My friends would do the same thing, then we'd meet up, usually on a Friday or Saturday night, and we got drunk. Our favorite form of drinking was to buy some *Country Club Stout* malt liquor, and a bottle of *Ripple* or *Arriba* rotgut wine, and that would do it. It was almost guaranteed to get me drunk and sick. I knew it was time to head home after I threw up. But, to be fair, not that many kids drank alcohol in my high school. Most of the kids I ran around with were, for the most part, from very dysfunctional families, mine being no exception.

None of us had a family life that resembled Ozzie and Harriet. Our parents were for the most part, invisible. Our parents didn't participate in our lives, ignored us for the most part, and seemed not to care about what we did or where we went, or whom we hung out with. So, we hung out together, feeling pretty much useless, with no future, and we drank. In the interest of full disclosure, I did play a lot of team sports, and was very good, thinking I'd get a chance to play professional baseball, but I didn't dedicate myself to the game, or to school in general. When I look back, I wonder how good I could have really been if a) I wasn't drinking and smoking, and b) my parents had participated in my life. OK, enough reminiscing.

Do you know what a CNS Depressant is? If you're a drinker, you've seen the results. If you drink too much, you'll often say or do things that, the next day, you wish you hadn't. A Central Nervous System Depressant screws up your ability to think or behave properly, whatever properly means to you and the law. In addition, your liver is damaged, your kidneys are damaged, and you are killing brain cells. If you've watched video of college kids on "spring break" you can see what happens when people drink to excess, and think they're just having innocent fun. I've encountered and dealt with alcoholics in my capacity as a drug specialist in the military, and in civilian life. I've had a family member that is an alcoholic who, gratefully, hasn't had a drink in over 10 years. But that family member had to reach rock bottom and make a choice, to live or die. This family member made the right decision, had a very loving and supportive family around them, got sober, went through the AA 12-step program. She made that commitment to never drink again, and stuck with it. That family member is now happily married with two kids, and life is good. Other people reach rock bottom and just choose to die, there is nothing anyone can do to "save" them.

I've worked with people who just had to have a couple of "joints" every morning; they were psychologically addicted to marijuana. Marijuana is not a harmless drug. It contains all of the tars and other garbage that gets sucked into your lungs just like cigarettes do. It damages several organs, and quite often leads to the use of other drugs. Methamphetamine will take over your life. You will stay up for days, forget to eat, forget to bathe, your teeth will rot while the drug is in the process of killing you. Crack cocaine was one of the worst forms of cocaine ever invented. People who get hooked on crack often cannot break the habit, and I've known people who died because they just had to have crack cocaine several times every day until it killed them. People inject and snort heroin, a very addictive drug that also can kill you. We then have all of the prescription drugs that are sold to patients legally, and often stolen by their children in an attempt to get stoned. There are hospital wards full of parents who are 100% addicted to prescription drugs. Oxycodone, and its derivatives, seems to be the pill of choice for a lot of people. Lately there are the designer drugs, like bath salts. No matter what law is passed to prohibit the sale and distribution of these drugs, the creators just change a molecule or two, and they're back in business. Some people still sniff glue or paint in order to get high.

So, from alcohol through the gamut of other drugs, one thing is clear, They Can and Often Do Kill You. Despite all of the information and counseling available, adults and children use and abuse drugs, and many die because of them. I remember people I knew who took acid trips on LSD (lysergic acid diethylamide) to open their minds. What they were doing was killing their minds, and the rest of their bodies. LSD had the added "benefit" of coming back to haunt the user years after they'd quit using it.

Someone please tell me why drug abuse is "cool." Are drunks cool? No, they're dangerous. Are stoned kids at a party cool? No, they're stupid. The more interesting question that seems to have dozens of answers is why people use and abuse drugs and alcohol? What happens in their brain that says, "I think I'll start drinking alcohol until I'm incoherent, and then take the car out for a ride? Why does a child decide to smoke marijuana, after being told and shown how dangerous it can be? Has our culture been dumbed down so far that common sense is no longer part of our genetic makeup?

Remember the '60's and '70's? This was the era of sex, drugs, and rock and roll. "Tune in, turn on, and drop out" was the mantra of one *Timothy Leary*, the major advocate for LSD, a drug that could literally blow up your brain. Marijuana was everywhere, too. An awful lot of young people answered the call, and jumped into the drug culture. A lot of people look back fondly on Woodstock. If everyone who said they were there actually attended, there must have been about two million people at that event. A bunch of hippies, druggies, and assorted hangers on assembled in Woodstock for a few days of music, drugs, constipation, overdosing, throwing up, dancing naked in the mud, and anonymous sex. Yeah, those were the days, huh? Many of those people from the '60's are now in politics, teaching at universities, and big business. What that era accomplished was legitimize the anonymous sexual revolution, coupled with lots of drugs. LSD, which was made popular as a drug that allowed people to really see the truth, the light, the future, whatever, was actually a mind altering drug that gave some people such serious mental problems from which they never recovered. Others would have "flashbacks" years later, and be unable to function in their suits and ties. Many of these people, who were kids at the time of the "revolution, have spoken about how terrible family life was in their younger day. hey were left to run free, run wild, just go do it. Sound familiar?

We're now into 2012 and looking forward. Have you checked the statistics on how many kids are taking heroin, methamphetamine, ecstasy, cocaine, smoking marijuana, and stealing their parent's prescription drugs? The numbers are staggering. Kids are exposed to drugs everywhere. They can buy drugs at school, at the local burger joint, at middle-and-high school events, everywhere. And they're pretty cheap, too. New, designer drugs, have hit the market almost daily. The police can't keep up with all of the new ones. The doctors can't, either. How many of you with children aged 10-18 absolutely know that your kids are doing drugs? Hold up your hand, and let's see. I don't see too many hands. Some of you are being fooled.

I've spoken to parents whose children are drug users and abusers. Their children got so hooked on drugs that they were stealing from their parents to buy drugs. They were pawning everything they could in order to get drugs. Some parents have thrown their kids out of the house, made them find another place to live. They tried to get their children into a good drug rehabilitation clinic and were rebuffed. As a former drug education specialist, I learned that every drug abuser has to find their own gutter before they make the decision to either get help, or die.

Many parents make a big mistake when dealing with their children's drug abuse. One mother had thrown her son out of the house because he was stealing everything of value. But this same mother would meet her son for dinner once a month. The mother would pay for dinner, and then give her son money to "help out." She said she just wanted to help her son. I suggested that she change that statement. Instead of saying she just wanted to help her son, she should say she just wanted to help kill her son, because that's exactly what she was doing. If you give a drug addict money, they aren't going to use that money to buy decent food, or find a clean place to live. No, they're going to go buy drugs. This mom was helping her son get drugs.

The peer pressure and availability of drugs today is overwhelming. If an impressionable child is in a bad home where he or she is ignored, has parents who are more interested in themselves than their children, there is a good chance the child will often look for a family at school or join a gang on the street. These kids are not kids you'd want your child associated with, but you're too busy with your life, so the child is finding a family of his own. Young kids may well give up on the future. Not everyone will end up making $200,000 a year as a scientist. But there are a lot of good paying jobs out there if the kids don't give up. I know my parents told me I'd never amount to anything, I shouldn't even think about going to college because they weren't going to pay for it, and I wasn't bright enough to make it. Wow, there's a vote of confidence. How many kids today are living in the same conditions? Kids have to see a future, dream of a successful future, be encouraged to pursue that dream, and understand why education is so important for the future.

There are a huge number of children today that live in broken homes, with no father or mother figure. Some kids never know who their father is. When a single mother with one, two, three, or four kids, no husband, and has to work two jobs just to get enough money to feed everyone, and pay the rent or make the house payments, how much time does she have for each child? Much of the time, the kids are left to fend for themselves. The mother is almost invisible. There is no accountability in the home. The kids could end up taking care of each other because mom isn't home very much. Given the temptation of drugs in school, on the streets, and no role model in their life, it's easy to see how a child can just give up. Often, the temptation to resist drug involvement is too much without help. Children seek, want, and need stability. If they can't get support, love, and stability at home, they'll look elsewhere.

Look inside the poorer communities, where an overwhelming majority of households are single parent, usually a mother. Quite frequently, the parent has no job, and lives on welfare and food stamps. There are no fathers in sight. As the children are growing up, what do they see all around them? They see poverty, failure, people who have given up. How many of them say, "Not me. I'm going to get straight A's, go to college, and become a doctor, nurse, executive?" Some may believe that at first, but that dream is easily destroyed when the reality of day-to-day life sinks in. The race-baiters don't help. They never miss an opportunity to tell black American kids that life isn't fair for them, education isn't fair for them, there are no jobs for them, and they need the government to give them more money.

Look at the suicide rates for teenagers today. The suicide rate has been rising steadily for years. Kids with 70 years in front of them have already given up and want to die. Why they want to die is a good question. No one has figured it out yet. I believe it's because too many children grow up, with no love, stability, or clue as to what they're supposed to do. Some kids see nothing in front of them, no future, no way out or up, just a bare existence. They just give up and kill themselves. Other kids don't want to die, but they do. They die in gang fights; they die from drug overdoses. The body count keeps rising, and drugs are right in the middle of it.

The facts are easy to see. More and more kids are doing more and more different kinds of drugs. Criminal gang membership is rising every year. These "*gangbangers*" are family to many kids today. That the gangs rob, murder, rape, do drugs, and many die before they're 25 seems not to matter. These kids never believed that they had a future, anyway. What do we need to do in America to turn this problem around?

When kids watch TV or go on the Internet to follow movie and music stars, what do they see? They see movie stars drunk, on drugs, in fights, sleeping around, getting married, getting divorced, committing adultery, but they're rich. Music stars, mostly in the Hip-Hop and RAP arena also dress like gang members, do drugs, carry guns, and they're rich, too. Could these people become role models for youngsters who don't have a role model in their homes?

Here's a caution to married couples. If you are busy, don't have much free time, or if you don't want to be bothered with dedicating at least a portion of your life to your children, DON'T HAVE CHILDREN! I can find no law that says you are required to have children once you get married, so don't have children that you're going to ignore. They are not Barbie dolls you can discard when you get tired of them. If you have children, the television, iPhone, X-Box,

Tweeting, and FaceBook do not replace you. You actually have to spend time with them, a lot of time with them. Your responsibility is to give them stability, lots of love, lots of attention, involvement in their school, helping them chart a path for the future, and help them learn how to make good choices and avoid bad ones. Any of you parents paying attention out there? You could give this same advice to the rising number of young girls who think it's just the coolest thing to get pregnant and have a baby at age 15, 16, or 17, with no father, no home—except their parents' home—and no income. What are you doing? Babies are not toys.

Next, the courts need to start handing out very harsh sentences for anyone who sells any form of illegal drug. No more pats on the wrist, no more probation. If someone is selling drugs, they are selling death. Treat it that way. Any parent who hosts a party for their children, and allows them to drink, do drugs, or have sex is, in my opinion, guilty of reckless endangerment, and should go to prison for at least 10 years. No more of these so-called "hip" parents who think they're doing a good thing by having the drinking, drug use, and sex in their house, instead of some hotel. These are dumb people. They're useful idiots as far as their kids are concerned. If they supplied the alcohol or drugs, add 10 years in prison.

This will never happen, but it should. Every parent with a child in school should absolutely attend Parent-Teacher conferences, PTA meetings, and demand the syllabus for each class their child is taking. They should also have to sign a document, once a quarter, stating that they have read and understand the grades given to their child, along with any recommendations made to them by the school. They must acknowledge that they will follow those recommendations. No more absentee parents. If you have children, you must be involved in their lives.

Lastly, every parent with one or more teenaged children should buy and use a home drug testing kit, and use it. Tell you child that you're going to test them, and if they fail, they will either get into counseling and rehabilitation, or all privileges will be taken away. Quit trying to be their friend, and focus on being their parent.

Some People Should NOT Become Parents

Across this nation, millions of children are taken into foster care because the parents have proven themselves to be unable or unwilling to parent. Sometimes it's drug-related, sometimes it's physical abuse, and sometimes, abandonment. We've all seen and read about these stories about these types of issues with parents. There are other types of bad parenting that don't get as much attention. Here are a few stories I've heard about.

A father thinks it's great to teach his son how to play Texas Hold'm poker at age 10. And not just play once, but numerous times. On many occasions, the father will pay the entry fee so his son can play in a "friendly" game at someone's house. The child is 10, and the gambling continues until the child attends high school. The child gets involved in gambling with his friends, with his father's support. The child's gambling increases to football picks, basketball game picks, and the habit continues to grow. When the child gets to college, there may be a credit card involved in some online gambling. Perhaps, the child places bets on college or pro football games with a bookie. The child gets into deep debt, and then what? The father may not connect the dots of what he has taught his son, and now there's serious money at stake. However it turns out, it's not good for the child or the father. It all started so innocently, just a little poker game with father and son. Should children be learning to gamble at the age of 10?

I know of parents who take their children to the movies. What could be more innocent than going to the movies as a family, right? These parents take their children to the theater, buy tickets for that great G-rated movie, but once inside, the whole family heads into that R-rated horror or blood and guts murder movie. The children are under 12. What have they taught their children? It's OK to cheat? Those movie ratings don't matter? The kids learn that if mom and dad break the rules, then rules don't really matter. In some cases, they not only sneak into one R-rated movie, they sneak into another one after the first one ends, cheating the theater out of ticket money. Other parents just drop their children off at the theater, with money for tickets and junk food, and the kids have learned the ropes. They buy the tickets for the G-rated movie, go in, buy their soda, popcorn, and candy, and just walk into the R-rated movie. When that movie is over, they just wander over to another R-rated movie, and spend the day at the movies. Sounds like cheap babysitting to me. Please don't tell me it's the theater's responsibility to keep watch on all of the kids in those 18-screen multiplex theaters; it's not going to happen.

Did you know that, at least in Arizona, there is this service called Respite Care? I didn't know either until just a few years ago. I found out when I became involved in a foster care case involving a mother and son. No, there was no father anywhere around. It seems that the mother dropped the child off at this respite facility because she was going to have some kind of surgery, and didn't have anyone to care for the child. So, the foster care program provides this service. In this case, the mother had been living in Washington State, and then moved to Arizona. After 30 days, the mother was supposed to pick up her son, but she didn't show up. It took several days, many phone calls and, finally, an investigator to track down the mother. When they finally found her, she wouldn't pick up her son, saying that he was mentally unstable and had tried to have sex with her. The child was taken into foster care. I found the story totally without merit, but was fighting Child Protective Services to get the truth. I had investigated and found that the mother had been using drugs while in Washington State, and had been a prostitute. The son told me he used to be in his room in their apartment while his mother entertained men in her room. CPS didn't want to confront the mother or do anything about it. I also found out that the mother had paid cash for a condominium in Phoenix, right in the middle of the area known for prostitution. She said she used money she received from the sale of her home in Washington State. I found out that she never owned a home in Washington State or anywhere else. There were also several gaps in her history she couldn't explain. CPS would not investigate. Meanwhile, the son was in a foster care group home, and we became friends. He knew his mother had used drugs, knew that his mother had been and, maybe was still a prostitute. He wanted nothing to do with her. This young man was really messed up. He was stuck in a foster care group home that he hated, but didn't want to live with his mother. My first question is why did this woman even have a child? Given her line of work, I'm sure she understood how birth control worked. What does the future have in store for this young man who, through no fault of his own, is caught in a trap? Where was the boy's father in all of this? CPS didn't care who the father was, or where he was. They never seem to care about the missing fathers. CPS knows that there is this endless supply of taxpayer money to pay for everything. Why bother getting child support from the father?

Then we have parents who are so lax, they allow their children to drown in their backyard pool. How did they just fall asleep for a few minutes while their little 4-year old daughter managed to get out the back door, open the pool fence gate, and dive into the pool? Most of these parents don't get prosecuted because, the story goes, "They've suffered enough with the loss of their child." No, their daughter is dead because they didn't keep track of her, and because their nap was more important. As far as I'm concerned, they should be prosecuted for involuntary manslaughter, and sent to prison for about 20 years. But, if there is no other parent, what happens to any living children? Every year in Arizona, there are anywhere from 10-20 small children who die needlessly in backyard swimming pools, most of them with security fencing.

If their parents would only behave as parents, those children would still be alive. Why so some people have children if they're so inconvenient?

Have you ever seen kids playing outside, for hours and hours, never going inside? I have. In a couple of cases, they were outside because the parents were gone to the store, and locked the house so their children couldn't get back in. What kind of parent does that? The kids are just inconvenient, so they lock them out.

Every year in my state, parents are caught and, in some cases, arrested, for leaving their children in the car while the parent goes inside "for just a minute." In Arizona, children have died during the summer because a parent has forgotten their baby in the car seat, in the car, with the engine turned off so there was no air conditioning. The outside temperature might be 105 degrees or higher. Inside that car the temperature would rise to over 120 degrees within a very short time. The parent feels oh so badly that their baby is dead, but they were just gone for a few minutes. To me, that's also involuntary manslaughter. In one case, a woman left her child in the car, asleep, parked outside a bar, while mom was inside, partying. She didn't want to leave the child at home alone, though that happens, too, so she left the baby in the car while the she goes into the bar to have a few shots. What is wrong with these people? The sad part is that these parents, criminals all, rarely go to jail. They get tickets, they get probation, they may pay a fine, but there's no jail time. That is criminal.

What about parents who allow their 12-year old daughters go to a concert hall the night before, and stand in line all night in order to get tickets for some musical event? Is this a good idea? As for me, my daughter would not be allowed to go spend the night in some ticket line at the age of 16 let alone at the age of 12. What kind of parenting is that? You can bet that if something happened and their daughter was kidnapped and later found dead, those same parents would be all weepy in front of the cameras, demanding that the police find the killer. That's too late, folks. The girl is dead. As far as I'm concerned, those parents contributed to the death of their daughter by allowing her to be in position to be kidnapped and killed. Shouldn't they be charged with a crime, too? If law enforcement would crack down hard on parents such as these, there's a good chance incidents like these would be dramatically reduced.

I've met many of these parents, and you have as well. These are the parent who don't want to parent their child(ren), but want to be their best friend. It's the job of a parent to say no, say no again, and say no again. Children want their own way all the time. It's the adult's responsibility to make good choices for their children, and teach them how to make good choices, not just turn them loose. Parents should be raising their children not indulging them. Children will always push the limits; they subconsciously want to know, what is the limit? It's a parent's job to set the limit, and stick to it. If there is no limit, then the child is in charge and will do whatever he or she wants. Where is the parent? Sometimes parents have to appear to be the bad guys, so the child knows who the adult is, who the child is, and who makes the rules.

Children have no "right" to privacy if they're living in their parent's home. The child is not the equal of the parent. Parents set the rules. There is no hiding of "things" in the house, and using "privacy" as the means to keep it away from their parents. Parents who allow this are fools. We've all read the stories of young girls who "met" some really cool guy online, and ended up arranging to meet him. That young girl ends up missing, and is later found dead. The parents didn't know their daughter was in chat rooms, on the web, looking for cool boys. Those parents who give a child in their house the right to privacy are fools. The child is totally dependent on the parents for everything, and don't have the judgment to make good decisions all the time—nor do a lot of adults. Parents should check their child's computer, check their cell phone, and inspect their room, if they believe that it's necessary. Parents also have the right to administer home drug tests, if they suspect that the child is using drugs. The child doesn't get a vote. Today, we have parents who have no idea who their child is communicating with, what web sites they're visiting, or what chat rooms they've joined. That's a recipe for disaster. Someone has to be the adult, and it's not some 13 or 14 year old. I also required that my children say "Yes sir" and "Yes Ma'am" or "No sir" or "no ma'am." Showing respect when they're young will carry over into adulthood. I know you've met or know parents who have children that call them by their first name. So my sons call me John but never call me Dad? Really? If you're not going to be a parent, who do you think is going to instill discipline, self-control, respect for authority, good values, and good morals? Are you the parent or their "buddy"?

How many car accidents have you seen covered in the news where the children weren't wearing seat belts, were thrown from the car, and their skulls were crushed. The parents may or may not have survived, but the children are dead. If the parents survive, shouldn't they be charged with contributing to the death of their children? I think so. Now, back when I was younger, there were no seat belts. My parents just tossed us in the back seat, all three of us, and off we'd go. We traveled across the country, sitting in the back seat with no seat belts. Fortunately for us, we didn't have an accident and get tossed out of the car. But even today, if you drive around farm country you might often see a bunch of kids in the back of a pickup truck, driving on the side roads without seat belts. Heck, I see pickup trucks rolling along with four or five kids in the bed of the truck, an accident waiting to happen. With pickup trucks, of course, there are no seat belts in the bed of the truck. But I do think there's a law that prohibits children from being in a vehicle without a seat belt.

Do you have guns in your home? I do. I have several guns ranging from revolvers to semi-automatic hand guns, to a 12-gauge shotgun, to a 7.62 semi-automatic rifle. They're placed all over the house, with one in my car. There are only two of us living in the house; my wife and me. My wife knows how to handle a gun and how to shoot one. However, when grandkids come to visit, and we have 14 of them, those guns are rounded up and stored safely away. Our grandkids cannot get to them. I'm sure you do the same if you have guns in your home. Unfortunately, a lot of parents have guns in their home, and kids can stumble upon them. They may be sitting on a closet floor, maybe on a shelf, or maybe just a rifle leaning against a corner of the room. Children all over the country get hold of their parent's guns and end up shooting themselves, shooting a friend, or shooting a parent. It happens in Arizona all too frequently. Except in very unusual circumstances, the parents are never charged with child endangerment. Even if the child shoots a friend, the parent's don't get charged, but the child does. Where's the justice in that? These are stupid parents; way too stupid to be having children or having guns lying around.

Alternative Energy—Ready in About 25 years?

With great fanfare, and a lot of your money, the president and General Motors designed and built the Chevy Volt. How far can the Volt go on a full battery charge? At most, 40 miles, then it has to switch to gasoline. Is this car of much use to working people? How about families with three or four children? It was a failure while it was still on the drawing board, but they kept spending our money to build it. Now, the Volt is on hiatus, production stopped for a while. I wonder what happened to the autoworkers who built the Volt? People won't buy it, despite the propaganda spewed by proponents. There's also one major fact that the propagandists leave out when talking about electric cars. If you buy one, how do you recharge the battery? You plug it into a wall outlet in your garage, right? What happens to your home electric bill? It goes up, way up. Where does that electricity come from? It comes from the power company, and how do these companies generate that electricity, mostly from coal and oil to run those power plants. So, wouldn't it be more proper to call the Volt the Coal/Oil car? Are people so ignorant that they believe that electricity just appears magically when you turn the lights or TV on? No, it comes from coal, or oil-powered generating plants. To be fair, there are some power plants that generate their electricity from hydro-electric technology, but the vast majority of electricity comes from coal and oil.

Look at solar power. Again, this administration has "invested" billions of our dollars in private companies to build solar panels. Why? If solar is so good, why does the government have to pick winners and losers? The private sector would be building solar power panels if there was a profit to be made. And yet, here comes the government is, playing investor. The company that appeared in the newspapers and on TV and radio was Solyndra, but there have been others, all bankrupt now. Having received over a half-billion tax dollars to build solar panels, the company went bankrupt. The main reason was that China was building solar panels a lot cheaper than Solyndra could build them. There are a lot of solar companies in America, yet this administration picks Solyndra to receive government largess. Could it be because one of the major campaign money "bundlers" for this president is a major investor in Solyndra? Naw, must be a coincidence. And the fact that the Chinese were building cheaper solar panels was known before our money was given to Solyndra. This looks like simple crony-capitalism to me. Then, when Solyndra was going bankrupt, there was this meeting where the private investors were put at the top of the list to get whatever money was recovered from the bankruptcy, and the taxpayers were moved down the list. This, by the way, is very illegal, but they did it.

You can bet that if there is a technology that can be developed and sold for a profit, private companies are working hard on it, with their money, not ours. There are hundreds of solar companies working on the technology, but it's not ready to make a significant impact on our energy needs. I like solar. I met with my city's government, and wrote to the state government about solar. And just for the record, there is no such thing as "renewable" energy. Energy cannot be created or destroyed; it can only be transformed to be used in other ways, but it can't be renewed. Evidently the ruling class in Washington flunked that class in school.

I asked why, in a state like Arizona, with all of its days of sunshine, isn't every home built with solar on the roof, and the cost bundled into the price of the home? The city fathers where I live practically laughed at me. That makes way too much sense, they said. I believe that if a city said that all new homes would contain solar panels, the power companies would have gone nuts because that cuts into their profits. It was a political decision, not one that would take advantage of the sun's energy to help people.

Take a look at windmill power. The first two things that come to mind are a) the environmentalists want to love it, but on windmill farms, thousands of birds are killed because they get sucked into the blades and chopped up. There are also some self-anointed, powerful people, like the Kennedy's, who said that "windmills are great, but you can't put them anywhere that disturbs people's view of the ocean." When windmills convert wind energy into electrical energy, where does the electricity go? It goes to certain homes or businesses. What happens when the wind isn't blowing? The electricity flow stops, and the power company has to take over. There is no battery technology available today that can store electricity in sufficient quantity. That technology is still being researched and developed, and has been going on for decades. If you play golf, look under the seat of an electric golf cart. You'll find four, five, or six storage batteries in there. It takes that many batteries to power a golf cart for about two rounds of golf. How many storage batteries would it take to store the electricity needed to power a small city? Quit laughing. Yes, to power small gadgets there are a lot of little batteries available now, but they only store a small amount of electricity. You get the idea. Washington has no clue.

The ability of batteries to store large amounts of electricity hasn't arrived. It's going to take some years to develop that storage capacity, but the government, in its zeal to force "alternative" energy on us, is trying to force us out of our gasoline-powered cars.

You also need to understand that, according to many scientists who study oil reserves and accessibility, there are approximately one to one and a half trillion barrels of oil under America's land, or under its waters. That's enough oil, at today's consumption rates, to last the United States 150-200 years. You should also understand that we have enough natural gas to last this country so far into the future there are no estimates when it would run out, but it's under the ground, and the government doesn't want us using anything that's under the ground. With that much oil available to us, why aren't we drilling for it while the private sector continues to research and develop alternative energy products? If you look at the partial list of products derived from refined oil, they number in the thousands. Will windmills solve those product problems? No. Will solar panels solve those product problems? No. Are there synthetic products available, that are not oil-based to replace all of those products? No. Can we make tires without using oil today? No. Yet the ruling class in Washington has this perverse obsession with wind, solar, and electric cars. That obsession is the enemy of the people.

Electric cars are really oil/coal cars. Windmills kill birds and the electricity produced cannot be stored. When the wind doesn't blow, there's no electricity generated. Solar panels work, but are still very expensive, and have the same storage issues. By the way, when you put one or two solar panels on your roof, even if just for your water heater, there is a small electric motor installed that is used to move the water up to the solar panels, and back down to your water heater.

Any politician paying attention or doing some individual research would say, "Let the technology keep advancing, but in the meantime, get the oil out of the ground and use it to keep the American economy moving forward." Don't say, "We can't drill our way out of these high gasoline prices. We need alternative forms of energy." Political leaders, mostly on the left, have been saying the same thing for 40 years. Do you realize how much more oil we'd have in this country if we had been drilling all this time? We wouldn't have to pay countries that don't like us trillions of dollars over the years for their oil. Why do we allow the head of the Energy Department to say that he believes that our gasoline prices should be equal to the prices in Europe, that is $8-10 per liter. Why is it a good thing for Americans to pay the same for anything that some other country or region pays? This guy should be tossed out of office for general ignorance reasons. The Department of Energy has been around for over 35 years and that's the sum of their intellect?

Voting is Our Civic Duty

Please note that I said 'citizen," not just anyone who happens to be in the country when elections are held. It's supposed to be one man, one vote, and that person needs to be a living person. Just think about that for a minute. Since I was a child, and that was a long time ago, I learned that voting is not only a civic duty, it's one of our precious rights as citizens. As an American, you have a right that most countries don't have, the right to cast a ballot for the candidates of your choice for elective offices. When I was young there was no early ballot, no provisional ballot, no registering to vote over the Internet. When you went to the polls you showed your photo ID, were checked in, given your ballot and a place to complete it. You could get an absentee ballot if you were going to be away from your polling place on Election Day, but that was it. You registered to vote by getting a form, filling it out, mailing or taking it to the proper office, and showing proper ID. On Election Day, it was your duty to show up at the polls, show your ID, sign in, and vote. Those were the days when citizens took voting seriously.

What we have today is a circus. There is voter fraud everywhere, and I believe that the left encourages voter fraud to the maximum extent possible. Each election more dead people vote than the previous election. Citizens are now whining that it's just so inconvenient to vote—can you come by and fill out my ballot for me, after I wake up from my nap? It would be funny if it weren't so sad. A large number of Americans are just too lazy to go to the polls. People who are in town, and working, vote absentee because they just can't stand the thought of standing in a line at the polls for 10 minutes; it's just so tiring. Our civic duty has become a chore that a lot of people just can't handle. Typically, only about 60% of eligible voters even bother to cast a ballot. If it's an off-year election, only about 30-35% of eligible voters bother to vote. After the election, those that didn't vote are the ones crying the loudest against this or that person who got elected. My view is, if you didn't bother to vote, shut up.

And that statistic even includes all the dead people that voted, and all of the illegal aliens who managed to vote, too. There are people in my neighborhood who never vote, don't know who the president is, and couldn't care less. All they care about is going to work, getting a paycheck, paying bills, and entertaining themselves.

There are so many ways to vote now without the sheer drudgery of actually going to the polls, voter fraud is occurring all over the nation. You can even register to vote on the Internet, get an "early" ballot, fill it out when it arrives, mail it back, and no one has ever seen you, verified your identity, or your eligibility to vote. There are people who set up phony addresses and phone numbers, and fill out online registration forms in the names of various people, using these phony addresses and phone numbers. There was a major problem in the Tucson, Arizona area, yet the state attorneys didn't follow up. Now we have the Attorney General for this administration coming down hard on any state that dares to make it a requirement that anyone showing up to vote, must produce a photo ID. Their position is that it's discriminative against, are you ready for this, Mexicans. You see, thousands of Mexicans in Texas have no driver's license or photo ID of any kind, so that requirement discriminates against them. This happened in another southern state. That state was willing to pay for a state-issued photo ID for anyone who wanted it, and the DOJ still came down on them. If I'm not mistaken, you have to have a photo ID to cash a check, open a bank account, get on an airplane, rent a movie at Blockbuster, and any number of other activities, but thousands of . . . . Mexicans . . . . don't have a photo ID of any kind? This is insane. Where does the DOJ get the authority to order a state to not require a photo ID to vote? This is an outright attempt to enable voter fraud by the Attorney General of the United States, and we know why. The current president's chances of reelection are growing dimmer each passing month. They will do anything, including fraud, bribery, foreign campaign contributions, whatever it takes, to steal an election. One detail we should all notice—Republicans don't do voter fraud; they don't try to intimidate states into allowing voter fraud, they don't make up laws to intimidate opponents. These are all tactics of the leftists, Democrats, Marxists, Socialists, take your pick; it's the same people.

There have been cases where people who owned two homes, in different states, would register to vote in one state, and request an absentee ballot. Then, while they're in the other state, they register to vote and go to the polls, thus, voting twice. That's a crime, but since there's no national database, few ever get caught.

One of the best things that could happen in this country, regarding voting is if every state enacted a photo ID requirement. And, every state tell the DOJ to go fly a kite. If the DOJ sues them, let them. If the DOJ tries to fine those states, don't pay. It's time states upheld their right to sovereignty, and make their own decisions regarding voting, border security, education, and a whole host of other things. Stand up to a tyrannical government, and refuse to allow them to dictate what states can and cannot do.

Immigration, Legal and Illegal

This is just a follow up on the earlier topic on our undeclared war with Mexico.

Do any of you ever watch the National Geographic Channel or the Discovery Channel? There are documentary shows on those channels with names like Border Wars, Drug Wars, and similar titles. If you watch a few episodes, as I've tried to encourage our Secretary of Homeland Security to do, you'd see that our southern border is as porous as a spaghetti strainer. Our border patrol personnel are under siege on a regular basis. They are trying as hard as they can to stem the flow of human smuggling, drug smuggling, and money smuggling. They estimate that they are able to stop about 10-15% of that smuggling activity. They confiscate tons of marijuana, cocaine, methamphetamine, heroin, and pills, yearly. Yet the federal government says, "Nothing to see here, move along," and put their collective heads back in the sand.

Several states, having grown tired of waiting for the federal government to enforce its own laws, wrote legislation to enforce those federal laws as a sovereign state. Their reward was to get sued by that same Attorney General, who has decided that if he's not going to enforce federal laws, he's not going to allow any state to enforce them for him. Arizona kicked it off with the highly publicized SB1070. The great majority of Arizonans said, "It's about time" when that legislation was passed and signed into law. Inasmuch as Arizona spends approximately $1 billion each year on illegal aliens, they believed, rightfully so, I say, that this is an expense that should not occur, and would not occur if illegal aliens were not in Arizona. Other states have also crafted and passed similar legislation. The Attorney General sued them, too. A liberal judge in Arizona issued an injunction against some of the aspects of SB1070, but some of it is in force today, and the entire SB1070 law went before the Supreme Court. That court tossed out almost all of SB1070 except for the provision that police officers in a state may, when legally stopping a vehicle, or in the course of other lawful stops and, having probable cause, may ask the people to provide identification. If they cannot, they can be detained until their legal status is determined. If they are here illegally, they must notify ICE. But, because of the federal decision to NOT deport illegal aliens if they haven't committed a crime, they will be released. What we have, then, is a decision by the federal government to refuse to enforce existing federal law. The President says that not deporting the children of illegal aliens is "The right thing to do." Clearly this is a case where the sovereignty of a state has been nullified. Two things come to mind when I read this ruling.

- It's now a national imperative, if for no other reason, to oust the current President in favor of his opponent, and demand that federal law be applied everywhere, not selective enforcement.
- The Supreme Court has made it clear now that they are a political body. The makeup of the Supreme Court and its politics will forever now be dependent on which party holds the presidency. Kagan and Sotomayor were certainly political picks, and the Republicans in the Senate did not have the spine to filibuster those nomination, so I fault the opposition party for that.

Throughout all of this, we should have learned a few things. The first is that our borders are porous, so we have no real way to control them. Billions of tax dollars are spent on the border patrol and all of their equipment in the fight against illegal aliens, human smugglers, drug and weapon smugglers, and money smugglers. As a nation, we are not secure and safe; this is the fault of the current Attorney General of the United States.

One thing we have been able to determine is that the vast majority of illegal aliens are uneducated and unskilled. We also have learned, to our chagrin, that some of them bring diseases with them. We have also learned that these illegal immigrants smuggle drugs with them when they sneak across our borders. We have learned that groups of people have been brought into the United States by people we call "coyotes." People wanting to sneak into the United States will often, somehow, pay these coyotes to sneak them in, and the price is high. Once across the border, they are picked up in trucks, taken to a city, put in "stash" houses, and then dispersed to various cities across the country. Not all of them are just here for a better life. Many of them are criminals from Mexico and other countries, who believe that crime pays better in America than in their home country. We know this is true because nearly 25% of Arizona's state prisons are stocked with illegal aliens who have committed felonies. The volume of robberies, such as carjacking, home invasions, domestic violence, child abuse, and sexual assaults has risen dramatically with the invasion of illegal aliens.

In addition to the criminals who sneak across the border, there are people who speak no English, but believe that they are entitled to receive welfare payments, food stamps, free medical care, free education for their children, and subsidized housing. Most of whatever money they earn is in cash, paid under the table by unscrupulous businesses so it's not subject to taxes. Companies looking to hire illegal aliens for lower skilled jobs will ignore the E-verify system so they can plead ignorance when caught hiring illegal workers. Some states will even issue driver's licenses to illegal aliens, not requiring them to provide any form of identification, or take a test.

Each state needs to empower their state and local law enforcement officers to arrest and incarcerate illegal aliens, wherever they are found, and hold them in jail until ICE takes them and deports them. If ICE refuses to take custody of them, put them in the county jail until ICE does take custody. It would be very helpful if states would change the charge for breaking into the United States from a misdemeanor to a felony. Here, in Arizona, it's been suggested that the state build a tent city jail similar to the county sheriff's tent city jail in Maricopa county. For every day an illegal alien has to be held in that tent city jail, located near the southern border, the state bills the federal government for the full cost of holding them.

What do our children and grandchildren have to look forward to in America if tens of millions of people can invade our country, take up residence, and demand to be taken care of just because they escaped capture?

Is America a Melting Pot or Stew Pot?

I'm sure you have noticed that when you call government offices and many businesses, you are asked by the auto-attendant to press 1 for English. Just why is that? It's simple, really. We have so many people in our country who cannot and will not speak English, they have forced America to adapt to their language demands, and we acquiesced. The language in this country is English. If you don't know how to speak it, learn. Until then, let people who understand and can speak English speak for you. There are many stores that hire bi-lingual employees to deal with non-English speaking customers. I know that the Walmart where I often shop is full of non-English speaking customers, and the cashiers all have to be able to understand and speak Spanish to accommodate them. If they don't, those customers will take their business elsewhere. The message is clear, you accommodate our language or we'll go somewhere that will. Does that make sense to you? Me neither.

Why do schools have to provide special classes for children who cannot speak, read, or write English? Let me tell you a short story. My wife immigrated here when she was about six or seven years old. She spoke no English; she couldn't read or write English. No one in her family could read, write, or speak English, either. They immigrated here under the sponsorship of a mid-Western church. Her parents enrolled her in school, and, when school started, they dropped her off. Within 6-8 months she was speaking, reading, and writing English at grade level. The teachers and the other students helped her learn. This was in the 1950's. It's called immersion and it works. But, today we have children enrolled in school and they have special classes just to try to teach them English. Those classes can last for years and years. What's the incentive for those children to learn English? None. But Americans will spend billions of dollars, almost begging them to please learn English. In many cases, the parents of these children have no English skills at all, and only speak their native language at home. So the child is being taught the English language at school, but at home, he or she has to speak their native language or the parents won't understand, which violates the immersion principles. This is stupid. But the upside is for the teacher's union. They cause extra bi-lingual teachers to be hired all over the country just to teach English to those students who need it, but those classes are short periods of time at school. The rest of the time the students are in classes where English is spoken, and they're not able to keep up.

In San Jose, California some years back, a friend sent me an e-mail after he had gone to the polls. He informed me that there were ballots available in 32 languages for voters. That's 32 different ballots, in 32 different languages, to vote in an American election. Someone please explain that to me. These "voters" can't read, write, or speak English, but are allowed to vote in the language of the country they left in order to come here. When Spanish-speaking people apply for a driver's license in Arizona, they can take the test in Spanish, not English. Can people who don't read, write, or speak English understand road signs, speed limit signs, turn instructions? If not, why are they allowed to get a driver's license? This makes no sense.

Medical Marijuana is another Oxymoron

While in the military I was given a collateral duty. I was to be one of a few people who would be a Drug and Alcohol Education Specialist (DAES). I spent two months in school, about 320 hours, learning the pharmacology of all the drugs known at the time, as well as everything possible to understand about the effects of alcohol. It was, to say the least, a very enlightening two months. When the classes were done, I was the identified specialist at every command where I served. I've heard every excuse for using drugs and alcohol that can be invented. I have also worked as a volunteer inside two state prisons, and one paid position as a computer instructor in a federal prison. In the state prisons, I worked for a prison ministry, assisting convicts who had proven that they wanted to turn their lives around. Between the one-on-one sessions, and general interaction with about 80 convicts, about 75 of them were in prison for offenses that involved drugs and alcohol. I also worked as a volunteer, serving on a Foster Care Review Board for two years, and another four years as a court-appointed advocate for kids in foster care. Between the prison experiences and the foster care experiences, I again heard just about every excuse possible for using meth, alcohol, crack, heroin, marijuana, PCP, you name it.

Anyone who tells you that marijuana is "medicine" is lying to you. There is absolutely no scientific evidence that marijuana contains any medicinal qualities. Arizona passed the Medical Marijuana initiative in 2010, though it still hasn't started operating in any meaningful way.

There are questions about whether the vote was somehow rigged, since it took so long for the final vote to be released, but that's another story. What I'm suggesting to you is that you ask anyone who wants medical marijuana, or just ask yourself, the following questions.

1. If medical marijuana is medicine, why hasn't it been submitted to the FDA for approval?
2. If medical marijuana is medicine, why aren't doctors prescribing its use? What we see are some doctors who sell <u>recommendations</u> for use, for a hefty fee.
3. California has had medical marijuana as a lawful enterprise for some time, and it's a nightmare. In general, the users of medical marijuana are in the 18-30 age group. Does that mean these younger people are the ones needing this "medicine" much more than people in their 70's? Someone please explain that to me.
4. Medical marijuana dispensaries sell marijuana under literally dozens of names. If medical marijuana is medicine, why are there so many names for medical marijuana? If different kinds of medical marijuana contains varying levels of "medicine," shouldn't the doctor recommending the use of the drug also tell the "patient" which brand to use, how often, and how much per dose? Wouldn't medical marijuana be the same for all? Help, I'm confused.
5. What is the name of the so-called medicine in medical marijuana? It can't be THC. THC is an acknowledged hallucinogen—it gets you stoned. So what is the medical ingredient in medical marijuana, and how much of it do I need? Ask that of a proponent of medical marijuana, and watch their expression. Priceless.
6. When someone buys medical marijuana, do they receive a label on the container that tells them what the proper dose is, how many doses to take each day, and any possible side effects, like hallucinations, urge to eat snacks, sleepiness?
7. If I roll my own marijuana cigarettes, how much medical marijuana should I put into each one? If I eat marijuana cupcakes or cookies, how much marijuana should be contained in each cupcake or cookie?
8. Is the dosage the same for someone who has headaches as someone who has glaucoma?
9. If I am smoking medical marijuana, is it legal for me to drive a car or operate machinery? If so, because it's medicine, if I have an accident and destroy property, or kill someone, is the taking of medical marijuana a legitimate defense?

10. If I take marijuana and go to work and, while there, I cause an accident because my judgment is impaired, and people are hurt or killed, is the use of medical marijuana a legitimate defense?

11. If I have a medical marijuana card, can I smoke my medicine at work or on company property, even though cigarette smokers cannot?

12. If I were somehow arrested for a crime and sent to jail or prison, and I possess a medical marijuana card, does the jail or prison have to give me my medical marijuana because it's a medicine?

13. If I'm at home, consuming my medical marijuana, and somehow cause a fire that destroys my apartment building, is my possession of a medical marijuana card a legitimate defense?

14. If I'm a student attending college, and I need my "medicine," can I light up a marijuana cigarette and smoke it inside a building or classroom, or outside? I know that the smoking cigarettes is illegal on college campuses, but how about the smoking of medical marijuana?

15. If I'm a police officer, member of the FBI, DEA, CIA, a Congressman, or President, and I have a marijuana recommendation card, can I take my medical marijuana while on the job? I mean, after all, it is medicine, isn't it?

16. If I'm a commercial pilot, can I take my medical marijuana while I am flying an aircraft with 200 or 300 passengers onboard? I mean, after all, it is medicine.

Ladies and gentlemen, medical marijuana is an absolute lie. If you were to ask the questions I listed above to any of the advocates of medical marijuana, they would run away from you so fast you'd see a vapor trail. It's nothing but a ruse to get marijuana into the mainstream, and it's wrong. Marijuana consumption affects your memory, affects brain cells, can cause lung, liver, and kidney problems. They call it medicine because when you consume it, by whatever means, the THC gets you "high," and you don't feel the pain as much. That's not medicine by any reasonable definition. People say that OxyCodone, Vicadin, Percocet, and other pain killers don't work for them, but at least you know what's in them.

For those people who voted to legalize medical marijuana in their state, you've been fooled, badly. It's a lie.

R. Eugene Spitzer

Hollywood and Gomorrah

As you can tell from the topic title, I have little use for 90% of the garbage that is released by Hollywood (Hollyweird). I read movie reviews that inform me that these movies or shows are intended for people possessing single digit IQs.

Have you ever watched a television show on the TLC Channel called, "Toddlers and Tiaras"? Many people I know refer to the cable channel that carries this terrible show as the pervert channel. Child perverts no doubt love the show; you can almost hear the saliva dripping from their mouths when that show is on. The focus is on little girls, some as young as four or five, all dressed up in short dresses, lots of cleavage, if a 4-year old can be said to even possess cleavage, push up bras, lipstick, wigs and hair extensions, all the makeup, prancing around on a stage, making sexual gestures, competing with other little girls for the chance to win a $10 trophy. I watched an episode of that show, and I noticed one thing in particular; 90% of the mothers were very "full-figured" ladies, and when they spoke, I wondered if their family tree ever forked. These women, primping, or is it pimping, up their daughters to look and act as sexual as possible in order to win a trophy. These mothers evidently have such empty lives, that they seem to be living their lives vicariously through their children. That's sad. And the girls don't really have a choice in the matter. What 4, 5, 6-year old is going to say, "No thanks, mom, I'd rather play with my Barbie dolls and my friends." These little girls are also given various soft drinks, anything loaded with lots of caffeine in it to "boost" their energy on stage. Delightful. As a believer in capitalism, this show has a right to be televised, but no one is obliged to watch. I'd like to know just how many people, other than child perverts, and lonely mothers, tune in to this show. Perhaps, if more people would contact the sponsors of this child perversion excuse for a television show, and tell them they won't be buying their products, they'd get the message. What effect does this kind of activity have on those little girls? What happens when they're no longer toddlers? Do they graduate to senior toddlers, and keep on prancing? I hope school doesn't interfere with their pageant schedule. I've heard rumors that there is a companion show being developed that features little boys. I'm assuming that this is a kind of preparatory show for future stars at Chippindales male strip clubs.

There's another show on cable TV called "Dancing Moms." It's not about mothers dancing; no, it's about moms primping up their little girls so they can dance on camera, fighting for a similar $10 trophy. The same comments from Toddlers and Tiaras apply to Dancing Moms. And the TLC channel also has a show called "Sister Moms." This a show that celebrates polygamous

180

marriage, even though polygamy is against the law. It's just a laugh a minute as the ladies discuss who gets to sleep with the "husband" on any given night. What a laugh-a-minute show.

There's this disgusting show on the MTV cable channel called "Jersey Shore." Until recently it featured this one person, "Snooki." This little, fat, drunken slut, proudly so it seems, makes a small fortune just for being herself on this reality show. Because she's now pregnant from a man to whom she isn't married, she doesn't appear as often, thank goodness. The rest of the cast isn't much better. They all seem to have the morals of feral cats. When kids watch shows like this, what do they think? What parent would want their kids watching this drivel? Most people who actually live near the Jersey shore don't like the way their neighborhoods are being portrayed by this bunch of misfits.

The Internet is full of sites that focus on the glamorous lives of the social misfits of Hollywood, and the kids eat it up. How many magazines do you see on the shelves at the checkout line with all kinds of salacious headlines about who is sleeping with whom, who is getting divorced, who is entering rehabilitation for one addiction or another. We all know that the "fashion" trends of these movie "stars," tend to drive the trends for kids, especially girls. How many women dressed like Madonna when she was on top of the charts—not sure for what, since she couldn't act, and her singing was marginal. Then there was the Britney Spears era, with millions of young girls dressing just like Britney. They thought that her fashion was just the best. and her life was so exciting. I guess those crotch shots of her getting out of a car were just what her fans wanted to see and mimic. Britney lost custody of her children, spent time in jail, and had a nervous breakdown were all just food for the grist mill that is Hollywood. And, there's the number one no talent, zero contributor to society, Paris Hilton. She lives off her daddy's money, pretends to be sophisticated, and looks at her pornographic video as a sign of liberation. Come on, tell the truth; do you think her IQ reaches triple digits? And Nicole Ritchie, another Hollywood no talent woman who is most famous for just showing up at parties, drinking, doing drugs, and sleeping around. I guess that's a talent. And don't forget Alec Baldwin. This man, who clearly demonstrates through his comments, and behavior, that he has little respect for his former wife, or for his own daughter. Baldwin, who goes on television and says truly ignorant things regarding the former President. I think he's a decent actor, and does some good commercials for a credit card company, but when he opines on anything political or social, he shows himself to be a dunce. He seems desperate for attention at any cost. I won't go to any movie he's in, and I don't watch that silly TV show he's on. I can't lower myself to his level. I'm sure you can rattle off a few dozen other actors that need to just do their job and go away. They're not that bright.

I have adopted the attitude used in a book written by a very nice lady, Laura Ingraham, "Shut up and Sing." For some inexplicable reason, when some people amass wealth, by whatever means, they come to believe that money makes them smart. They shoot off their mouths about matters that are a complete mystery to them, but they believe they know the answers. Fortunately, most of these limited talent individuals just do their job, collect their money, and disappear until the next movie or TV show. For those who open their mouths and confirm what we all believed about them, shut up and sing.

Then there are such shows, in prime time, as "Working Girl," "Two and a Half Men," "Two Broke Girls," "The Big Bang Theory," "Modern Family," and many others that are devoted to young people hooking up for casual sex, with some laugh lines tossed in. Prime Time television has become Slime Time television.

There's also a television show devoted to the joy of being a high school girl with a baby and no father. Oh, the laughs keep on coming.

And don't leave out the so-called reality TV shows. They are too numerous to count. They are not really unscripted shows. "Survivor," "Big Brother," and all the rest, are just scripted shows that pretend to be reality. The shows follow a script, the purpose being to put people in bad situations, pit one contestant against another, and are, in my opinion, a tremendous waste of time.

We can't leave out some of those classic movies that Hollywood is foisting upon us. There are such gems as "Hangover," "Hangover 2," "Jackass," "Jackass 2," "Everyone is All Right," which tells the hilarious story of how two homosexual women who have children and, occasionally, allow the father to visit them. They wanted to call it, "It's a Wonderful Life" but that name was already taken by a real movie. In June, another Adam Sandler bomb was released, "My Boy." Even the most liberal movie critics said they had to take a shower after reviewing this disgusting movie, but Hollywood keeps on paying this guy millions to churn out losers. And here we thought the movie, "Jack and Jill" was as low as Sandler could get, he's lowered himself even more. Amazing. My guess is that it goes to DVD in about two weeks.

Just look at the inhabitants of Hollywood. Could you intentionally put together a more dysfunctional group of people if you tried? Actors and actresses bed hopping, drug indulgence, alcohol overloads, unruly behavior, arrests, rehab, total meltdowns, and they think they're just so cool, and so rich. It's always been a source of amusement to me when these actors jump in front of a microphone to extol the virtues of Hugo Chavez (Sean Penn), and Barbra Streisand who, by the way, has maids to take her clothes to an exclusive laundry and dry cleaning service, telling us that Californians should dry their clothes on clothes lines to save energy. One of my favorites is Martin Sheen. He never graduated from high school, but he knows what's best for America, and that would be for you to give your money to others. He won't be giving any money away himself, but you should because he says it's the right thing to do. After all, he did play a President on a television show, so he should know, right? Then there's the acknowledged socialist, Ed Asner. He knows that Socialism is the best form of government for the United States. Then there's Tim Robbins ranting against the war, blaming America for all of the world's ills, but you don't see him spending any of his millions to help solve any of those problems. No, he's telling you to give your money for causes he supports. You can count on the Hollywood millionaires showing up for some telethon or another, volunteering their time to answer phones, pleading with you to send your money in to fight one crisis after another. But if you do a little digging, they don't donate their money, and they don't check to be sure that the charity actually uses the money donated to help the cause. No, they're too important for that. George Clooney is a huge hypocrite. He loves the current President; he believes that the President is doing a wonderful job, but can't list anything, won't list anything the President has done that has helped Americans. Do you think someone like Clooney gives a hoot in hell if gas goes to $20 a gallon? When you've got $50 million or so in the bank, what things cost is of no concern to you. Does Clooney ever go to a grocery store? Give me a break. He has servants to take care of such mundane tasks. He's too busy throwing parties, dreaming up some movie "project" to enrich himself even more. There are the Kardashians, who have absolutely no talent or skill to do anything, but they have a marvelous marketing crew around them to make them appear famous. They're famous for being famous, but they contribute nothing to society. But you'll see them on the nonsensical "entertainment" shows on weeknights, sitting on the couch, talking about their new perfume, their new reality TV show, their new husbands, divorced husbands, all the truly important issues of the day. Do any of you care, really care at all, what the Kardashians are doing, or saying? If I see them on the schedule for a show, I skip the show. I consider them to be empty-headed bimbettes.

And just to finish off this topic in style, let's look at the list of "celebrities" who have died from drug and/or alcohol overdoses:

- **Bridgette Anderson,** dead at 21 from "accidental" overdose of drugs and alcohol;
- **Scotty Beckett, dead** at 38 from a "suspected" overdose of barbiturates and alcohol;

- **Brittany Murphy, died** in 2009 from pneumonia caused by multiple drug intoxication, and iron-deficiency anemia;
- **Marilyn Monroe, dead** from an overdose of barbiturates;
- **Jim Morrison, singer** for The Doors, died at age 27 from an overdose of heroin that caused a heart attack;
- **Dana Plato, died** of an overdose of prescription drugs;
- **Anissa Jones,** died of a drug overdose which was, according to the coroner, the worst he had ever seen;
- **John Belushi,** died of an overdose of a cocaine and heroin injection;
- **Anna Nicole Smith,** died of an overdose of chloral hydrate and various benzodiasepines; after several failed suicide attempts,
- **Judy Garland,** died of an overdose of barbiturates; River Phoenix, died of a combine heroin and cocaine overdose outside a restaurant owned at the time by his friend, Johnny Depp;
- **Bradley Nowell,** died of a heroin overdose;
- **Jimi Hendrix,** died of respiratory arrest caused by alcohol, barbiturates, and vomit inhalation;
- **Janis Joplin,** died of an overdose of heroin and alcohol;
- **Corey Hamm,** died of pneumonia caused by a weakened immune system from years of drug abuse;
- **Sid Vicious,** committed suicide with an overdose of heroin;
- **Heath Ledger,** died of an overdose of prescription drugs;
- **Chris Farley,** died of an overdose of injected heroin and cocaine.

Those are just a few of the many Hollywood and music "celebrities" who have died, all of them through drug and alcohol abuse.

What Happens to the Money You Give to Charity?

Companies support charities and ask their employees to contribute. Every time there's a disaster anywhere in the world, you can count on charities to run ads asking for your money to help the needy. Well, here are some evidently very needy people. These are the salaries and perks paid annually to the heads of some charities.

- American Red Cross, Marsha Evans, $951,937 + Expenses.
- United Way, Biran Gallagher, $675,000 + Expenses
- UNICEF, Cary Stern, $1,900,000 + ALL expenses including a Rolls Royce

Then there are charitable organizations that help millions of people. Take a look at what the leaders of these charities make.

- Salvation Army, Todd Bassett, $13,000 + housing
- American Legion National Commander, $0 salary. All donations go to help veterans and their families
- Veterans of Foreign Wars, $0 salary, all donations go to veterans and their families
- Disabled American Veterans, $0 salary, all donations go to help veterans and their families
- Military Order of Purple Hearts National Commander, $0 salary, all donations go to help veterans and their families
- Vietnam Veterans Association National Commander, $0 salary, all donations go to help veterans and their families

Do you notice a disparity between these charitable organizations? You won't see movie stars and rock music stars running a telethon for the organizations that help American veterans. No, they only spend their time and energy working for charities that pay their leaders millions of your dollars. You might want to ask yourself just where does the money go when you donate? There is a website that will keep you up to date on how charities perform. Try http://www.charitynavigator.org.

All This Focus on Sex

As I gained maturity, I came to understand and believe that a man and a woman having a sexual relationship was an important expression of love and commitment. Somewhere along the way I lost track of the change in understanding of sexual activity. It seems that now, in the "enlightened" age, sex has become a recreational activity, like bowling, golfing, soccer, and going to a movie. You won't hear much about the sexually transmitted diseases (STDs) that have accompanied this sexual revolution.

The term, "*hooking up*" has now come into common use for a boy and girl, or a man and a woman or, I guess a man and a man, or a woman and a woman, getting together for the sole purpose of having recreational sex. There are now web sites devoted to helping men and women hook up for sex, no commitment. There's at least one web site that offers hook ups for married people who just want some sexual fun with no commitment, and your spouse need never know. Isn't that great? Young people hooking up today often don't know each other's last names, or anything about them. A former president of the United States, Bill Clinton, was quoted as stating that oral sex isn't really sex, and many high school and college kids now believe that to be true. Yes, this is the same womanizer who had long affairs and quickies with any woman who would stand still long enough, and his wife never uttered a word.

With that attitude in mind, you can see how the whole issue of contraception takes center stage in many conversations. Women who go looking for anonymous hook up sex want to be sure that they are on "the pill," or that whatever man they hook up with is wearing a condom. There doesn't seem to be much concern about sexually transmitted diseases, somehow believing that the pill or a condom makes them safe. There's never a shortage of ignorance with people who think this way. Then you look, again, at attitudes. Having sex just for the feel good aspect is what counts; women have sex with boys or men they don't know or particularly like, because they want that good sexual feeling. Just watch a few episodes of "Sex and the City" and you'll get the idea. The whole idea of delayed gratification or commitment is lost on these people. They want sex when they want it, with whomever they want it with, and don't tell them any of that nonsense about sexual activity being an expression of love. That's so 50 years ago to them. This also tells us a lot about the attitudes people have for one another.

When a man looks at a woman as being only good for one sex, what do you think his marriage prospects are for the future? If he were to get married to some woman who is evidently not very selective in husband-hunting, how will she be treated? If a woman only looks at a man in terms of whether he's a "hunk," or someone she'd want to have sex with a few times, what does that say about her marriage prospects? I've read about, and even known, a few women who have been married five or six times, and they're in their 40's. What if children were conceived during these marriages? How are they going to view the world, through their mother's eyes, their father's eyes? Do they develop a view that a woman is only good for one thing, or a man is only good for one thing?

Let's consider abortion in its various forms. There is the pill to keep a woman from getting pregnant, and condoms to keep the male from impregnating the woman. Many married couples use contraception for all kinds of reasons. It's too soon to start having babies. They're getting older, have some children, and want to prevent more pregnancies. While those actions may be at variance with the teachings of their faith, they have the choice. That's one of the things that most religious teachings provide; we all have free will to follow or not follow all of the church's teachings. But now, as a society, we have to deal with the issue of abortion. There is a pill commonly available called, I believe, RU486, which has now become the "morning after" pill. The intent is clear. If, after having sex, a woman believes she may become pregnant, she takes this pill, and that stops any pregnancy from occurring. This pill is available almost everywhere, and many times it can be obtained free of charge.

There are sonograms that show the development of a baby, a fetus, at less than 10 weeks of age, in the womb. You can clearly see the arms, legs, torso, head, and there is a heartbeat. The pro-abortion crowd doesn't want you to see that sonogram, and they don't even acknowledge that it exists, but it does. But women can choose to abort (kill) that baby. There are organizations in America where abortions are free, paid for by others. One of those organizations, Planned Parenthood, performs about 340,000 abortions each year, and gets millions of dollars from the government—you and me—to pay for them. Not long ago, in Nebraska, there was a man, called "Tiller the Baby Killer" who performed thousands of abortions, many of them late term, and even partial-birth abortions. The current Secretary of Health and Human Services, Kathleen Sebelius, was the governor of Nebraska back then, and protected Tiller. Draw whatever conclusions you wish from that association. Then there's the issue of having an abortion at three months, six months, eight months. At eight months an unborn baby could survive outside the womb, but it doesn't matter. If a woman wants that pregnancy terminated with an abortion, step right up, and it's done. There's even this process called "Partial Birth Abortion" where the delivery of the baby is begun, but as soon as the head of the baby emerges from the womb, the doctor punctures the brain and sucks out its contents. Not that many years ago, in Illinois, a state senator had no problems with Partial Birth Abortion. He is now President of the United States.

All sorts of rights have been granted by the government to all kinds of people except one group, the unborn. They have no rights. They have no right to be born, no right to breathe, no right to live. It's all about women's rights. The right to have sex, the right to have unprotected sex, the right to get pregnant, and the right to have the baby killed for any reason, or no reason. To the hundreds of thousands of couples out there who would love to adopt a baby, tough. These women want those babies dead. What kind of America agrees that killing the unborn is just a choice, and that the unborn baby has no right to live? If you're pro-life instead of pro-death, you are a target for ridicule. Is that what we've become as a nation? Is this a national attitude to which you want to subject your kids and grandkids?

Some Clarity Regarding Homosexuality

As with a lot of contentious issues, homosexual marriage is no exception. I have worked with, worked for, and managed homosexual men and women over the years. As far as I'm concerned, they are either co-workers, bosses, or part of my team. I don't care about their personal, private lives and lifestyles. I like or dislike homosexuals based on their work ethics, and ability to get along. These are the same standards I follow when dealing with heterosexual men and women. So, when I state that I am opposed to legitimizing homosexual "marriage," many supporters of homosexual marriage call me a homophobe. It's a ridiculous statement, but the intent is to stifle free speech and opinion if it doesn't agree with their agenda. The great majority of Americans have no issues with homosexual people. We're not interested in what goes on in their bedrooms. I don't appreciate heterosexual men and women telling me all about their sex lives, and I don't want to hear about homosexual sex lives, either. The bottom line on all of this is that there is a difference between people who happen to be homosexual and their private lives. I don't believe that men should be having sex with other men; I think it's anatomically impossible. It's the behavior that most people have a problem with, not the individual person. So, homosexual rights advocates, do you understand now?

For the homosexual supporters and lobbyists, there is one overwhelming goal. Homosexuals want the right to be "married." Once that right is conferred, homosexuals can then claim that their lifestyle is normal. That's what this fight is all about. The majority of Americans do not believe that two men can be married, nor can two women. When this President stated that he referred to the Christian Bible and "The Golden Rule" as justification for personally supporting homosexual marriage, he must have forgotten a more specific reference. For those of you who have a Bible, open it to Leviticus 18:22, which says, "You shall not lie with a male as you would lie with a female; it is an abomination." The President must have missed that passage, or intentionally ignored it.

The homosexuals and their supporters often exhibit conduct that hurts the cause. For example, in June, a reception was held in the White House to celebrate homosexual pride. A group of homosexuals from Philadelphia attended. The band was playing, and good food was available to all. The attendees were then given a tour of the White House. When the group reached the hall where a portrait of former President Ronald Reagan was on display, the homosexual attendees thought it would be great fun to pose in front of the portrait, with their back to the painting, and "flip off" Ronald Reagan. A pair of homosexual women then posed in front of the portrait, and had a nice, deep kiss while giving their middle finger salute to the portrait. They thought this behavior was so meaningful that they posted these pictures on Facebook, and several media outlets picked up the story. Somehow, homosexuals think this helps their cause?

Let's be clear about one major point, no one has a "right" to be married. If it were a right, you wouldn't have to get a license from the state. Marriage has, for centuries, been a religious celebration and confirmation of the relationship between a man and a woman. To the best of my knowledge, that formation ceremony has not been canceled. Not a man and a man, not a woman and a woman, not a man and his goat, not a woman and her poodle, not a man and five women, not a woman and five men. No, marriage is a religious ceremony between a man and a woman. A couple wishing to get married can apply for and obtain a marriage license, get their blood tested, and get married by a judge at city hall, or in some major production at a Church or a bowling alley. Anyone with the authority to administer marital ceremonies can perform that ceremony, and it can be as drawn out or as short as the participants want it to be. Anyone ordained to conduct a marriage ceremony also has the right to not perform the ceremony. It's up to the individual. No one can force an ordained person to perform a marriage ceremony.

Note: I call them homosexuals because that is the word that defines their sexual preference. The homosexuals took control of the word, gay, because they didn't like being called homosexuals, but it doesn't change anything. There's one organization, LBGT, that encompasses all kinds of lifestyles that are, shall we say, different from most people. Lesbian, Bi-sexual, Gay (homosexual), Transgender (LBGT) tries to convince everyone that one out of 10 people in the country, 10%, fall into one of those categories of people. It's a lie. Almost every objective estimate says that perhaps three out of 100 people (3%) fall into this category. In a country of 300+ million people, that's still quite a few folks, except in places like the Castro and Noe Valley in San Francisco, where the percentage is much higher. So, this 3% of the population wants, and gets, protected class status. If you hurt a homosexual, that's a hate crime. If a homosexual hurts you, that's not a hate crime. Get it? Homosexuals claim that they have the right to marriage just like heterosexual people. On the face of it, that's a lie because, as I said, marriage is not a right. What the homosexual lobby is trying to do is to force heterosexuals to accept their sexual behavior as normal, just like heterosexual behavior and, grant them all of the privileges enjoyed by heterosexuals. These could include marriage, joint ownership of property, or medical benefits for each other, and so on. Well, except for that marriage thing, they've pretty much gotten their way.

While we are continually inundated with all this propaganda about homosexuality being perfectly normal, there are these things called "Gay Pride Parades." Have you ever seen one, or seen video of one? The one in San Francisco will ruin your whole day. This parade seems to go on for hours. These people wear costumes to accentuate their genitalia, and there seems to be a very large contingent of folks who are, evidently, totally confused about their gender, so they try to cover all their bases with their outfits. It's disgusting, it's obscene, it's stupid, but they're expressing their "pride" in your face. And all the while, the propagandists are shouting for acceptance. They have even convinced some members of Congress, but as we all know, members of Congress aren't necessarily the sharpest pencils in the box. They'll go for anything if it gets them money for their reelection campaigns and votes.

Homosexual proponents keep insisting that homosexuals are born that way but, try as they might, not one scientist can find any homosexual gene in the DNA. If homosexuals are born that way, why are some successful in changing to heterosexual? Anyone remember an actress by the name of Ann Heche? She was the main squeeze of Ellen Degeneris for some years. After the breakup Ann met a man, got married, and had some kids. If you're born homosexual, how can you switch to heterosexual, without therapy, without a pill? There are many other stories just like this one, but you get the point.

I have an idea that will resolve any doubts anyone might have about homosexuals being just as normal as heterosexuals when it comes to sexual activities. (you may want to skip the next paragraph if you're queasy about sex.)

I would like the U.S. House of Representatives, U.S. Senate, and the Capitol of each state to schedule a hearing on homosexuality. It should also be televised on all the nighttime shows, like Leno, Letterman, Kimmel, Fallon, and so on. Just a little side note here; Leno has said repeatedly that he thinks homosexual marriage is fine with him, but he, too, isn't all that bright. At this hearing, two events will take place. First, two homosexual men will enter, disrobe, and proceed to have sex. One man will put his sexual organ into an orifice of the other man that was anatomically never intended for that purpose. They will then get up, thank everyone, put on robes, and leave. For the second event two homosexual women (that many call lesbians) will enter, disrobe, and one will strap on a male sex organ device, and proceed to have sex with the other woman. When they're finished, they will get up, thank everyone, put their robes on, and leave the stage. When these two events are over, each body will vote on whether this form of sexual activity is as normal as heterosexual sexual activity. When that vote is taken, in the U.S. Congress, and in every capitol in the United States, we no longer need to discuss whether homosexual activity is "normal," do we?

As far as homosexuals having the "right" to marry, it's a non-starter. No one is stopping two men from living together, and doing whatever they want in the privacy of their bedroom, or any other private place. The same applies to two women. No one really cares, but they shouldn't go around demanding that heterosexual Americans "accept" them. Pay attention now—homosexual behavior is the problem. It is NOT acceptable to a vast majority of Americans. For Christians it's an abomination. It's not the person; it's the behavior. Get over it.

Then there is this whole issue of openly homosexual men and women serving in the military. What a boneheaded decision this has been. Just think about it for a minute. Those who served in the military, especially the Navy, will certainly understand this. Openly homosexual men go through boot camp with men, those people with whom homosexual men prefer having sex. They shower together, use the same toilet facilities. What could possibly go wrong? Next, they are assigned to a unit and off they go for more training and possible deployment. If it's the Navy, and they are sent to a ship, they have to be happy beyond belief. Now they will be berthed in compartments where the bunks are stacked up three or four high, separated from the bunk next to them by about six inches. Again, they share shower facilities, toilet facilities, and you know they're not unhappy with this arrangement. For the heterosexual sailors, knowing that an openly homosexual man is in the shower with them, sitting in the toilet next to them, sleeping perhaps six inches away from them, they are not happy. I served 20 years in the Navy, and I can tell you one thing for sure; if you want to destroy morale on a ship, have several openly homosexual sailors sleeping and working amongst you. There was more than one incident of a homosexual sailor thinking he was welcomed by another sailor, proceeded to sneak over to his bunk in the middle of the night, and attempt to perform oral sex on him, only to discover that his assumption was wrong. The sailor woke up yelling, and within seconds, literally every man in that berthing compartment was attempting to kill the offender. It took the ship's master-at-arms force to drag the homosexual sailor out of there and lock him up in the brig for his own safety. The military is a male, testosterone-driven force, that does not accept what they consider deviancy in their midst. "Don't ask, don't tell" worked, worked well, but the pinheads in Washington, and a pandering President, having absolutely no knowledge or understanding, decided that they knew better. But I have a suggestion that may solve the problem.

On a base, where the women and men are housed separately, the homosexual men are allowed to live with, sleep with, and shower with the heterosexual military men. To make it fair, the heterosexual men are welcome to live with, sleep with, and shower with the women. Makes sense, doesn't it? If men who prefer sex with men are allowed to live with other men, shouldn't heterosexual men be allowed to live with women, their preferred sexual partners? This should apply on ships, too. On those ships where women are serving, open up those living quarters for heterosexual men, so they can live in there. It's only fair, isn't it? This should be a no brainer. Let's ask Congress to pass a law.

On a sadder note, the following countries allow same-sex marriage:

- Netherlands
- Belgium
- Spain
- Canada
- South Africa
- Norway
- Sweden
- Portugal
- Iceland
- Argentina

Fortunately, in America, 32 states have voted overwhelmingly to not allow same-sex marriage regardless of what Obama says. North Carolina recently passed a state Constitutional Amendment, with over 60% of the vote to prevent some federal judge from overruling their vote, so same-sex marriage is dead in North Carolina.

Gender Squabbles

Every spring, starting around the first week of April, the feminists start whining about the Augusta National Golf Club in Augusta, Georgia. This course has been the site of the Professional Golf Association's Masters golf tournament, and has done so for decades. Augusta is a privately owned golf club, created and maintained with private money. There isn't a nickel of taxpayer money involved in the operation of this club. It was started by men, and its membership is comprised of men. It always has been. To the feminists, this is war. The fact that there are women-only golf clubs matters not at all to these ladies. A few years ago, the feminists organized a protest outside the gates of Augusta National Golf Club. The problem was that their protest was being held over a mile away from the entrance to the course because Augusta National Golf Club owned all the land immediately outside the entrance. Very few feminists showed up, and the protest frizzled. In 2012, the feminists started whining again because the new CEO of IBM was now a woman. Over the decades, Augusta National has invited the CEO of IBM to become a member, but there are qualifications that have to be met. The first qualification is that whomever is invited must play and love golf. The new female CEO of IBM doesn't play golf, and doesn't much care about golf at all.

As soon as the feminists started wailing and whining, you knew we'd be hearing from the political class, and they didn't disappoint. Our current President said that August should allow women to become members, paying no attention to the fact that the club is a private, not a public club. Then the GOP Presidential candidates chimed in. And the story would not be complete without a few comments from the TV pinheads, Katie Couric being one of them.

During her little screed on TV, she never mentioned that Augusta is a private club where membership is by invitation only, based on a set of rules, one of which is that the club is for men only. These members not only love golf, they also pay the bills for this private club, and it can cost millions of dollars of year to keep the course in great condition. It's also never mentioned, by Couric or any of the other talking heads that women play golf at August all the time, as invited guests. A private organization determines its own rules for membership or access and, if they decide to restrict access or membership to men, or to women, it's no one's business. Anyone who is protesting a private company deciding on its own rules of operation has no understanding of the word, private. There are thousands of golf clubs around the country that are to people that meet the standards of access and membership. Is that fair?

Yes. If Katie Couric wants to do something, she should build her own private golf course, and restrict access or membership to whomever she wants.

We've heard for years, from leftist women, that men and women are essentially the same. Well, not so fast, ladies. Why, in the women's professional basketball association (WNBA) is the ball smaller so women can control it? Why are there no women's baseball teams? Women play softball not baseball because their arms aren't strong enough for baseball. Why are there no women professional football players? This is because women aren't strong enough, big enough, or fast enough. Why does the ladies professional golf association (LPGA) play on courses that are hundreds of yards shorter than what the male professionals play? This is because the women can't hit the ball as far as the men. There are other examples, but you get the idea.

Women as Street Police Officers, Firefighters, and Combat Warriors

Before you read this and get all riled up, perhaps a little clarification is necessary. Women are great creations. They are superior to men in many ways. My wife and I have been married for decades, and she is a fantastic person. She has her career, yet she is still my partner, and a great friend. We do lots of things together. But you know, sometimes she'll come to me and say, "I need you to do your man thing." It'll be some task such as lifting something heavy, helping move something heavy, and other, similar tasks. I drive the power lawnmower around, prune trees, and assorted yard work. She is a far superior cook, is much more nurturing and loving with our 14 grandkids than I am, and still does her best at work where she is very well liked and respected. We have different roles and, I believe, that was the intention all along. Even looking back at the caveman era, the roles were different. Men were hunters and gatherers, and the women gave birth to and nurtured the children, kept the cave livable, and prepared meals. Moving forward into this century, some roles have changed. Women are a much larger percentage of the workforce than ever before. Some husbands choose to stay home and raise the children. It works for them, but it's not a mandatory shift in roles as some would have us believe.

Considering men and women, there are the obvious anatomical differences, but there are other differences. Neither gender is superior or inferior; the genders are just different. There are some jobs for which a very strong physical person is needed. There are other jobs where either gender could do them well, and there are some jobs where a woman is better suited. So when I hear all this blather from these feminists saying that men and women are the same, I wonder just where they get their information or, as I suspect, is it just propaganda to support some agenda. Whatever their motivation, they are wrong, and always have been wrong. Anyone who pays the least bit of attention to objective facts understands that.

I remember, and maybe you do, too, some years back when the feminists, with able assistance from Washington, decided that women should be able to be firefighters. No more of this men-only club. They wanted us to believe that women are just as qualified to be firefighters as men. And the law made it so. Women could now compete for firefighter jobs in fire departments all over the land, and it was good. Well, not quite. What was discovered was that, first of all, 90% of the women applicants could not meet the physical standards demanded of the job. No problem. The standards were lowered so women could meet them. They didn't have to lift as much weight, didn't have to drag heavy hoses as far, things like that. The intent was to lower the standards in order to get women into fire houses across the land. How does this play out? Well, first of all, most fire houses are staffed with firefighters who work long shifts, sometimes 24 hours or more, living in the fire house, sleeping in a small room with cramped quarters. Women didn't like that. They needed separate showers, separate sleeping quarters. What to do? Well, give in of course. Spend taxpayer money to accommodate the female firefighters. So, in the end, does this less than noble experiment prove that women are just as good at firefighting as men? I don't think so. I believe it's an accommodation to a voting bloc, feminist women.

Look at one scenario. There's a fire in your apartment building, and you're stuck up on the 10th floor. There's smoke and fire everywhere, and you're screaming out the window for someone to help. Here come the fire trucks. You're waving out the window of your apartment, shouting for help. The fire truck extends the ladder, and here comes a firefighter. It turns out to be a female firefighter. She weighs, oh, about 130 pounds. You, unfortunately, weigh about 220 pounds. The female firefighter gets up to you, takes a look, and says, "Sorry, you're too heavy. Stay right here, and another firefighter will be right up." Is that what you want to hear? Of course not. There are standards for firefighters, not separate standards for men and women. Or, do they have to change assignments so no female firefighter goes up a ladder to rescue people; only the men do that. Women don't have to haul heavy hoses into building and up staircases; leave that for the men. Is that what we want? Female firefighters is a dumb idea, and should be rescinded.

Let's look at women as patrol officers for various police departments. Patrol officers drive or walk an area, responding to calls, trying to catch bad people who have committed crimes or are in the process of breaking the law. Some of them are very large people, some are on mind-altering drugs, and many are armed. The feminists, once again, demanded that women be police officers, working the streets, dealing with all of these bad folks. Now, to be fair, some female police officers are quite capable of taking down a bigger person, and take no guff from anyone. But quite often, it doesn't work out so well. I was involved in one, albeit minor, incident where it was clear that the female officer was undecided on what to do. Briefly, here it is. We have neighbors across the street, both of whom are elderly. The woman has a son from a previous marriage. The son is in his mid-40's, and has been an alcoholic and drug abuser since he was 15. He has been arrested numerous times, and served time in jail in at least two states. He convinced his mother that he was straightening out, but needed a place to live for a short time until he got a job. She relented and agreed. Her husband advised against it, but the son moved in.

He had his own room, ate their food, and they drove him around to various places. Well, it soon turned out that he was still drinking, and one day, he got very drunk. He decided that he didn't like his step-father, charged and head-butted him, dislocating his step-father's nose, and bloodied him up. His mother called me, and I went over to try and calm things down. The son knew me, and knew that if he tried to assault me, I would hurt him badly. After 30 minutes it was clear that the son was out of control, and might well assault his step-father again. So, I told the son I was calling the police, and I did. The son ran next door and hid. The police came, two officers, but couldn't find him, so they left. Ten minutes later the son returned, laughing at us and telling us no police were going to arrest him. I managed to get out of sight and called the police again, and they arrived, with the son unaware they were there.

The female officer came in and confronted the son from about 10 feet away. The son was verbally abusing his mother, and the female officer tells the son to please calm down, get down on the carpet, and place his hands behind his head. The son points his finger at the female officer, and te;;s her to (expletives deleted). She keeps trying to talk to him; he keeps telling her to (expletive deleted). At that point, the male officer walked in, walked over to the son, grabs him and takes him to the ground. The son attempted to resist, and the officer administered a short shot from his Taser®. The son is now whining that he has a bad heart which he does not. Handcuffs were applied, and he was taken to jail. The female officer didn't say a word. If the male officer had not been there, and the son had wanted to, he could have charged that female officer, and done great bodily harm to her.

When I need a police response, I need a police response. I expect the police to do everything they can, within the law, to take the bad folks down, arrest them, and get them away from me. There are many roles women can fill in the police department, but going up against some crazed 300-pounder on the street isn't one of them. The street is a physical environment more often than not. The police often have to exert strong physical force to subdue suspects. If women can't meet the physical requirements, the same requirements men have to meet, get them off the street.

How about women in combat? Have you seen some of the video of our combat warriors in Iraq and Afghanistan? Of course you have. If you paid attention, you saw these combat warriors running, climbing, going after the enemy, avoiding enemy fire, all kinds of vary dangerous things, and they also had a pack on their back that weighs, give or take, about 70 pounds. They also tote their rifles, bulletproof vests, and wear helmets. Now, as some have suggested, let's put a female in that attire, toting that 70-pound pack, running, climbing, chasing the enemy, evading the enemy. Do you think those women are an asset or a liability? How many women do you know who could endure that for months on end? I don't know of any. What I could envision is those female combat warriors having to be protected, assisted, slowing the pace down, and putting everyone in more danger. Is that what we need? What if a male combat warrior is wounded? Can the closest warrior, perhaps a female, put that man on her back and carry him out of danger? Or does she have to call for someone else to carry that wounded soldier out of harm's way?

What do you think an enemy like we're facing now would do if they were to capture a female combat warrior? They have clearly demonstrated that they have no problem with beating, murdering, beheading or, if it's a female warrior, raping her, then shooting them and hanging their bodies on a lamp post. Is that what we want to see?

I spent a little over a year in Vietnam in 1969-1970, on the ground, in the mud, in the jungle. During my tour, we were under fire repeatedly in our base camp. The enemy attempted to overrun our camp numerous times. Bullets, rockets, and mortars were flying everywhere. When I was in camp and not out on a mission, I wanted to know that the foxhole I shared had someone in there with me who could carry me out of there if I was wounded so badly I couldn't move on my own. What I did not want to have was a foxhole partner who couldn't even drag me out of harm's way. I also wanted someone with me who didn't think twice about fighting back, lobbing grenades, and going hand-to-hand with the enemy, if the situation arose. War is a terrible thing. War means killing; it doesn't mean thinking about fighting. You fight or you die.

I didn't fight for my country, my flag, or my family at those times. I fought for my brother in arms—we took care of each other, trying to be sure we all came home alive. That would be my biggest fear, that my team would have someone we couldn't count on when it really got hairy, someone who might freeze, someone who wouldn't fight with me and for me so we both came home alive. Combat is no place for anyone who can't do their job as well as every other person there. It's a physical business; it's not a desk job. Men and women are different.

You may also have read about incidents in the Navy where the Navy was directed to, and determined to, qualify females as fighter pilots. Several women made it through flight school and qualified for fighter pilot training. A long time later it was discovered that grades had been "adjusted" to ensure that the women graduated on to the next level. While in pilot training, one female pilot in particular could not pass the test to land her fighter on the deck of an aircraft carrier. She was given more and more opportunities to pass that test. She was given way more attempts than male pilot trainees were given. Unfortunately, on her last training flight, she panicked and crashed on the flight deck. Several flight deck personnel barely avoided injury or death, the multi-million dollar plane was destroyed, and the female pilot trainee died. The facts were covered up for a long time, but eventually the truth came out. This lady was not suited, physically or psychologically, to be flying fighter jets from the deck of an aircraft carrier. She should have been washed out in the classroom, but in their zeal, and being under orders to qualify women as fighter pilots, she was pushed through, and she died as a result. All of this just to somehow prove that women can fly jet fighters as well as men. Yet the people responsible for pushing this lady through went unscathed.

For those paying attention, can you count how many females make it through qualifications and training to become Navy SEALS? How many females make it through to become Army Rangers? The standards for those units are not lowered so females can pass. No, these units cannot lower their standards or they put every mission in jeopardy. There's a lesson to be learned there, but the feminists seem not to be paying attention.

Is America Becoming an Entitlement Society?

Have you gone back and read our founding documents? I have. In particular, one of our founding documents, the Declaration of Independence, says, in part, "We hold these truths to be self-evident, that all men are created equal, that they are endowed by their Creator with certain unalienable rights, that among these are Life, Liberty and the pursuit of Happiness. That to secure these rights, Governments are instituted among Men, deriving their just powers from the consent of the governed." I'd be willing to wager serious money that most members of Congress could not recite that declaration, or understand what it means.

First of all, that statement clearly spells out that our rights come from our creator, not from a government. Government does not, and should never been allowed to, endow citizens with anything. What government has done over the past 200 years or so is to take rights away from us, which they cannot legally do, and defy anyone to curtail their actions.

When you look at the ending words of that declaration, you get another, very clear understanding, if you believe in our founding documents. Notice that the statement doesn't guarantee happiness. There is no guaranteed outcome, but our creator endows us with the right to pursue happiness. Then there's that pesky "life" word in the statement. If our creator endowed us with the right to life, how can the government sanction abortion or euthanasia? Isn't an abortion the termination of life? Isn't euthanasia the termination of life? Isn't the execution of a convicted murderer the termination of life? Of course they are. But government not only sanctions the termination of life, in many instances it demands that citizens pay for that termination. Is that what our founding documents intended for us? Of course not. Yet government has not only sanctioned death, but encouraged it.

So, the government has created the right to kill the unborn. Let's just toss out that right to life declaration. In the government's zeal to appease a certain group, they have sanctioned the killing of the unborn. Those unborn babies have no right to life.

Over the decades, mostly since the 1940's, entitlements or social programs have been increasing in frequency and duration. Well, actually, when the government creates some entitlement, they rarely ever get rid of it. Not only that, they put more money into it each year. Social security was never part of any government authority; they invented it as a means of taking money from taxpayers and spending it on things they liked. No one who has contributed to social security through their payroll taxes has ever received one penny of interest on those contributions. If citizens were allowed to take the money that is confiscated by the government and put it in interest bearing accounts, even a passbook savings account that they controlled, they'd be a lot better off. Social security was "invented" by government because, at the time, most people didn't live beyond age 66 or 67, A retiring citizen couldn't start drawing social security until they were 65. When that person died, all money due him or her reverted to the government. What a good deal for the government. When the government gives you your social security payments each month, they tax it, too. The government taxes your money when you earn it, then when you get some of that money back, they tax it again. You can look at it as the 'vigorish' the government charges for giving you your own money back. But, it's an invented right that is forced on you if you work. Well, my understanding is that the Congress doesn't participate in social security; they have their own retirement system, which you can't participate in because you're not a member of the ruling class.

Then there's the invented right to receive money if you lose your job, called unemployment insurance. You contribute to that unemployment insurance fund, and so does your employer. The number of weeks you can receive money has been steadily increasing over the years. While you work, you and your employer each have money taken by the government in case you lose your job. It's not a lot, but it's forced on you, nonetheless. If you resign your job or if you're fired for cause (because you screwed up), you get nothing. The government keeps the money. When you lose your job, through a layoff of some kind, you are eligible to go to the government, fill out some forms, and then start receiving payments after a couple of weeks. The payments vary depending on how much you were earning when you worked. Again, the government decided to grant you a right that they control. You might get $100 each week, or $50 each week. At one time, you were required to look for work each week, and demonstrate to the unemployment office that you did indeed look for work. No more. You are told you can get unemployment benefits (benefits?) for 26 weeks, then 52 weeks, now up to 99 weeks, and you don't have to do a thing. Just remember, when the government grants a right, they can take that right away.

How about the invented right to receive welfare payments, food stamps, and subsidized housing? Yes, the government created these rights, too. Just go down to the local welfare office, fill out some forms to verify that you're broke, and voila, here come the welfare payments, food stamp credit card, reduced rent or free housing. You don't even have to be a citizen. You can be in this country illegally, and get those benefits. Why you can even go to the local hospital emergency room and get free medical treatment. Did you ever wonder where the money comes from to pay for all of this? You do know it's not "free," don't you?

If you're in this country illegally, you also have the "right" to send your children to American schools for free, Yes, free. They won't even ask if your child is here legally. You need not have any concerns; the taxpayers will fork over the money for this "free" education.

In America, the amount of money you can earn and still be considered to be living in poverty continually rises. People can be living in an apartment, with heating and air conditioning, have a big screen TV, iPhones, a video game machine, and a couple of cars in the carport, and be considered poverty-stricken. This is your government in action. Raise the poverty level high enough and we'll all be on welfare!

Some years back, the government decided that it was unfair to make people on food stamps actually have to carry stamps. So they came up with the food stamp credit card. People on food stamps aren't supposed to be buying beer, liquor, or tobacco products, but they do anyway. Who is going to stop them, the government? You must be kidding. They just grant rights, pass laws, and head back to the clubhouse. They don't enforce anything. This means that you and I are paying for people on welfare to be able to be well stocked with beer, booze, and smokes. What a country? If you asked the recipients if it bothered them at all that other people were paying for their welfare, they wouldn't care at all. They don't care who pays as long as it isn't them. What do you think their incentive is to actually go look for and find a job? I've run into some people at grocery stores that are some of the most obnoxious, arrogant, rude people I've ever encountered, and every darn one of them was using food stamps. Many of them are morbidly obese. Yet there are they, filling their shopping carts with every kind of fattening food possible, lots of snack foods, beer, wine, booze, and a carton of smokes, and then out comes the food stamp EBT card. They are slow, and some try to steal extra food, are loud, and often berate the cashier for not letting them steal something. I actually saw one welfare lady, in one of those electric carts because she had to weigh 350 pounds, pick up a dozen donuts in a box, then go over to the individual donuts in a case, pull out four or five, and stuff them inside the donut box, trying to steal a few extra treats. I walked up to her and suggested she try exercise instead of stealing donuts, and she tried to run over me with her cart! I did, however, find a supervisor, and pointed out the lady who was stealing the donuts. I don't know if they did anything about it.

So, just how much are citizens entitled to in this beautiful country? If you added up all of the welfare payments, food stamp cards, subsidized housing costs, free medical care, and free education for illegal aliens, it would amount to well over $500 billion per year. That's money that you and I are paying because, despite what many think, the government has no money except that which they confiscate from you and me. This country is nearly $16 trillion in debt, borrows $0.40 of every dollar the government spends, and the waste, fraud, and corruption are rampant. Our ruling class in Washington isn't interested in rooting out all of that waste, fraud, and corruption. Why should they? They'll just add some taxes somewhere, and keep on tossing money at every perceived problem, real or imagined.

Let's not leave out those young college kids. A Valencia college professor in Florida conducted an experiment with his students. He asked each of them, about 80 students, mostly sophomores, to write a short essay to describe what "The American Dream" meant to them. He picked up their essays and took them home to read and analyze. He discovered, much to his surprise, that 80% of the students, about 64 of them, described The American Dream this way:

- Free tuition for as long as they are in college, even if they stay in school to get their Doctorate degree. They shouldn't have to pay anything for their education. In addition, they should receive free healthcare the entire time.
- Upon graduation, they should receive a guaranteed job paying them the money they deserve.
- They should receive extra money to invest for their retirement.
- They want "the rich" taxed, with the money going to them so they have plenty of disposable income.

Now you know why they're in school. They've been indoctrinated into the leftist, socialist model by their leftist, socialist professors. They have no idea where the money comes from, so they ride free, and they don't care. The American Dream means they're entitled, and to hell with everyone else. Wow, has that dream changed. I was somewhat surprised they didn't demand a free X-box, 25 video games of their choice, and a designated student to take tests for them.

What we're talking about here is communism. This vision of everyone sharing everything, no matter who works and who doesn't seems very logical to the weak-minded. People who don't understand Communism very well might be surprised to learn that under this form of government, everyone works, or they starve. No slackers. Everyone is the same, with a couple of important distinctions. First, what if some people just don't want to work. Do they get the fruits of other people's labor? Well, according to those college students, yes. If everyone is the same, and the government, or ruling class, distributes to those who need from those who have, who enforces that rule? Oh, the ruling class leaders, of course. According to the Karl Marx model, there can be no middle class. There can only be a working class, the peasants, and those who control them, the ruling class. Who gets to move from the working class to the ruling class? No one. The ruling class selects its leaders from the families of the ruling class families. They, however, live like royalty. Ruling peasants is hard work, don't you know. The laws don't apply to them, either. Laws are for the peasantry, not for the rulers.

There is also welfare fraud, social security fraud, and Medicare and Medicaid fraud, yet somehow, the government can't seem to find it. There's a lot of workmen's compensation fraud, too. This is another invented right. If you work for a company, and slip and fall when you step on a crack in the concrete, you go to the doctor and tell him or her that your back hurts so bad you just can't work. You can't even straighten up or bend over. Because it's so hard to diagnose back pain, many employees file a claim, and the doctor has to accept the statements from the employee. Employees, who can no longer work receive Workmen's Compensation payments. Some insurance companies that now employ investigators who follow people on this compensation to see if they are truly unable to work. On a Huckabee show one night, one of those investigator companies sent a spokesman who said that of all the cases they're hired to investigate, about 70% of them turn out to be fraudulent claims. People who commit this fraud, and get caught, rarely ever go to jail. They're just taken off workmen's compensation and fired.

What Was the Original Purpose Behind the Affordable Care Act?

We know that our youngest citizens always think everything should be free, or at least an awful lot of them do. That's why they're in school. They really don't understand the concept of what free means. Most young working people don't buy into their company's healthcare plan because, like a lot of young people, they'd rather keep that premium in their pockets, or spend it on other things. I felt that way when I was a young man, but I was in the Navy, and healthcare is part of the deal, such as it was. I learned what the "practice" of medicine really means.

We hear all the time about how so many people can't access healthcare, or afford healthcare insurance. The numbers range from 20 to 50 million depending on which Democrat you ask. When some research was actually performed, the results were quite different. It was determined that over half of those supposed 50 million people were illegal aliens. The actual number of citizens that didn't have healthcare insurance dropped considerably. Then, after some more digging it was discovered that several million people that were counted in that "no access" category were rich people who paid for medical services received, and had no use for health insurance. When all was said and done, the actual number of people that couldn't afford healthcare insurance was less than 10 million. So, to take care of those 10 million people, this President decided that America needed the Affordable Care Act, lovingly referred to as "*ObamaCare*." Actually, a new label emerged to describe this act, the "*ObamaDoesn'tCare*" tax act. I heard Herman Cain use the term, and it seems appropriate.

This act, which is about 2,700 pages in size, contains all kinds of stuff that nobody in Congress ever read or understood. Private meetings were held by the House and Senate, consisting only of Democrats. Then, when it appeared that the bill would not be passed by the Senate, some sweetheart deals were made with specific senators to secure their vote. The *Louisiana Purchase* and the *Cornhusker Kickback* are a couple of the terms used. All during the bluff and bluster campaigning for this bill, the President must have said at least 150 times, "*No one who makes less than $250,000 will see their taxes increased one dime*." Actually he didn't lie. Your taxes won't go up one dime; they're going up by hundreds, maybe thousands, of dollars each year. When it came time for the vote in the House, then Speaker Nancy Pelosi, walked the carpet with some huge gavel that looked like it came from a carnival midway, and announced that "We have to pass the legislation so we could find out what's in it." Huh? Not one Republican in the House voted for it; not one Republican in the Senate voted for it. The bill was crafted and passed only by Democrats.

Immediately there were challenges to the bill that eventuated in 26 states suing in federal court on the grounds that the ACA was unconstitutional because it contained a mandate that every citizen would have to buy healthcare insurance or face heavy fines. This mandate also included all businesses. Meanwhile, little portions of the bill began to be implemented as the lawsuit wended its way through the courts, ending up on the Supreme Court docket. On the last Thursday of June, 2012, the Supreme Court announced its decision. By a vote of 5-4, most of the ACA was deemed constitutional.

The majority opinion, penned by Chief Justice John Roberts, says, in part, that the Congress has the power to levy taxes, and the majority decided that the Affordable Care Act (ObamaCare) mandate is not Constitutional under the Commerce Clause, but is a tax for NOT doing something. All this time, Senators and House Representatives were promised that this bill was not a tax. That was a lie. This decision is now a precedent that can be used for decades.

- If the government mandates that all Americans must buy an electric car or a hybrid to conserve energy, and if you opt not to do that, you can be 'taxed' for not buying that car.
- If the government says that everyone should have an iPad to improve communications amongst citizens, and you don't want or can't afford an $800 iPad, you're free to not buy it, but you will be taxed for NOT buying that iPad.
- The government could decide that beef is not healthy and, therefore, citizens will not raise, sell, or consume beef. Ranchers can decide to grow the beef and sell it anyway, and people can decide to eat it, but both will be taxed for eating beef that was grown and sold against federal law.
- The government can decide that golf courses need to charge an additional $15 per person for each round of golf to fund national parks. Golf courses can opt not to charge that fee, but then be charged a tax for not collecting that additional fee.

You see where this is going? The federal government can now tax you for doing something AND for not doing something. Now, after nearly three years, some details of the bill are coming to light. It was revealed that there are 21 new taxes included in the bill.

If the ACA is not repealed, there are $800 billion in taxes starting in 2014, with an additional $500 billion taken from Medicare, all to help fund the thousands of bureaucrats who administer the act, and the additional IRS agents to enforce the act. There will be regional boards set up to make decisions on whether or not this or that medical procedure will be performed. For example, I'm a senior citizen who needs a hip replacement based on a diagnosis by two or three doctors. The medical procedure recommendation must be submitted to this board (which some call a *Death Panel*) that will decide whether I can have that procedure. This is a procedure similar to that used in Canada and England. In many cases that procedure will be denied because a) it's expensive and, b) the recipient is old. As the current President once said, "Sometimes instead of a heart transplant, maybe it's better to just give that old lady a pain pill." What compassion.

Who will pay that $1.3 trillion, which is just the beginning? We all will. The middle class is going to take it right in their wallet.

Corporations will decide early on to pay the tax (it's really a fine) and not follow federal law, but the tax increases exponentially in the following years, making it impossible for corporations to offer health care for employees, so they will drop it, forcing employees to go to government healthcare exchanges to get some kind of healthcare coverage. You will get a lot less, and pay a lot more for it. Any business with more than 50 employees will face the same fate.

All citizens should be outraged at this decision, and start bombarding House and Senate members to start the process of repealing this draconian law. Remember, this healthcare bill was supposedly created so as to take care of the approximately 10 million uninsured. But the ACA is over 2,700 pages long. This is typical Washington politics. Use a hammer to swat a fly. I am encouraging the Arizona Governor, and all of the state legislators to begin writing Nullification and Sovereignty declarations or legislation. These acts will simply deny implementation of the Affordable Care Act in the state.

There is also a provision in the act that says that young people will have to pay for a healthcare insurance policy. However, if they can't afford the price, the government will help out. What? You have to pay, but if you say you can't pay the American taxpayers will pay the premiums for you?

Remember what the current President promised us? "*I will TransformAmerica.*" He just didn't tell us what he would transform America into before he was done. Now we know. If he is not stopped, our Constitution may be shredded and left in a trash can. This President has already said he won't enforce most laws against illegal aliens, and gave 1.2 million illegal aliens the right to stay here and get work permits. Is anyone paying attention?

The one thing you need to remember is that the leftists never go away. The left picks out a certain target and starts attacking it, trying to change it or destroy it. When people who believe in the Constitution start fighting back, the left sends out other minions to start attacking another freedom, another right, trying to change or destroy it. The attacks come from all sides, and the left is very patient; they never stop; they never give up. They just keep attacking. Look at your children, grandchildren, and great grandchildren. What kind of America do you want to leave them? Are you willing to just roll over and give up? Are you willing to get involved and try to save the greatest country in the history of the planet for them? You better think about just what you'll be leaving behind.

Where does FREE Stuff Come From?

I gave a speech a few years back at a local high school. I had been invited by a student with her teacher's permission. My topic was the difference between Democrats and Republicans. Two classes were combined for my speech, and there were about 80-90 students in attendance. Everything was going along fine until I asked the class, "How much money does the government have?" I called on several students, and almost all agreed that the government has all the money. They can print more if they need it. I then explained that the government does not produce any products, essentially provides no services, and does not "earn" money. What the government does is take money from working people in the form of taxes. They then distribute that money on various programs, defense, energy exploration, and so on. I then asked them to check with their parents and ask them how much money is taken from their pay in the form of taxes. I also mentioned that the very school they attend is paid for with taxpayer money. The chairs, lights, water, computers, everything is paid for with taxpayer dollars.

Then I asked the students about the cost of education, and if they thought college should be free. Almost every hand shot up in the air. I then explained to them what free would mean. If college were truly free, then the people who construct the building work for free. The materials needed to construct those building would have to be donated. All of the landscaping would have to be created and maintained for free by some number of people. The lights, heat, and air conditioning would have to be free as well, provided by the utility companies. The authors of the textbooks would have to donate them to the colleges for free, the publishers would have to print them, and truckers transport them for free, too. The school administration employees would have to work for free, and the instructors and professors would have to work for free, as well. All of the equipment used in the classroom, such as computers, servers, printers, blackboards, whiteboards, paper, and everything else would have to be donated, too. So, if college is free for the students, how many people have to work for nothing to provide that free education? You could see lights coming on in the eyes of several students. They were starting to understand that there is no such thing as a free education. No one at any college would get paid a nickel so you could get a free education. What if you were an employee at that college? Would you go to work every day, and get paid nothing so the students could go to school at no cost? Is that OK with you? What if you spend two years writing an excellent textbook that colleges are going to use, but you will receive nothing for your two years of work? Is that OK with you?

So, I asked again, "Should college be free for students?" Now, only about one-third of the student's hands went up. I then called on one of the students who still wanted a free college education, and asked why? "College students are the future. Working people, especially the rich, should be happy to pay for our education." I then asked, "Do you think that the last generation of college students believed they were the future, too?" "Yes" was the reply. Well, I said, "Many of those people are the ones you want to pay for your college education so you can get a free ride. Is that fair?" He had no answer.

The Constitution spells out what we are endowed with from our creator. We are not entitled to free stuff; we're not entitled to a free education; we're not entitled to free healthcare; we're not entitled to free money. All of these entitlements, or rights, were created by, and continue to be created by the government in an effort to pander for votes. If you pay attention, you know that they don't ever worry about what an entitlement costs, or how to keep fraud and corruption out of it. They don't care. They believe their job is to spend every nickel the government takes in, and more, to buy votes from various groups. That's why we're all broken down into groups and classes. First of all, we're easier to control and secondly, we can be targeted by the government for handouts or denial. But the whole entitlement program has gone totally out of control, and you can blame the political class for the problem.

Are Role Models Important to Children?

I kind of understood what a role model is, but I thought that I should look it up. "True role models are those who possess the qualities that we would like to have and those who have affected us in a way that makes us want to be better people, to advocate for ourselves and our goals and take leadership on the issues that we believe in. We often don't recognize our true role models until we have noticed our own personal growth and progress."

When children are born and begin to grow, they are constantly learning. Much of what they learn isn't accomplished in some government school. What they learn and mimic comes from people around them, and what they see on television. Charles Barkley, a former professional basketball player, often said that kids should not look at professional athletes as role models. Instead, they should look to their parents as role models. That's all well and good, but for a young man who plays sports, who will he be looking to as he dreams? It usually isn't mom or dad. It's some professional athlete. I played a lot of basketball as a young man, and was pretty good at it, but I didn't idolize some professional basketball player. I look at professional basketball today and think, these are grown men playing a child's game in short pants. Yet the media treat these basketball players as if what they do on a basketball court really matters. Several of the players have tattoos all over their bodies; others wear earrings, and several of them father children all over the country with different women. Who would want them as role models? You could apply the same comments to baseball and football players.

Some of what kids learn is basic, such as walking, talking, and getting potty-trained. But children are also learning how to behave. Some children do destructive things, and the parents correct the child, and teach them that a particular behavior is wrong. When a child behaves well, praise is given. But as children get even older, they look at the people around them to see what they do, and they may well start to mimic that behavior, good or bad. Peer pressure is often a destructive thing. Many kids who would otherwise never try drugs, or get into drinking, do so because their supposed friends talk them into it. If parents aren't paying attention to who their kids are hanging out with, there can be severe consequences. So just where are the role models for kids? It should be their parents, but more and more we're seeing children born into homes with only one parent, usually the mother. There are a lot of fathers out there who won't "man up" and do what's right by their children. If mom is working two jobs just to get enough money to pay the bills and put food on the table, how much time does she have to spend with her child(ren)? Is the absent father going to be the role model for a child? How about a two-parent family that is always fighting, and there's physical abuse? Is that the role model for the child(ren)? Is the drug dealing father going to be the role model for their son? I knew a man who was in prison when we met. He knew he had to change. He had a wife and four kids, and this was his third trip to prison. We worked together for nearly two years. During that time, he shared much of his early life with me. He'd tried drugs for the first time when he was just 14 years old. How did this happen? Well, his father was the local drug dealer, and he believed that his son would get into drugs anyway, so he wanted to be sure that his son got good drugs. So he showed his son how to shoot heroin, at the age of 14. That man's father was his role model, and he had to fight through that for 20 years before I met him in prison. Or, a young man I met when I worked with foster children who used to sit in his bedroom while his mother was prostituting herself with men in the next bedroom? He never met his father. He was learning about life from his mother the prostitute. Then were those kids whose mother was a meth-head, never around, no father anywhere in sight. There are parents who both work, get home late, so their children are what we call "latch key" kids. They come home to an empty house, fend for themselves, do whatever they want, and the parents are essentially oblivious. The parents don't go to their children's events, don't attend parent-teacher conferences, and don't even look at the report cards. They don't know who their kids are hanging out with, or what they do on the computer or their cell phones. But these are the kinds of parents who will just be so utterly shocked when one of their children gets arrested for burglary, or for getting drunk and driving someone's car into a building. Are these kids looking at their parents as role models, and will they end up in a marriage where they don't care about their kids, too? Should policemen or firemen be role models? That sounds good, except when the media runs stories about this crooked cop or that fireman who steals. The child forgets that for every 2,000-3,000 good policemen and women, and firefighters, there's one or two that make the headlines. How about children born into second or third generation welfare families? What do they see all around them? What do they hear from their parent or parents? Life isn't fair, I couldn't afford to go to college, I had to quit high school and get a job, you'll never get anywhere in life. How does that shape a child's dreams and aspirations?

If you're a parent, a grandparent, or a great grandparent, what are you doing to ensure that those children have role models to emulate in a positive way? If you think it's someone else's job to provide role models for those kids, don't be surprised when they turn out with multiple tattoos, drug addicted, and arrested for dealing death. You are their role models whether you like it or not. Can school teachers be role models? Sure they can. Some teachers can inspire their students to work hard, aspire to attend college, and go on to greater things. Unfortunately today, too many government school teachers are just going through the motions, and don't really care about the students. It's just a job.

When Did Climate Change Begin?

Did the earth get colder and warmer before Al Gore discovered it? I think the record is pretty clear on that subject. Geologic records and about 500 scientists have determined that the earth has gone through cooling and warming periods many, many times before humans ever inhabited this planet. How could this be? The simple answer is—are you ready for it . . . . nature.

The south and north polar caps have increased and decreased in size forever, despite our presence on the planet. The temperatures around the planet have risen and fallen throughout the centuries. It is incredibly presumptuous for a few people, including Al Gore—who knows practically nothing about science, or much of anything else, to blame climate change on the existence of man, especially Americans.

Some of you may remember a document called the Kyoto Protocol. It has the United Nations fingerprints all over it. It's one of their conventions. It was adopted in 1997 in Kyoto, Japan, thus, the name attached to it. It's been ratified by almost every member country of the United Nations except for the United States and a very few other countries. When it was brought before the Congress during the Clinton administration, they informed the President that the Kyoto Protocol was going nowhere, so don't even bring it up. The Kyoto Protocol is, more or less, an attempt to get the rich countries (America) to agree that the richer countries needed to pay the poorer countries because of all the pollutants they spew into the air. The Kyoto Protocol has never really gone anywhere in our country, but the leftists keep threatening to bring it up again. The true purpose of such a treaty is simply to confiscate money from rich countries and give it to poorer countries, with the United Nations taking a slice. It is purely baloney. Redistribution of wealth, writ large.

Let's talk polar bears. First of all, there are more polar bears than ever on the northern polar ice. Glaciers form and fall all the time. This whole environmentalist gibberish is a pack of lies. The environmentalists manufacture some facts, and useful idiots, such as Al Gore, keep repeating them.

If you remember some years back, the environmentalists were dead set against the Alaska pipeline because, they said, the caribou would be harmed. What happened when the pipeline was created? The caribou loved that pipeline. In really cold weather, the caribou can be found all around the pipeline, keeping warm!

You do remember that back in the 1970's many of the scientists who are telling us now that the earth is warming because of human activity. These are the same scientists who, back then, were telling us that the earth was going to enter an ice age. They lied then, and they're lying now. There is no objective science to support their claims. The question to ask is why are these scientists wrong so often? The answer is easy. Many research firms depend on government grants in order to keep doing research, and keep paying themselves and their employees. When the government tells a research firm that they'll get their grant, they also imply or outright tell those scientists what they want the research to conclude. That makes perfect sense to me. How about you?

If you've noticed, the environmentalists changed the name of the calamity they said would befall us from Global Warming to Climate Change. They discovered that Global Warming just wasn't getting through to the weak minded. They changed the calamity to Climate Change because people understand weather getting warmer and cooler. Heck, most of us live through those conditions every year. If your area has an unusually cold winter, it's caused by climate change. If your area has a warmer than normal summer, that's caused by climate change as well. To them it's a win-win campaign. But again, it's all lies.

The whole climate change rant is just a scam. Its purpose is to extort money from the United States in order to redistribute it to third-world countries. When you look at the countries that are exempt from climate change rules and regulations, you will see China and India on the list. China brings a new coal plant online just about every week, and spews more pollutants into the air than America, month after month, but they're exempt. India gets the same exemption. If it's about "global" climate problems, why are some countries exempt from any regulations?

Do you remember reading or hearing about carbon credits? They were all over the news a few years ago. Essentially, a company could purchase a carbon credit which was, in essence, permission to emit a metric ton of pollution into the air. Guess who owns or owned a carbon credit company? Why, what a surprise; it was Al Gore. He would sell carbon credits to companies who were emitting pollution as determined by the Environmental Protection Agency (EPA. Again, this was just a scam to suck money out of companies as punishment for daring to emit pollutants they identified. The carbon credit companies traded carbon credits on the carbon credit exchange, so some smart, rich, insiders could make money buying and selling carbon credits. No one has ever explained how carbon credits do anything for the air quality. They don't. It was all a scam perpetrated on companies all over the world to extort money from them.

The EPA has been used as a tool by government administrations to create and enforce laws that couldn't be done working through the Congress. The stories of EPA overreach are legend. Just recently, a married couple had bought a lot in Idaho. It was landlocked. They wanted to build their dream home. They had all the surveys done, applied for and received all of the permits, and hired a company to begin construction. Not long after, the EPA arrived on the scene and declared their property a wetlands. They were ordered to return the land to its original condition, including all plants. The EPA also ordered the land owners to obtain, plant, and maintain plants that were not even natural to the area. Remember now, none of the other homes around them were subjected to these draconian EPA edicts, only this one lot, with no water anywhere around it or on it.

The landowners filed a request for a hearing. The EPA denied their request, saying no hearing would be held. The EPA also ordered the land owners to pay $75,000 for each day the land was not returned to its original condition. The landowners then hired a lawyer and took the EPA to court, and they lost. They appealed to a higher court, and lost. The case finally made its way to the Supreme Court. After several years, and tens of thousands of dollars in legal fees, the case was heard by the Supreme Court. It didn't take them long to issue a decision. The EPA was told, in no uncertain terms, that what they did was unconstitutional, and that the landowners could do with their land what they wanted, with no interference from the EPA. The final outcome has yet to be determined, but just think about it for a minute. If this couple had not had the money to spend to fight the EPA, and their determination not to let the government run over them, they would have lost everything. What if this was your son and his wife, or your daughter and her husband? Would you want them to have to go through all of this just to build their home? They broke no laws, they obtained every permit, they did everything right, and the EPA comes along, puts a boot on their necks, and says "we don't care." That's tyranny, folks.

The EPA is carrying out the essence of the Cap and Trade bill that the President couldn't get through the Congress. He just tells the EPA to start coming up with rules and laws, none of which are subject to Congressional approval or oversight, and away they go. Who suffers? We all do.

Finally, when you think about it, how can a bunch of environmental zealots actually "protect" the environment from other humans? Most companies try to be good citizens and neighbors. Not all of them, but most of them. As technology improves, as it has forever, companies will buy better methods of cleaning pollutants from their factories. Why should an organization come along and start dictating to private businesses what they must do or else be fined or, perhaps, even shut down. Is this the America you want to leave for your kids and grandkids? I sure don't.

People that Contribute Nothing to Society

Each of us could probably write down a long list of people that fit the description of this topic. I chose to select just a few to illustrate a point. You may have seen some of these people on television, or heard them on the radio. I certainly have, but I seek them out because I believe in keeping an eye on the insane. These people are useless because they contribute nothing to society except obscenity, lies, and promotion of drugs and alcohol. They are people with low self-esteem, often deservedly so, narcissistic, contribute nothing to the world around them, are unhappy, and usually very ignorant. They attack others with whom they disagree, slander people, and typically use foul language to try and get attention. Others believe they are very important, that what they have to say is very important, and believe they are adored by the little people. I was going to title this topic, Useless Human Debris, but I wanted to be nice.

Al Gore

We all know that Al Gore took credit for creating the Internet, one of his bigger whoppers. He also said that he and his wife, at the time, were the couple who was the basis for the movie, "*Love Story*" until the writer of the book came out and said that was a lie, too. Poor Al Gore is a man in a desperate pursuit of something that would make him relevant. He is one of the few men who served for eight years as the Vice President of the United States, and then lost the election for President.

Gore served in Vietnam as a writer for the *Stars and Stripes* newspaper, and never came anywhere close to combat, yet wrote and spoke of carrying a weapon, and standing a post. This was obviously a figment of his imagination. Gore was also the only military man I'd ever heard of who served in Vietnam who had his own personal security detail. He didn't serve a full tour, opting to come home early. Wow, we had that option? Dang, missed another memo.

Gore entered and dropped out of a Seminary. He didn't even try to get a master's degree after finishing his bachelor's degree, with less than stellar grades. Yet, Al Gore was touted as the "intelligent" man when compared to George W. Bush, who achieved his MBA at a prestigious college. When he literally yells and rants about global warming, oops, climate change, we should all be suspicious. This is a man who constantly preaches to us about lessening our carbon footprint, then takes off in his chartered jet aircraft, or travels the roads in a chauffeur driven limousine.

I am very critical of these so-called late night shows, like "The Tonight Show," "Late Night with Dave Letterman," "Late Night with Jimmy Fallon," and the "Jimmy Kimmel," show. I remember people like Johnny Carson and Red Skelton. They could tell jokes that were more like short stories, but were always funny. They didn't need obscenities, and they didn't need to pick on someone else just to try and get a laugh. When I think of people like Lenny Bruce and Richard Pryor, on stage, with every foul mouthed word known to man, ridiculing everyone he could think of, and calling it comedy, it makes me sad. The whole issue of comedy seems to have degenerated into trying to get a laugh by a) swearing and b) making fun of other people. Do any of you remember Jerry Seinfeld? He was funny, and his stand-up acts contained no foul language at all. But now we have a whole generation of people calling themselves comedians who aren't funny, but they are crude. There's a TV show called "Saturday Night Live" that takes great pride in making fun of everyone and everything. And that show has been on the air for a long, long time.

Bill Maher

I have occasionally watched this Bill Maher character, and I immediately put him in the Useless Human Debris pile. It became clear to me that if this ignorant fool didn't use obscenity-laced rhetoric, no one would pay any attention to him. He has nothing intelligent to say. Maher is, supposedly, a Cornell University-educated man who, evidently, didn't take any classes on civil discourse. I'm sure Cornell would like to disavow any association with him. He also seems to have only a passing knowledge of an English sentence that doesn't contain at least one obscenity.

Now, to be fair, not many people care about anything this little, swishy gnome says. Even ABC banished him from a show called "Politically Incorrect" many years ago. He was too obscene for the ABC brass to stomach. Now he does a once-a-week show on HBO for a few weeks each year. But, while he is on the air, he misses no opportunity to be as obscene as possible all in the name of comedy. The only problem is that he's not funny. The laughter sounds like a recorded laugh track. He has guests on this little known show. Typically, it's two or three far left loons, and an occasional conservative, whom he uses as a "whipping boy." I think he likes that "whipping boy" phrase.

He has referred to conservative women as MILFs (Mother's I'd Like to (bleep)." He's had one guest who said he'd like to have angry sex with a male conservative man running for President. Boy, what a knee-slapper that was.

We do need to understand that Bill Maher, after spewing his venom, runs back and hides under his desk, or says, "Hey, I'm a comedian" as cover for his slimy comments. I should also note that no woman will be seen with him unless, I'm betting, she's getting paid to do it. He's never been married, which comes as no surprise. When you see him, or when he speaks, you understand why.

First of all, Bill Maher is no comedian and, most importantly, because he's not funny. He's crude, and can't seem to complete a sentence without an obscenity or two thrown in. His sleazy speech is aimed at anything conservative, Christian, or Republican. He slanders anyone who espouses conservative or Christian views. His audience, small though it is, seems fully enthralled by his obscene comments. Fortunately, very few people see or hear him. America is all the better for that.

Bill Maher recently said that he isn't betting on the day that Dick Cheney dies. No, he just would like to know so he can book the party and caterer. Isn't that cute? He has called Sarah Palin the C___ word, to roars of laughter.

This is a little man who needs a spanking and then sent to bed without his gruel. Wait a minute; skip the spanking; he'd probably like that.

We need to be clear about the purpose of late night shows, such as *The Tonight Show, Late Night with David Letterman, Jimmy Kimmel Live*, and *Late Night with Jimmy Fallon*. They were invented decades ago by television producers to be *"shill shows."* There are other shows like these late night shows, but their purpose is the same. The host is there as the warm up act. They supposedly do some comedy, maybe some skit, and then bring on the guests. The shows exist so that movie stars can come on and tell everyone how wonderful they are, what a great vacation they had in the South of France, and just finished this wonderful movie—"Let's show a clip." These shows bring on millionaire athletes, millionaire musicians, and groups to give them *"exposure"* to the audience. I've noticed one thing about these shows that some of you may have missed. These guests never appear when times are really bad. For example, take Tom Cruise. When he was going to marry Katie Holmes he was on all the shows, hopping on couches, and gushing. When he had a movie coming out he was on those shows gushing about what a great movie it is, shot on location here or there. But when times went bad for Tommy Cruise, he asks that we respect his and Katie's privacy.

David Letterman:

This 65-year old meets the definition of "*Dirty Old man.*" Not that long ago it was revealed that Letterman had made it almost a condition of employment for women who wanted to work on his show to have sex with him. This had been going on, supposedly, for many years. Even after he had a child with his girlfriend, and even after he married his girlfriend, his sexual appetite for female employees seemed to continue unabated. He gave a sort of apology, and the CBS network didn't even blink. As long as they're selling high-priced advertising, Letterman can do whatever he wants. It's interesting to note that almost every year Letterman gets an award for his show even though he's up against Jay Leno, who beats him like a drum in the viewer ratings.

This is also the man who, on one of his shows, stated that "The Palins attended a Yankee baseball game at Yankee Stadium and, in the 7th inning, Sarah's daughter was "*knocked up*" by Alex Rodriguez." Of course the audience was delighted.

It is estimated that this sex pervert makes about $30 million per year for hosting his TV show on CBS.

Letterman has demonstrated, in his own words, that he dislikes conservatives and especially Republicans. When he has Democrats on his show, he almost falls to his knees, similar to what he put those women through, I'm guessing, ingratiating himself to his leftist guests. When a Republican is on his show, Letterman seems to challenge everything that is said.

Letterman is a man who attended and graduated from Ball State University, but I have to wonder just what classes he took. He stammers a lot, can't seem to form a complete sentence, and can only speak reasonably well when he's looking at his teleprompter. Where have we seen that tendency before?

During interviews, Letterman displays that distorted, fuzzy intelligence for which he has become famous. That is, he doesn't know what he's talking about, but tries to throw in a few multi-syllable words to appear smart. Few people buy the act, and he's easily embarrassed by guests when they correct him. Television would be better off without him, but at least we know where a lot of weak-minded people are at that time of night.

Jimmy Fallon

Fallon's main claim to fame, insofar as I can tell, is the promotion of drugs and alcohol. He never misses a chance to talk about drunks and people who are stoned. His audience, most of whom, I suspect, are in one of those two states, is just delighted. This show is what passes for entertainment late at night. It took him until 2009 to finally graduate from college, so academia doesn't seem to be his strong suit. On one of his shows, he invited Michelle Bachman to be a guest. When she was introduced the show's band, The Roots, broke out into a song titled "Lying Assed Bitch." Wasn't that clever? No one on the show paid any price for insulting her that way. However, when a Democrat is a guest on the show, Jimmy falls all over himself to grovel and seek approval. His primary claim to "fame" seems to be that he can imitate the voices of other people. Wow, that's impressive. I have a 10-year old grandchild who can do the same thing, so the sky's the limit for him. Fallon seems to be a man suffering from stunted mental growth, a man forever stuck in childhood. His jokes are seldom actually funny, and he loves making fun of all things conservative, Christian, or Republican. Sound familiar? You know, I've never heard Fallon, or any of the other late night "entertainers" ever make a joke about Islam. The butt of these jokes seems always to be Christians. It's always easier to make fun of Christian people. Christians don't resort to violence when they are the butt of jokes. Some zealots of other religions threaten and carry out violence against anyone that makes fun of their faith.

Jimmy Kimmel

Jimmy Kimmel, who is about 42 years of age, was born in Brooklyn, New York. His first TV gig was hosting a show called, "Win Ben Stein's Money." It was canceled after two seasons. His TV gig now is "Jimmy Kimmel Live," which has been on the air since 2003. The first inkling we get of Kimmel's values is when he said that David Letterman was his idol. He did a stint on HBO as an NFL professional league prognosticator. He, like the others in these late night time slots, struggles for laughs by saying ridiculous things about conservatives, Christians, and Republicans. Like the others, he has a small following of mindless young people who will laugh at anything when they're a little stoned, and Kimmel seems to like them that way. He contributes nothing to society, and is paid handsomely for doing nothing worthwhile.

There are many other people who are, sort of, famous but add nothing to our society, like Jay Leno, Conan O'Brien, all RAP musicians, all Hip-Hop musicians, Barbra Streisand, James Brolin, Susan Sarandon, Tim Robbins, George Clooney, Wesley Snipes, Nancy Pelosi, Harry Reid, and the list goes on. They really do nothing to advance our culture, but a lot to degrade it.

Are We Safe From Terrorism?

I can remember, not too long ago, when I could arrive at the airport about 20 minutes before my flight, walk in, check in, and walk onto my plane. That was before the murderous attacks of September 11, 2001 by 19 Middle Eastern terrorists, most of them from Saudi Arabia, and all of them Muslim. Now, we are warned again and again to arrive at least two hours ahead of time. Why? Well, our infinitely organized and efficient government decided that we had to increase airport security so they invented the Transportation Security Administration (TSA). Yes, another government agency. You, too, can become a TSA security agent if you have a high school diploma and have never been convicted of a felony. I mean, how much training do you need to grope people? The TSA spends about $9 billion dollars of our money each year, and in return we get to be folded, spindled, and mutilated and, oh yes, groped. They can put us through machines that blow up women's skirts or put us in a plastic container where X-rays look right through our clothes, so a TSA agent can enjoy him or herself looking at our "naked" bodies. There have been several TV stories that report on how easy it is to get weapons through airport security, but look at who we're dealing with.

They don't profile; that wouldn't be fair. I know, the terrorists declared war on America, and all of the attackers of 9/11 were Middle Eastern men of the Islamic faith, but in America we have to be fair. Profiling, though very effective, would just not be fair. So, the TSA does random searches, with no regard for the age, gender, or ethnicity of the traveler. Anyone from one week old to 105 years old is ripe for a frisk. Searches have been conducted on old, infirm grandmothers, with their walkers, down to two-month old babies in bassinets. The TSA, after all, is non-discriminatory; they'll molest anyone. Many TSA agents have demonstrated that giving them power and control is not a good idea. Some of them don't believe that the rules for their job apply to them. They do what they want. I mean, come on, they have to have something to do for those eight-hour shifts. Remember, they are a government agency, so we know that intellect, efficiency, and professionalism are not necessarily a part of who they are.

I have also watched stories on television, and heard them on radio, where passengers have had their genitalia massaged, many ladies have had their breasts groped, and people with a cane have had that cane disassembled, all in the pursuit of security. I don't fly much anymore, but when I do, and they want to pat me down, I have no problem with it. While the agent is running his hand up and down my leg, I usually let him know how I feel. I'll say, "Oh, that's good; don't stop; yes, you're almost there; is this as good for you as it is for me?" The TSA agent doesn't much care for my attempt at conversation, but I've noticed that my pat downs don't last very long.

The TSA put restrictions on how much liquid we can carry in any bottle; we have to use a certain size clear plastic bag to hold our toiletries (no large tubes of toothpaste), and don't even think about carrying a bottle of water or a can of soda with you through security. You could be subject to "enhanced" interrogation. They will, of course, confiscate your water, and then tell you to buy your water or soda after you've gone through security. Wow, what a deal. And don't forget to bring your photo identification with you. You may not need a photo ID to vote, but you can't get on an airplane without it.

And, related to terrorism at airports, have you noticed the rise in craziness by flight attendants and even pilot in the past few months? What is going on? Did that pilot get a bad dose of LSD during his layover? Some flight attendants have lost it as well, while the plane is 37,000 feet in the air. This is not a good thing. But I've also seen how pilots live while they're flying. I'm referring mostly to commuter commercial pilots. They have to travel to some city, get their plane, fly it to some other city, layover for 8-10 hours, then get another plane, and on and on it goes. Considering the skill they need, they're not paid very much. Trying to get some sleep, real restful sleep, seems difficult, if not impossible. Some pilots stay in what can only be called "pilot flop houses" for a few bucks, where they share the room with up to 10-15 other pilots coming and going all night. Or they sleep in the pilot lounge on the couch. After a while, is it any wonder some pilots are just so tired, so stressed, they lose it and have a breakdown? It sure doesn't surprise me. The life of a commercial airline pilot is not as glamorous as we might think. But the airlines, always chasing the bottom line on, cut expenses wherever they can. So, pilots are overscheduled, barely staying inside the FAA rules on time off between flights, with no concern as to where these pilots get their rest. Flight attendants aren't treated any better. One flight attendant who works for a commercial airline says that he makes, after taxes, about $10,000 per year. People on welfare make a lot more than that. Why would anyone do that job?

Flight attendants have to put up with all kinds of idiot passengers, like Alec Baldwin, who refused to follow the rules. The stories are legion about how unruly celebrities behave on commercial airline flights. Then you have other passengers who drink too much, can't control their bowels, refuse to turn off electronic equipment, and make life for the flight attendants a living hell. We're very good at holding people who have nothing to do with writing the rules responsible for those rules. Yes, some passengers are stupid, arrogant idiots who should be banned from all airlines, but I know one thing: When I fly I want the flight attendants and the pilot, co-pilot, and navigator sober, alert, and extremely competent, so I arrive at my destination alive.

But think about this for a minute. The government, in its infinite wisdom, is attempting to close the barn door after the horse is long gone. The terrorists used airplanes to crash into the twin towers, the Pentagon, and a fourth plane was intended to be crashed into who knows where before the passengers brought it down in Pennsylvania. But once terrorists use one method to attack us, they watch and listen to how we respond. That we needed better security at airports before 9/11 is obvious. It's just that the TSA is, like a lot of government agencies, inefficient. The terrorists usually move on to other methods of attack. But once we're attacked and a few thousand people are killed by some other method, you can bet that our government will be right on the case with more stupid procedures. Folks, that's a reactive government not a pro-active government. Here are just a few ways in which dedicated terrorists could attack us pretty easily:

- How about a large 18-wheelers, full of fertilizer and other chemicals crashing into a major building in any one of a hundred cities? Could that happen? Of course it could. How about terrorists just dropping a few gallons of some poisonous liquid into a city water supply? Could that happen? Of course it could.
- How about a coordinated attack at major malls in 10 of our largest cities? At a preset time, five or six terrorists, with automatic weapons, enter each mall and start mowing people down.
- What if, I love to play what if scenarios, terrorists bought a few small, single engine aircraft through front men, then loaded them up with some poisonous gas, and drove it over a few football stadiums, and crashed onto those fields, and released the gas?
- What if the terrorists filled those planes with dirty nuclear devices and crashed them into those football stadiums?

- What if a terrorist organization was able to hack into the power grid on the East or West coast, and bring it down? There would be no power to 75-100 million homes and businesses would be a success for them, right?

The bottom line is that, with our porous borders, and inability to get surveillance and wire taps on suspected terrorists without a warrant, we are not safe. We may be safer, but we are not safe. We won't be safe until the terrorists are all captured or killed. That will never happen. Because our federal government refuses to control the border, we have no way of knowing how many terrorists are crossing into our country on any given day.

So, as always, life contains risks. Terrorism is an added risk, and a very real one, but there is no such thing as safe.

What Makes "Diversity" So Wonderful?

American Heritage Dictionary says this about Diversity: The fact or quality of being diverse, different. A point of respect when things differ. Variety of multiformity, "Charles Darwin saw in the diversity of species the principles of evolution that operated to generate the species, variations, competition, and selection."

That's not very helpful. Let's apply diversity to various parts of our culture, shall we?

Does diversity in the workplace mean that we have to hire people of all races, genders, religious faiths, non-religious people; people from any and all countries? By doing this, America gains what? Does a company that sets quotas to hire so many men, so many women, so many white people, so many black people, so many Mexican people, so many Filipino people, so many Columbians, and so on, add value to the company? Is the company allowed to insist that all employees in America speak English, or is that just unfair? Just a wild thought here, but how about hiring the most qualified people for the job, period? Having people from all these cultures and geographical locations means that all company literature must be printed in how many languages, six, maybe seven? And, the computer software used on those company computers must have an interface for each of the various languages? And, if there's a cafeteria, do the menus have to be printed in six or seven languages, and provide culturally-sensitive meals, too? What about religious practices? Do those employees who are directed to pray six or seven times a day have to be given a place and the time to practice that faith? And, how do you determine who to hire for an opening? Do you hire the right race, gender, or ethnicity in order to meet the quota? Does that add to the productivity of the company? Gee, what if an employee displays a cross on their desk, and it offends someone of another faith? What if a Satanist displays a replica of the devil on their desktop, and it offends other employees? What if an employee wears clothing that replicates their homeland, and no one can tell who the employee is because their face is covered? What does the company do?

What language is used by employees to communicate with each other, with management, with customers? What language is used to write reports? If you insist that all employees speak and write English, is that fair?

Do you see this going anywhere? Or, is the company so busy accommodating the diversity in their employee population that productivity is negatively aff4ected, maybe to the point of non-profitability, and the company has to let some people go? How does the company decide which employees to lay off? Do they do it by quota?

Now, take diversity and apply it to your neighborhood, your city, your state, to the entire country. America is such a wonderful place that people from all over the world want to come here. Do you hear of people trying to immigrate to China, Russia, Iran, Libya, Pakistan? No, people want to come here. America receives over a million legal immigrants every year. No one knows how many people break our laws and sneak into the country. Many years ago, people who immigrated here assimilated into the American culture. Why do we have people from all over the world immigrate here, to America, and then demand that we acknowledge their language and culture? Why, in Dearborn, Michigan, are Muslims fighting to throw out the U.S. Constitution in favor of the Islamic Sharia Law? Is this the diversity all these people are talking about? So many people who have come here for the American dream refuse to learn to read, write, or speak English. They demand that Americans allow, support, and accommodate the culture they left behind. So, we now have Barrios, Chinatowns, Little Vietnams, Japantowns, and on and on. Is this a good thing? We have multiple generations of people, legally living within the United States who can't read, write, or speak English. They prefer to speak their native language while in the United States, and we have to accommodate them. How many courthouses have to provide interpreters of multiple languages for immigrants doing business there? There are thousands of them, and we pay for the bill. We now have citizenship ceremonies given in languages other than English. This is diversity that is good for America?

Take a look at some of our high schools and colleges. In some colleges, students of a particular faith have demanded that they have separate dormitories. There are students who demand that special accommodations be made on school property to accommodate their religious faith. They want to be segregated. How is this diversity good for America?

We have butcher shops that refuse to sell certain kinds of meat because it's against their religion. There have been cab drivers who refuse to pick up passengers who have a dog, or who are carrying liquor because it's against their religion. We have had schools that attempted to fly the flag of a foreign country above the flag of the United States. Is this what diversity is all about?

We have fast food restaurants where employees speak little or no English. We have supermarkets that cater to foreign language-speaking customers. English isn't the language of choice in these stores in the United States. Please explain to me how diversity is good for America.

How can any clear thinking person look at all of these special accommodations, and think it is good for America? While I think we should all be tolerant of differences between people, it certainly does not seem to be the attitude of very many immigrants who come to our country.

If Americans who deplore what is happening speak up, they are often harassed and called names. That's shameful. Our own government seems powerless, or spineless, and won't even make English the language of government in America. That's really shameful.

Here's what I think needs to happen. All ballots should be printed in English. If you can't read English, go learn it; this is America, and we speak English here. It's not racist, it's American culture. Legal immigrants have no right to demand that Americans cater to their culture. Get over yourselves. Either assimilate into the American culture, or leave. The United States is not a melting pot any longer. No, it has become a stew pot, with clumps of isolated cultures all over the place, all demanding that we be tolerant of them, but offering no acceptance of our culture in return.

The current President of the United States said, "Americans should learn to speak Spanish." Just a quick note here: the President cannot speak Spanish or any other foreign language, but he wants you to learn to speak Spanish. What is even worse, the audience applauded wildly when the President made this comment. He never said that Spanish-speaking people in America need to learn to speak English. Gee, maybe we should also learn to speak Vietnamese, German, French, Italian, Chinese (all dialects), and a few others so the foreigners who immigrate here won't have to be bothered with that pesky English language. What kind of boneheaded comment is that from the President?

So, why is diversity good for America? If you want to know about the culture of another land, study it, go visit that land. But when you're in America, act like you're an American. Immigrants swore allegiance to the United States when they became citizens. People born as citizens of the United States have no reason to start hyphenating their names. Citizens are Americans, not partial Americans. Show some respect; show some pride; show your allegiance.

Here's a short story to illustrate a point. I was in Germany some years back, and had the opportunity to meet and speak with many people during my stay. What I heard was that a lot of immigrants had been pouring into Germany, mostly from Turkey, asking for asylum, but having no identification of any kind. But the German government welcomed them in. The government also provided them with welfare and free housing, mostly in large apartment complexes. These immigrants, who were not allowed to work by law, made no attempt to adapt to the German culture. There were hundreds of incidents where the police were called because some immigrants had a nasty habit of doing their bowel movements out the window of their apartment, and it was causing a real stink, literally. They couldn't be arrested, so the government had to hire people to clean up the feces all over the ground, and the immigrants kept on doing it. The immigrants, who had begged for asylum, began demanding that restaurants serve food that met their cultural needs, and sell clothing that met their requirements. They wanted the government to conduct business in their language, and the list of demands went on and on. The cost to the German taxpayers rose higher and higher just for dealing with "immigrants." Some of the younger Germans finally got fed up, and a number of fires in those apartment complexes started breaking out. After a time, the police knew it was the German youth that were setting the fires though no arrests were made. But many of the German people wanted these asylum immigrants out, and the atmosphere has remained hostile since. Do you see some similarities between what is happening in Germany, and what is happening here?

Is Capitalism Doomed in America?

Read this article by a Russian columnist, Stanislav Mishin, who writes for *Pravda, RU English,* and see if you agree. This column was published on the web in April of 2009.

"It must be said, that like the breaking of a great dam, the American descent into Marxism is occurring with breathtaking speed, against the backdrop of a passive, hapless citizenry.

True, the situation has been well prepared on and off for the past century, especially the past twenty years. The initial testing ground was conducted upon our Holy Russia and a bloody test it was. But we Russians would not just roll over and give up our freedoms and our souls, no matter how much money Wall Street poured into the fists of the Marxists.

Those lessons were taken and used to properly prepare the American populace for the surrender of their freedoms and souls, to the whims of their elites and betters.

First, the population was dumbed down through a politicized and substandard education system based on pop culture, rather than the classics. Americans know more about their favorite TV dramas than the drama in Washington, D.C. that directly affects their lives. They care more for their "right" to choke down a McDonalds® burger or a BurgerKing® burger than for their constitutional rights. Then they turn around and lecture us (Russia) about our rights, and about our "democracy." Pride blinds the foolish.

Then their faith in God was destroyed, until their churches, all tens of thousands of different "branches and denominations" were for the most part little more than Sunday circuses and their televangelists and top protestant mega preachers were more than happy to sell out their souls and flocks to be on the "winning" side of one pseudo Marxist politician or another. Their flocks may complain, but when explained that they would be on the "winning" side, their flocks were ever so quick to reject Christ in hopes for earthly power. Even our Holy Orthodox (Russian Orthodox) churches are scandalously liberalized in America.

The final collapse has come with the election of Barack Obama. His speed in the past several months has been truly impressive. His spending and money printing has been record setting, not just in America's short history, but in the world. If this keeps up for more than another year, and there is no sign that it will not, America at best will resemble the Wiemar Republic and, at worst, Zimbabwe.

These past two weeks have been the most breathtaking of all. First came the announcement of a planned redesign of the American Byzantine tax system, by the very thieves who used it to bankroll their thefts, losses, and swindles of hundreds of billions of dollars. These make our Russian oligarchs look little more than ordinary street thugs in comparison. Yes, the Americans have beaten our own thieves in sheer volume. Should we congratulate them?

These men, of course, are not an elected panel but made up of appointees picked from the very financial oligarchs and their henchmen who are now gorging themselves on trillions of American dollars, in one bailout after another. They are also usurping the rights, duties, and powers of the American Congress. Again, Congress has put up little more than a whimper to their masters.

Then came Barack Obama's command that GM's (General Motor) president step down from leadership of his company. That is correct, dear reader, in the land of "pure" free markets, the Amrican president now has the power, the self-given power, to fire CEOs and we can assume

other employees of private companies, at will. Come hither, go dither, the centurion commands his minions.

So it should be no surprise that the American President has followed this up with a "bold" move of declaring that he and another group of unelected, chosen stooges will now redesign the entire automotive industry and will even be the guarantee of automobile policies. I am sure that if given the chance, they would happily try and redesign it for the whole of the world, too. Prime Minister Putin, warned President Obama and the United Kingdom's Tony Blair, not to follow the path to Marxism, it only leads to disaster. Apparently, even though we suffered 70 years of this Western sponsored horror show, we know nothing, as foolish, drunken Russians, so let our "wise," Anglo-Saxon fools find out the folly of their own pride.

Again, the American public has taken this with barely a whimper . . . but a "freeman" whimper.

So, should it be any surprise to discover that the Democratically controlled Congress of America is working on passing a new regulation that granted the American Treasury department the power to set "fair" maximum salaries, evaluate performance, and control how private companies give out pay raises and bonuses? Congressman Barney Franks, a social pervert basking in his homosexuality—of course, amongst the modern, enlightened American societal norm, as well as that of the general West, homosexuality is not only not a looked down upon life choice, but is often praised as a virtue—and his Marxist enlightenment, has led this effort. He stresses that this only affects companies that receive government monies, but it is retroactive and taken to a logical extreme, this would include any company or industry that has ever received a tax break or incentive.

The Russian owners of American companies and industries should look thoughtfully at this and the option of closing their facilities down and fleeing the land of the Red as fast as possible. In other words, divest while there is still value left.

The proud American will go down into his slavery without a fight, beating his chest and proclaiming to the world, how free he really is. The world will only snicker."

Even from as far away as Russia, people see what's happening here in America, and can explain it quite well, don't you think. I'm pretty sure that people like Nancy Pelosi, Barbara Boxer, and Harry Reid are incapable of understanding this this letter unless it is read to them by an interpreter. Almost everyone on the left will absolutely deny that accuracy of this letter, but you get to decide. The people named here, and many who aren't named, don't want you to read this, or question what's going on because their plan hasn't been fully implemented yet. But the author makes a lot of sense and, remember, he's not writing for some lame stream media outlet in America. I hope you'll give this some thought, and decide to fight back.

Many of our young people are being indoctrinated in government schools, and by socialist-leaning professors in college. That indoctrination is very specific, but uses subtle methods, to convince the youth that Capitalism is unfair. What IS fair is Communism. Under a Capitalist system, people have opportunity, but no guaranteed outcome.

If you listen to what this President says, it is clear that he is a Communist. He says, quite clearly, that government provides all things. Small businesses are only successful because government allows them to be successful. A thought comes to mind. If a small business fails, is it because government made it fail, too? Think about his comment regarding the Ford automobile. Which came first, the car or the road? When Henry Ford came up with an assembly line process to mass produce Ford cars, the government had to respond by building roads. It wasn't the other way around. The government didn't decide to take our tax dollars and go build some roads, maybe some bridges, and then go to Henry Ford and say, OK, now you can build some cars. This President is just not the sharpest pencil in the box. No, he's a Communist. I used a term for him that someone else turned into a book title (I wonder if he owes me royalties?). I called this President the Manchurian President, and I still believe that's what he is.

Those that favor and teach Communism under many guises, preach that everyone should share everything equally, and the government ensures that. Everyone works, everyone has a place to live, has basic human needs, and everything is right in the world. Well, the first thing you find wrong with that teaching is that not everyone will work; not everyone can work. People have different skills, and can only perform certain jobs. Not everyone has the education or skill to work at jobs unsuited to them. There are also always some people that don't want to work, or if they do work, won't work as hard or as long as others work, but insist that they get the same amount of food, the same housing. and that their needs be met just like everyone else. What they don't mention is that people who won't work, or those who won't work hard are placed in Gulags where forced labor is the law. The other thing that comes to mind when discussing the beauty of Communism is that, under that model, there must be a ruling class, and there must be a peasant or working class, under the control of that ruling class. Without that, Communism can't function. If you listen to or watch some of the news about Occupy Wall Street or similar groups, one thing that pops into my mind is this—the "occupiers" want those who do work and earn money to give it to those who don't work and earn. That's what this whole 99% versus the 1% is all about. The 99%-ers, according to the occupiers, are left out of the wealth and freedom of America. That they are either in college, or not educated beyond high school, seems not to matter. In their view, it doesn't matter whether you're educated, experienced, and a hard worker or you're a high school dropout with no skills, no experience, and can't get a job other than minimum wage, which is yet another disaster for America. To them, the brain surgeon, who went into debt $200,000 or more to get the education and training, is worth no more than the person waiting on you at your fast food restaurant; both should share equally. Well, we know what that means—the minimum wage earner gets a big slice of what the brain surgeon makes for contributing less to society. This is where it all falls apart.

I followed events when the Berlin wall fell, and East Germany was reunited with West Germany. When the West Germans went into East Germany to see what they had to work with, they were shocked beyond belief. This Communist-bloc country was in total disarray. The factories had broken down and didn't functioning. The people were starving. The employees had been reporting to jobs where there was no work to do, just killing time, and drawing their government check. That money was barely enough to stay alive. There was little if any private ownership of anything; the government ruled everything. Germany was now united again, but the cost to the West German people was astronomical. All those people had to be fed and housed in decent living quarters. The factories had to be torn down, and new ones built. The currency of East Germany was worthless. Communism in the Soviet Union eventually had to crumble and fall apart, and so it did. Look at North Korea.

North Korea is one of the most brutal Communist countries on the planet. The people are starving, but the ruling class lives very well. Look at Communist Cuba. There are two kinds of healthcare; one type is for the rulers, the other type is for the working class. Working class healthcare is almost medieval. There are "reeducation camps" for those who speak out against the ruling class. This is Castro's Cuba, yet many believe it's a wonderful place. Those same people would never live there, but they think you'd love it there. In China, they kill the second child of any couple who dares to have that baby, and impose forced sterilization on many occasions. The ruling class lives and works in beautiful palaces and homes, but the working class live in hovels, living on what little rice and other crops they can produce. But China, at least, has seen fit to try some limited Capitalism, although it's under strict government control. Many American companies have their products assembled in China because the wage is so much lower than here. This adds to our unemployment disaster.

Over the decades, some non-enterprising people have started communes. Everyone lives together, works together, and shares. Those communes don't exist for the most part today because they fell apart as all Communist communities, states, and countries do.

There are people in the media, in positions of political power, and in education who insist that Communism is the salvation of America and, yes, the world. One World Order, under the control of the United Nations. What Communism does is suck the life out of people; Communism sucks the incentive out of people; Communism sucks the dreams out of people. Capitalism rewards those who work hard, save, get themselves educated, and pursue their dreams. That can't happen under Communism. Tell your friends.

Finally, What Do We Want to Leave Our Kids and Grandkids?

Here are some suggestions to turn our sinking ship called America around. If we all fight to make these changes, your kids and grandkids have a chance for a better life.

- Citizens, especially parents, get off your collective butts and pay attention. Government schools are not educating our children and grandchildren. If your children have kids, are you making sure that those grandchildren are getting a good education? Are you inserting yourself into your children's decisions if they are the kind of parents that just aren't raising their children to be productive adults but, instead, trying to be friends with their children? Why aren't you getting involved? Drag your children to school meetings, demand to see the course schedule, the syllabus for each class, and let the school know that there will be no, homosexuality is normal, nonsense taught in school. Get involved.

- This country needs parents that behave like parents, not parents who think that raising a child means feeding, clothing, and providing a bed for them.

- Do your kids and grandkids know what the Constitution is, and how this country works under that Constitution? Why not? How about the Bill of Rights? How about the Declaration of Independence? Why not?

- We need parents to hold their children accountable, and quit blaming others for the bad behavior of their own children. When your child assaults another student in class, or on a school bus, and the school calls you in, support the school. Your child needs to be taught that there are consequences for bad behavior, and you should support it, not make excuses so you won't be inconvenienced if that child is suspended. Be a parent.

- How many of you know who your local state legislators are? Why not? How many of you know who your Congressman is, your Senators? Why not? How many of you show up at townhall meetings and challenge your federal legislators and their votes? Why not? We need to demand, all of us, that government be held accountable for its behavior. When the Executive branch, the President, violates the Constitution, how many of you contact your members of Congress and raise hell? Why not? If just a few thousand citizens would inundate a Congressman or woman's office with demands for action, they will listen. Their instinct is for self-preservation. Get involved with your local legislators. Here in Arizona we currently enjoy a good majority of Republicans in both houses, but we've become complacent. Don't forget, the media is our enemy in almost every state. But the voices of the people speak volumes. Get involved. The one thing I can't stand to hear is—"I hope somebody does something about this." Too many citizens are way too detached from America. Quit thinking about yourself, and start thinking about the future of this country. Your children and grandchildren are depending on you.

- Our government can't produce a financial statement. It's beyond them, and they're not interested in even trying. Start writing all of your elected officials, and demand a balanced budget every year, or they're gone. Demand that they live within that budget or they're gone. No more debt ceiling increases. If we're not in a world war, live within your budget, or you're gone.

- How many children in school today, including college, can name their elected representatives for their state? It's appalling how few even know this. In a representative republic, you elect these people to speak and act for you. You and your kids and grandkids should at least know who they are.

- To eliminate the problem and expense of illegal aliens in your state, start demanding that representatives and the governor pass laws to prevent any illegal alien from receiving any support from the government, other than emergency medical care. Once that medical care is given, they are immediately deported. No welfare checks, no food stamps, no free housing, no free education, and no jobs. Once that law is passed, the number of illegal aliens invading our country will drop to a trickle. And, add a law that any company caught hiring an illegal alien will have their business license revoked for one year, per incident.

- No war declaration should be entertained unless the country we would fight is a threat to our national security. If the President insists on sending troops without the consent of Congress, deny all funding.

- Demand that any law that can be enforced against any citizen also applies to any member of government, including Congress, the Executive branch, and Judicial branch. If any member of Congress, the judicial branch, or the Executive branch is found to have lied under oath, they shall be charged with perjury and, if convicted, sent to jail. If any member of those bodies is served with a subpoena and refuses to immediately comply, they will be arrested and jailed until they do comply, and that includes the Attorney General of the United States.

- Demand that Child Protective Services be given the power, and exercise that power to garnish or attach the income of any child, under 18, or adult, if a teenage, unmarried girl gets pregnant. The amount garnished or attached would include all monies needed to adequately care of the child until that child reaches the age of 18. If the mother of the child refuses to provide the name of the father, she will receive no welfare or other payments until she complies. This would not preclude charging the male with sexual assault against a minor female, which, if found guilty, would result in at least five years in prison, regardless of their age.

- Demand that any parent of a child who either commits child abuse or neglect, or allows it to happen without contacting law enforcement, shall be tried and, if convicted, serve no less than 15 years in prison, no parole. Any monies earned while in prison shall be paid to CPS to cover the child's expenses.

- Demand a law that any person caught distributing, selling, or possessing more a legally banned substance be charged, tried, and if found guilty, sentenced to no less than five, but up to 50 years in prison. The age of the offender shall not be a legitimate defense.

- Demand that your state pass a school voucher law. This law should apply to every school in the state. Any parent can use one voucher per child to take those child(ren) out of a failing school and enroll them in a successful school. The amount of the voucher shall be considered a tax credit.

- Demand that education control be returned to the states. Dissolve the Department of Education. All education shall be implemented and controlled at the state level without exception.

- Parents should attend, en masse, school functions and demand that all teachers be administered a performance examination every two years. The examination should be administered by an outside body not affiliated with the government or the school system. The teacher must demonstrate their ability to understand and teach the subjects they are assigned in the classroom.

- Tell your state's education leaders that English Immersion will be the method by which non-English speaking students learn America's language.

- Contact your state legislatures and demand teacher accountability, and the end of tenure. Teachers should be paid for performance, not for length of service. Private sector employees must earn their pay, every working day; the same should be true for teachers.

- Parents must demand that all school education expenses begin with the classroom and the students. Once everything necessary for the students and classroom is completed, expenditures for teacher salaries, administrator salaries, and benefits can be allocated. No school or school district can exceed their budget. No budget overrides. Demand that each year every school publish a list of all expenses, itemized, and all salaries for each non-teacher employee. and then justify each of those positions.

233

- Petition the government and demand that each DES office add a grocery store and pharmacy to their facility. Anyone who qualifies for food stamps—which excludes illegal aliens—will instead, receive a photo ID card, with an expiration date, usually one to three months from date of issue. That Photo ID card can only be used to shop for groceries at the government stores. Those stores will not sell any tobacco products or any alcoholic products. The store will not sell any junk food, such as candies. sugary cereals, and similar products. The store will sell healthy foods and beverages. When the holder of the photo ID card enters the store, the ID is checked to ensure that a) it is not a forged card, b) it is still valid, and c) the person presenting it is in fact the person to whom it was issued. When the ID card holder checks out, the grocery total will then be deducted from the balance on the card for that period. Each state would save tens of millions of dollars using this program.

- Any child who is bullied while on the school grounds or on school transportation, who does not receive assistance or intervention from the bus driver or other school official, can file charges against the school for creating a hostile education environment. There are existing laws government bullying. Verbal attacks are assaults; physical attacks are called battery. Use them. Hold schools accountable.

- Any teacher found guilty of sexual assault, or conduct, with a student, shall be treated like every other sexual predator, and be sentenced to the same term in prison as any other sexual predator. That teacher shall also be banned from teaching in any school again. This also would apply to non-teaching employees of the school.

- We have to demand that any driver who is found to have been under the influence of either alcohol or an illegal substance be charged with at least one felony, and be sentenced accordingly. We will no longer tolerate probation or "light" sentences for first time offenders. Do the crime, do the time.

- We must insist on job skills training for anyone who is unemployed and receiving any benefits. Anyone who, for whatever reason, is receiving unemployment payments must attend job training classes. These classes will be taught by private companies, not government agencies, though state and federal government funds would be used. Anyone who refuses to take the training classes will not receive their unemployment benefits. There are no excuses for not attending. If child care is involved, the state unemployment system will pay for day care at a private company's facilities. Having to stay home because of the children is not a reasonable excuse.

- Demand that schools impose a dress code, from kindergarten through high school. No pants on boys that do not include a belt. No shorts, no tank tops. No display of underwear, male or female, no dress or skirt that ends above the knee. Girls cannot wear fishnet stockings, high heels, open cleavage, or excessive makeup. No student can artificially color their hair that presents a distraction to others. There will be no cell phones, iPads, or other electronic communications instrument on school grounds. Any child that acts out by threatening a teacher or other student will not be suspended. Instead, one parent of the child will attend classes with that unruly child for a week, every class, every school day.

- If any employee files a complaint with human resources that they are offended because another employee has a religious symbol on their desk, that complaining employee will be given two options: Take a different route so you won't come into eye contact with the offending symbol, or two, resign. Being offended is a choice people make, not something that is done to them. Being offended has gotten out of control with all this politically correct nonsense.

I could add to this list for another month, but I believe that the point is clear. Parents need to start behaving like parents, not their child's best buddy, and the giver of anything a child wants. Saying "no" is part of being a parent. The entire concept of the family unit is being destroyed in a number of ways. Those on the left believe that they should raise your children. When Hillary Clinton ghost-wrote her "It Takes a Village" book, she made that clear. When teachers say that the parents should just deliver their children to the school, and then butt out, that's another message. When there are more single parents today than we have ever had, that sends another message. When we have a government that is unrestrained in their zeal to spend, spend, and spend some more, on social programs that have proven not to work, that is another message. When we have so many Americans who have no pride in their country, no allegiance to their country, that sends another message. When we have nearly 50% of Americans of employment age, paying no federal income tax, that sends another message. When we have a government, at all levels, that believes that it "rules" the people rather than serve the people, that's another message delivered.

As citizens we have an obligation to stand up, speak out, and hold people and organizations accountable. This is our country, not theirs. If you won't get involved and let your voice be heard, quit complaining. You're one of those people who assumes that other people are fighting for you. You are those people. Freedom isn't Free. Get busy.

God Bless America !

About the Author

Mr. Spitzer was born in Shanghai, China of American parents. His father was in the U.S. Navy on a ship patrolling those waters. His mother took her daughter and, with other wives, went to Shanghai using a troop transport, then took up residence on a harbor houseboat where Mr. Spitzer was born. Everyone except Mr. Spitzer's father returned to the United States shortly before Japan invaded China.

Mr. Spitzer was raised in Northern California, graduating high school in 1958. He then joined the U.S. Navy where he served until his retirement in 1978. During that 20-year period Mr. Spitzer was in a collision at sea, served a full tour in Vietnam in 1969-1970, and returned to Vietnam again in 1975 to assist in the evacuation before South Vietnam fell. He was a translator bringing evacuees onboard his ship, and preparing them for transfer to merchant ships for a trip to Guam and the Philippines. During his 20 years of service Mr. Spitzer served as a Drug Education Specialist, Naval Instructor, and Chief in Charge of Communication at shore stations and onboard several ships managing up to 150 personnel at any given time.

From 1978 until his retirement from the private sector in 2003 Mr. Spitzer worked with several companies in the computer hardware and software industry in multiple capacities. He rose as high as Vice President at his last full time job. He managed training organizations, technical publication departments, software quality departments, and many others. He was often used to take over failing departments in order to bring those departments back to full productivity. In a part time capacity Mr. Spitzer also taught computer literacy at several community colleges and at a federal prison near Phoenix, Arizona. He also volunteered to work in a prison ministry program at two state prisons, mentoring convicts who wanted to change their lives, and was very successful. Mr. Spitzer continued his bowling activities learned while in the Navy, completing his career, because of back injury, with his final perfect game, and winning the City of Phoenix Championship.

Since he retired Mr. Spitzer has volunteered to serve on a Foster Care Review Board, and as a CASA (Court Appointed Special Advocate), where he worked with foster children and represented them in the juvenile court system.

Mr. Spitzer was an elected chairman of a Republican legislative district, and served on his city's Planning and Zoning Commission.

Mr. Spitzer lives with his wife of over 20 years in Arizona, enjoying golf, volunteering for causes in which he believes, writing letters and articles for local newspapers, and giving speeches around the state.